Subtle Subversions

Subtle Subversions

READING GOLDEN AGE SONNETS
BY IBERIAN WOMEN

GWYN FOX

THE CATHOLIC UNIVERSITY OF AMERICA PRESS
WASHINGTON, D.C.

Library of Congress Cataloging-in-Publication Data

Fox, Gwyn.

  Subtle subversions : reading Golden Age sonnets by Iberian
women / Gwyn Fox.

    p. cm.

  Includes bibliographical references and index.

  ISBN 978-0-8132-1528-0 (cloth : alk. paper)   1. Spanish
poetry—Women authors—History and criticism.
2. Portuguese poetry—Women authors—History
and criticism.   3. Spanish poetry—Classical period,
1500–1700—History and criticism.   4. Portuguese poetry—
Classical period, 1500–1700—History and criticism.
5. Sonnets, Spanish—History and criticism.   6. Sonnets,
Portuguese—History and criticism.   I. Title.

  PQ6055.F58 2008

  861'.042099287—dc22   2007049868

To my family,

and in loving memory of

Ben and Iryn

Two hearts, one soul, always

CONTENTS

ACKNOWLEDGMENTS

I am deeply indebted to a number of people who have supported me during my work on this project. I should especially like to acknowledge Mercedes Maroto Camino and Christine Arkinstall for their constant support, advice, and encouragement. I have also enjoyed the active interest and support of colleagues in the School of European Languages at the University of Auckland, especially Bernadette Luciano and Sarah McDonald. We are also lucky to have an excellent university library and a wonderful specialist subject librarian in Shelley Taylor. From further afield, I have been overwhelmed by the generosity, interest, and willingness to share ideas of professors Anne Cruz, Julian Olivares, Amanda Powell, and Lisa Vollendorf.

I should also like to acknowledge the financial support of the Foundation for Research, Science and Technology of New Zealand, the University of Auckland, and the Regueiro McKelvie Foundation.

INTRODUCTION *Revisiting the Baroque*

⁕

[N]othing is known about women before the eighteenth century. . . . Here I am asking

why women did not write poetry in the Elizabethan age . . . any woman born with

a great gift in the sixteenth century would certainly have gone crazed, shot herself,

or ended her days in some lonely cottage outside the village, half witch, half wizard,

feared and mocked at.

(Woolf 45)

VIRGINIA WOOLF wrote these words in her celebrated work
A Room of One's Own in 1929, expressing her frustration at the
lack of women's voices in history and literature. Yet, unrealized by Woolf,
across Western Europe women were writing in all fields of literary endeav-
or and trying to make their voices heard, even in that "Elizabethan" era.
We have only to think of Mary Wroth or Aphra Behn, in her own country; Louise Labé, in France; Gaspara Stampa or Moderata Fonte, in Italy;
and Maria de Zayas, Ana Caro Mallén de Soto, or Mariana de Carvajal in
Spain to see a small but distinctive body of literature written by women.
Nevertheless, it was not until the excellent scholarship of the last quarter
century began to address the lacunae left by a historiography written within a masculine framework of reference that women began to discover and
celebrate the extent of their own history and cultural production. Thanks
to this scholarship, we are becoming increasingly aware of the wealth of
cultural activity by women, produced in spite of long-cherished masculine
notions of biological determinism. Whatever the authors of moral trea-

tises and preachers wrote and said about women's lack of reason, women have shown across time that given the opportunity and the education, they are equal in reason and intelligence to their male counterparts and are only too keen to seize the opportunity to express their capacity for independent thought. If we consider the artworks of the likes of Artemisia Gentileschi, we can see that this equality extends also to the plastic arts. Furthermore, and as will be seen in the course of my analysis of their sonnets, the women I discuss here did not consider themselves to be in any way inferior to their male counterparts; instead they saw themselves as rational, confident, and important members of their social milieu.

The purpose of this book is to further the study of both women's history and their artistic production through a contextually based exploration of sonnets of love and friendship by seventeenth-century women in the Iberian Peninsula. I study principally the works of five women: four Spaniards, Catalina Clara Ramírez de Guzmán, Leonor de la Cueva y Silva, Sor María de Santa Isabel, who wrote under the nom de plume Marcia Belisarda, and Doña Luisa de Carvajal y Mendoza; and a Portuguese, Sor Violante del Cielo. In choosing these five poets, I am able to situate their works in relation to the widest possible sociohistorical background, for their lives span part of the sixteenth and almost the whole of the seventeenth century, and encompass both the religious and the secular worlds. Their works all show a clear awareness of and engagement with the argument about women, patriarchy, class differences, patronage, love, and the value of friendship. They therefore serve as a representative sample of the writings and attitudes of seventeenth-century Iberian women. At the same time, by restricting the scope of my study to five poets, I am able to provide a deeper appreciation of both their own attitudes and those that informed their thinking that would not be possible were I to produce a broader based selection.

In the course of this study and through the words of these women, I shall address the concerns raised by Gerda Lerner that women have always been forced to prove to themselves and others that they are capable of abstract thought and full humanity. Lerner contends that this necessity has skewed the intellectual development of women as a group, as they have had to turn their intellectual endeavor to counteracting pervasive patriarchal assumptions about their inferiority and human incompleteness (Consciousness 10–11). Moreover, literate women wishing to write always found themselves in an anomalous position: female loquacity was associated with promiscuity, whereas male eloquence was celebrated as the mark of an educated and distinguished man (Jones, "Nets" 1).

Women were considered by men to need constant surveillance in three specific areas: their mouths, their chastity, and their access to the entrance of the house. This connection between speaking and wantonness was common to legal discourse and conduct books (Stallybrass 126). The pressures on women to remain silent and enclosed, verbally, sexually, and scribally, can only have increased as print culture developed and there was greater access to both literary and religious models to inspire wouldbe female poets. Certainly, there is considerable scholarly agreement on the Counter-Reformation repression of women in terms of their education and independence, both physical and intellectual. For example, Paul Julian Smith has claimed that there were even fewer women writing in Spain in the Counter-Reformation period than elsewhere in Europe as a result of the Spanish obsession with domestic privacy that also prevented the publication of memoirs and letters (14). Similarly, Beth Miller notes that only three women of late medieval Spain—Leonor López de Córdoba, Teresa de Cartagena, and Florencia Pinar— left any substantial work and that few women in the Spanish Empire wrote in the seventeenth and eighteenth centuries (4).

In spite of these observations, the large number of women's poetry and prose works recorded in Serrano y Sanz's *Apuntes para una biblioteca de escritoras españolas* (Notes for a library of Spanish women writers) first published in 1895, indicates that women were writing and furthermore that their families and descendants felt sufficiently strongly about their compositions to retain them, hence leaving a discernible trace of women's intellectual powers, personalities, and education. What is even more surprising is that Serrano y Sanz, a nineteenth-century scholar, should have gone to the considerable time and trouble required to gather such a multitude of female writers under one reference. He too must have considered that such a body of work was worth preserving as part of the Golden Age's wider cultural and social fabric.

These women's works are readily available, both in manuscript form, at the Biblioteca Nacional in Madrid, and in various anthologies. They have attracted a rapidly growing body of critical interest: they have been included in anthologies and discussed in essays, journal articles, and, in the cases of Carvajal y Mendoza and Sor Violante, entire books. Some of the works of all of these poets appear in the most complete anthology to date of early modern women's poetry in Spanish, *Tras el espejo la musa escribe* (Behind the mirror the muse writes), edited by Julián Olivares and Elizabeth Boyce, which includes a very comprehensive and informative introduction.[1] Some poetry also appears in a 1989 anthology, *Antología poética de escritoras de los siglos VI y XVII* (Poetry anthology by women writers of the sixteenth and seventeenth centuries), edited by Ana Navaro. Gradually, more of their works are appearing in translation, as in Elizabeth Rhodes's *This Tight Embrace* and the present work.[2]

INTRODUCING THE POETS

The earliest of the poets is Luisa de Carvajal y Mendoza, born in 1566, in Extremadura, to a noble family.[3] The extraordinary nature of her life and vocation have ensured the production of many studies, commencing shortly after her death, when her confessor, Michael Walpole, first wrote the biography that began what he hoped would be the process toward canonization. Like Walpole's, the majority of these studies have been decidedly hagiographic. In 1632 another biography, based on Walpole's, was published: *Vida y virtudes de la Venerable Virgen Doña Luisa de Carvajal y Mendoza. Su jornada a Inglaterra y sucesos en aquel Reyno* (Life and virtues of the Venerable Virgin Donna Luisa de Carvajal y Mendoza: Her Journey to England and events in that kingdom). The fullest account of her life is that written in 1966 by the Jesuit Camilo María Abad: *Una misionera española en la Inglaterra del siglo XVII (1566–1614)* (A Spanish woman missionary in the England of the seventeenth century [1566–1614]). In the same year Abad published her *Epistolario y poesías* (Letters and

---

1. The detailed introduction to this volume provides information about the lives of women in the seventeenth century, as well as discussion of their poetic skills and achievements.

2. All the translations in this text are my own. I have lightly modernized the spelling in the Spanish verse.

3. Further details of Carvajal y Mendoza's life are included in Chapter 6.

poems). which included a biography and an introduction to her poetry. Abad's two studies, while detailed and scholarly, wholly endorse her militant fervor and strive to emphasize her saintliness, perhaps as a means to promote the cause for canonization, still in abeyance.[4] His interest in her poetry lies in its evocation of her religious calling and he does not offer any kind of critique of her poetic skills or her subject matter.

Carvajal y Mendoza's poetry is notable for its intensely passionate style, and has been highly praised for its artistic qualities. Margarita Nelken makes the following observation: "La propia Sta Teresa no ha descrito con más intensidad las emociones de la comunión. . . . Doña Luisa es la más ilustre de las escritoras religiosas del siglo XVII" (76; St. Teresa herself has not described the emotions of the communion with greater intensity. . . . Donna Luisa is the most illustrious of the female religious writers of the seventeenth century). More recently, Carvajal y Mendoza has been the focus of much detailed critical study. Her life and, less prominently, her poetry have been discussed in a number of articles and books, some of which I contend with in the course of my analysis of her poetry.

There is far less information available on the other poets, with the exception of Sor Violante del Cielo.[5] Although their birthdates are sometimes not known, or are debatable, all appear to have been born in the first decade of the seventeenth century. Leonor de la Cueva y Silva, daughter of a noble family of Medina del Campo, was the niece of the celebrated lawyer, courtier, and poet Francisco de la Cueva y Silva, for whom she wrote a funeral sonnet in 1621. Barely decipherable script at the end of her manuscript bears the date 1697, suggesting a very long life (ms. 4127 276).[6] Some of her sonnets indicate her determination to celebrate the nobility and valor of her line, perhaps as a means of elevating herself as part of the typical pursuit of patronage favor. However, she also writes sonnets that criticize masculine pretensions and hypocrisy, and others celebrating female fortitude, honesty, and moral courage. Her

---

4. Even Iberia Airlines, the national carrier of Spain, has attempted to lift Carvajal y Mendoza closer to heaven by naming one of its 747 passenger jets after her.

5. Most of the critical work on Sor Violante is available only in Portuguese.

6. Her manuscript, considered by Serrano y Sanz to be an autograph, is conserved in the Biblioteca Nacional in Madrid.

single extant play, *La firmeza en la ausencia* (Constancy in absence), extols women's loyalty and criticizes masculine abuse of power.[7]

Like Cueva, Catalina Clara Ramírez de Guzmán was born in an important rural center, Llerena, in 1618. Some confusion has arisen in anthologies over her actual birthdate since a sister, Catalina, is recorded as being born in 1611.[8] Two manuscripts of her work, numbered 3884 and 3917, totaling 118 poems, are held in the Biblioteca Nacional in Madrid. Ramírez's poetry is almost ethnographic in its detail about family life in an important country town. Although she writes few sonnets, her other works make interesting reading for their contrast with the received wisdom about women's plight in the period. She clearly enjoyed the fondest relationships with her large family, including her father and brothers.[9] Her poetry is lighthearted and entertaining, but also often acid and cruel in the style of Francisco de Quevedo, whose works she knew, according to Arturo Gazul (510). Her poetry was first published in 1929 by Joaquín Entrambasaguas y Peña, who included a detailed biography in his introduction. Other historians have also studied her life and that of her family, though not her works.[10] Ramírez also wrote a book entitled *El extremeño* (The Extremaduran), now lost.

Both Ramírez and Cueva lived all their lives in their respective towns. Ramírez never married, and while Cueva's marital status remains unclear, that she had the freedom to write a *comedia* (play) and to compose po-

---

7. This play has now been published several times. See Teresa Scott Soufas, *Women's Acts: Plays by Women Dramatists of Spain's Golden Age* (Lexington: University Press of Kentucky, 1997); also see Marina Subirats, Juan Antonio Hormigón, Felicidad González Santamera, and Fernando Doménech, eds., *Teatro de mujeres del Barroco* (Madrid: Asociación de Directores de Escena de España, 1994). It is not known whether *La firmeza en la ausencia* has ever been performed. There are also several articles discussing aspects of the play; these are detailed in Chapter 5, where I explore the play's sonnets.

8. This infant must have died before Ramírez was born. Although Entrambasaguas gives 1611 as her birthdate, her baptismal certificate reveals a birthdate of 1618. Gazul assumes the early death of the first Catalina, and that the parents named their next daughter in memory of the first. See Arturo Gazul, "La familia Ramírez de Guzmán en Llerena," *Revista de Estudios Extremeños* XV.III (1959): 522; and Antonio Carrasco García, *La Plaza Mayor de Llerena y otros estudios* (Valdemoro: Tuero, 1985) 108–9.

9. Gazul corrects an anomalous reference to Ramírez in Serrano y Sanz that indicates that she was the daughter of the eminent jurist and humanist Lorenzo Ramírez de Prado. She was his niece.

10. See Gazul, "Familia Ramírez," 499–577, and Carrasco García, *La Plaza Mayor de Llerena y otros estudios*, 98–135.

etry throughout her life suggests that she too did not marry.[11] It is, perhaps, this single independence that enabled both poets to write as openly as they do. The four sonnets exchanged by lovers of disparate social classes in Cueva's *comedia* show a clear understanding of the workings of class; in them she also underlines women's constancy and the possibilities for freely chosen, genuine affective relationships between men and women. The frank enjoyment in the love of her family that Ramírez displays is clearly to be seen in the poetry she writes to and about her family members, particularly to her brother when he is away at war, discussed in Chapter 3.

Of the remaining two poets, Marcia Belisarda was born in Toledo, according to Serrano y Sanz, though her birthdate is not known. Almost nothing is known of her life, other than that she entered the convent of the Concepción in Toledo. Her manuscript, number 7469, is conserved in the Biblioteca Nacional in Madrid. It is clear from the prologue and encomiastic poems that precede her poetry that she intended it to be published. She is unusual in reserving the sonnet form for her more playful and secular verse, where others, particularly Sor Violante, find its formal structure more suitable for works of religious devotion. Marcia Belisarda's work includes both religious and secular verse, in which she frequently celebrates the importance of reason over passion and argues for women's rational capabilities. She goes further in evincing the strong bonds of friendship that obtained within enclosed convent communities when she writes welcoming poetry to new nuns and her sad sonnet at the death of a friend, discussed in Chapter 4.

The last and most prolific poet in this study is Sor Violante del Cielo, born in Lisbon Violante Silveira de Montesinos. Although she is Portuguese, I include her works because she wrote many of her poems while Portugal was under the dominance of the Spanish Crown and because many of them are composed in Spanish. Furthermore, her feminine ap-

---

11. Ramírez's testament, which left the bulk of her estate to her brother, Pedro, was written in 1684, and notes her civil status as *doncella* (spinster). Entrambasaguas observes that she had several suitors and assumes that the son of the Almezquita family was the favored suitor, but that the relationship was doomed by the enmity that developed between the families. See Joaquín de Entrambasaguas y Peña, "Estudio preliminar," in *Poesía de doña Catalina Clara Ramírez de Guzmán,* ed. y notas por Joaquín de Entrambasaguas y Peña (Badajoz: Centro de Estudios Extremeños, 1930), 31–32. Further details of this enmity are provided in Chapter 3.

praisals of the patronage system and of extant masculine versus feminine roles in her cultural milieu show that women's literary and cultural history was a shared one across the breadth of seventeenth-century Western Europe and was not confined to Spain. Serrano y Sanz gives her birthdate as 1601, as do Olivares and Boyce, but in the introduction to a 1993 edition of Sor Violante's *Rimas varias* (Collected poems), Margarida Vieira Mendes declares that Sor Violante's birthdate was 1607, verified by sight of her birth certificate. If this date is correct, then Sor Violante's reputation as a child prodigy is well deserved. A play by her, now lost, was performed for King Philip III during his visit to Lisbon in 1619, when she was either twelve or eighteen years old, depending on the biographical information to hand. Sor Violante lived among the highest circles of Portuguese society, and she retained these contacts when, in 1630, she entered the convent attached to the Lisbon court, the most wealthy and luxurious convent in Portugal at that time. According to Serrano y Sanz, Sor Violante entertained friends there and continued to write poetry, activities that led him to conclude that she appeared to have no religious calling at all. I shall contest this view in the course of my discussion, for Sor Violante composed clever religious poetry that shows not only a full knowledge of spiritual matters but a deep faith as well. A collection of her secular verse, *Rimas varias,* was published in Rouen, France, in 1646, by the Portuguese ambassador to France, Vasco Luis da Gama, count de Vidigueira, whose wife, Inés, a close friend of Sor Violante, is the recipient of several poems. Serrano y Sanz also theorizes that Sor Violante entered the convent due to an unsuccessful love affair with the Portuguese poet Paulo Gonçalves de Andrade, with whom she exchanged a number of poems. This claim, which will be discussed in greater detail in Chapter 5, is refuted by Vieira Mendes.

After her death, Sor Violante's religious verse was collected in two volumes and published in Lisbon in 1733 by Miguel Rodrigues under the title of *Parnaso lusitano de divinos e humanos versos, compostos pela Madre Soror Violante do Ceo, religiosa dominica no Convento da Rosa de Lisboa, dedicado a Senhora Soror Violante do Ceo, religiosa no convento de Santa Martha de Lisboa* (Lusitanian Parnassus of human and divine poems, composed by Mother Violante do Ceo, Dominican nun in the Convent of the Rose, Lisbon, dedicated to the lady Sister Violante do Ceo, nun in the convent of St. Martha, Lisbon). The first volume consists entirely of sonnets and includes a twenty-one-sonnet cycle on the mysteries of the rosary, the only extant, thematically linked sonnet cycle written by a Spanish or Portuguese woman of the period known to date.[12] In addition to her published works, an eighteenth-century manuscript held in the British Library includes a number of Sor Violante's sonnets (Add. ms. 25353). Sor Violante continued to write poetry throughout her long life; her last recorded poetic works were two sonnets written to celebrate the birth of a new prince in 1689. She died in 1693.

Sor Violante has always enjoyed considerable fame in Portugal, and she appears in numerous studies and anthologies of Portuguese poets that stretch from the seventeenth century to the present day, almost all of which are available only in Portuguese. In Chapter 1, I engage with some of the conclusions drawn by a number of nineteenth-century scholars in regard to the nature of Sor Violante's religious vocation and her sexual orientation. Because of the variety and quantity of available verse by this nun, her works appear in almost every chapter except Chapter 6, although even here awareness of her religious verse style creates a foil for the fervent mystical sonnets of Luisa de Carvajal y Mendoza.

In addition to works by these five women, where they are particularly germane to the study of women's history and cultural production, I include sonnets from other poets, such as a poignant sonnet of desertion by Inarda de Arteaga that points to male fickleness and mutability, or the sonnets by the Mexican nun Sor Juana Inés de la Cruz on the death of her patroness. Sor Juana's works merit inclusion partly due to her extraordinary virtuosity as a poet, and also because, although she lived and wrote in the New World, Sor Juana was intimately acquainted with the workings of the vice-regal court in Mexico, an extension of the courtly existence of peninsular Spain. Furthermore, her sonnets to the vicereine are written to praise a representative of Spanish nobility and majesty and have little to do with the concerns of New Spain.

It is of particular note that none of these women married. This may have been by deliberate choice, as a means of maintaining a degree of in-

---

12. The mysteries of the rosary number fifteen. Sor Violante writes more than one sonnet on what must have been, for her, the most important mysteries, those concerning Christ's betrayal, Crucifixion, and Resurrection.

dependence, or it may have been due to the reduced number of males in Spain in the seventeenth century. Shifra Armon, for example, puts the disproportionate survival ratio between women and men down to men's long absences in the colonies and away at wars, high death rates among males due to those wars, and an inheritance system that made it difficult for any but the eldest son to wed, therefore reducing the probability of marriage for many young women (51).[13]

These women do not rail against enforced enclosure or masculine restriction on their activities. Rather, they celebrate their intelligence and wit in their verse. Furthermore, they actively, often openly, criticize the failings of others, both male and female. While this is particularly evident in Ramírez's verse, Marcia Belisarda also makes a strong critique of masculine pretensions, as she does, for example, in a pair of sonnets comparing the benefits of reason over appetite, to be discussed in Chapter 5. Similarly, Cueva's sonnet to an unfortunate *pretendiente* (suitor) explored in Chapter 1, shows familiarity with, as well as criticism of, the patronage system. Cueva's ironic presentation of the *pretendiente* does not disguise the fact that she fully understood the benefits of patronage, and wrote poetry that underlined her willingness to invest intelligence and effort in furthering the cause of her family within that system.

JOINING THE CANON

The choice of sonnets from among the variety of poems that these women write is particularly important as a means by which to demonstrate these women's affirmations about their capacity for reason. The sonnet is the preeminent form in early modern poetry in Western Europe. Probably deriving from the *strambotto* (an Italian eight-line verse form) at the hands of Giacomo da Lentino, a *notaro* at the thirteenth century Sicilian court of Frederick II, it was taken up with enthusiasm and developed first by Guittone and later by the *stilnovisti* (exponents of the sweet new style), particularly Guinizzelli, Cavalcanti, and Dante

13. On the Spanish population in the seventeenth century, see also Antonio Domínguez Ortiz, *La sociedad española en el siglo XVII*, 2 vols. (Granada: Universidad de Granada, 1992), 1: 101–3; and Jose Antonio Maravall, *Culture of the Baroque: Analysis of a Historical Structure*, trans. Terry Cochran (Minneapolis: University of Minnesota Press, 1986).

Alighieri. It is with Dante that the sonnet achieved a complexity and originality that would not be achieved again until Petrarch. Dante's and Petrarch's sonnets, more than any other works, cemented the sonnet into the Western canon as one of the major poetic forms.

Petrarch's *Rime* (Ryhmes) focus principally on his love for Laura, although he also includes poems with political and religious themes. With Petrarch the journey toward interiority, begun in Giacomo's earliest sonnets, comes to fruition in Petrarch's desire for the beloved, internalized into a study of the poet-lover's moods and attitudes in confronting the virtuous, strong, and ideal figure of the beloved. His example was followed by a number of successful Italian poets, including Bembo, Castiglione, Michelangelo, and Tasso. The sonnet form was rapidly and easily assimilated into Spanish, initially through the works of the Marqués de Santillana, who produced sonnets both amorous and religious, themes that were closely related in fifteenth-century Spain.[14] Later, the sonnet would be brought to its intellectual and artistic peak in Spain in the Golden Age sonnets of Lope de Vega, Góngora, and Quevedo.

As an extremely popular form of display among court poets and dedicated court amateurs alike, the sonnet constitutes an ideal format in which to uncover the skills of these women and the forces that motivated them to write as they did. Of all verse forms the sonnet provides the best opportunity to display wit, linguistic ingenuity, and knowledge, all combined in a tightly controlled, fourteen-line stanza, with strict requirements as to rhyme scheme. In early modern Spanish sonnets, the quartets are invariably rhymed ABBA ABBA, while some relaxation in the structure of the tercets allows a number of combinations. The tercet structures favored by these women poets are CDE CDE and CDC CDC. In addition, its formal requirements make the sonnet a more elevated style of poetry than the *romance* (a Spanish ballad), the *silva* (vers-

14. For detailed studies on the history and nature of the sonnet, as well as its principal early exponents, see Christopher Butler, "Numerological Thought," in *Silent Poetry: Essays in Numerological Analysis,* ed. Alistair Fowler (London: Routledge, 1970), 1–31; Paul Oppenheimer, *The Birth of the Modern Mind: Self, Consciousness and the Invention of the Sonnet* (New York and Oxford: Oxford University Press, 1989); Elías L. Rivers, ed., *El soneto español en el Siglo de Oro* (Madrid: Akal, 1993); Maurice Valency, *In Praise of Love: An Introduction to the Love Poetry of the Renaissance* (New York: Macmillan, 1958); and Ernest H. Wilkins, "The Invention of the Sonnet," *Modern Philology* 13 (1915–1916): 79–112.

es in strophic form with variable rhyme schemes), the *canciones* (poems in strophic form similar to the *silva*), *seguidillas* (a seven-line verse form with lines of seven and five syllables), and *octavas* (an eight-line stanza) also written in the period and practiced by the women in this study.

A scrutiny of verse by women in the period shows a preponderance of poems addressing various aspects of personal involvement in the fields of love and friendship, even allowing for love always being an important subject matter for poetry. Lerner observes that women poets are quite explicit in their self-identification, that they speak out of their own lives (*Consciousness* 168). In *The Creation of Patriarchy* she observes that creative women have struggled against a "distorting reality" where their literary works are buried under a literary canon based on the Bible, the Greek classics, and Milton. She notes that recent feminist literary criticism has introduced a way of reading women's works that shows powerful but hidden and slanted worldviews, expressed through a language of metaphor and symbol that is often subversive of the male tradition (225). The opportunities for veiled language and conceits provided by the sonnet form enable women to launch subtle criticism at the prevailing patriarchy without overtly upsetting the order of their personal lives or that of their families, who would suffer humiliation were they to achieve notoriety through their writings. This concern is relevant given the importance of class in Spanish society and the fact that these poets are all from the upper classes.

While the historical emphasis on assumed inequalities of gender restricted women to a single category, the fact that only women of the highest classes had the education and the leisure time to write poetry can restrict still further our access to the cultural production of seventeenth-century women. Women of the lower classes led very different lives from the women whose works are examined here; consequently, they have left fewer accessible traces in the record. Nevertheless, even here, recent scholarship has uncovered a wealth of information about nonwriting women, or women who wrote to defend themselves rather than writing conscious works of art.[15] Women in the dominant classes had conferrable assets of

15. See Elizabeth Lehfeldt, *Religious Women in Golden Age Spain: The Permeable Cloister* (Aldershot: Ashgate, 2005); Mary Elizabeth Perry, *Gender and Disorder in Early Modern Seville* (Princeton: Princeton University Press, 1990); Mary Elizabeth Perry, *The Handless Maiden: Moriscos and the Politics of Religion in Early Modern Spain* (Princeton and

status and wealth, privileges that further established the class structure and the status of the men who controlled it. As will be seen in the course of my analysis, these poets have much to gain from the very system that attempts to oppress and restrict them. At the same time, in winning prizes at national *certámenes* (poetry competitions), literate women make a statement about female equality and enjoy a degree of "chaste" fame. For example, a poet who is not included in this study, Cristobalina Fernández de Alarcón, achieved considerable fame and is mentioned in Lope de Vega's *Laurel de Apolo* (The Laurels of Apollo). She was particularly successful in national *certámenes,* with one of her sonnets securing sixth place in a poetry festival held in Seville in 1623 in which Juan de Jáuregui finished eleventh.[16]

Where literary purists may argue that nothing can be found in poetry except pure invention (and bearing Lerner's words in mind), I make no apology for using the literary works of these seventeenth-century female poets as conduits to a greater understanding of what opportunities may have been available to writing women. Since we are all conditioned by the circumstances into which we are born and raised, I contend that it is never possible entirely to divorce experience from literary production. Since women had to write within a masculine mode and within a society dominated by masculine ideas, anything written and kept by women has validity in helping to determine their sociohistorical context that may well not be the case for male-authored works.

Early modern society drew its inspiration and its code of living from the Church Fathers, from the teachings of the contemporary Church, and from pagan philosophers, as well as from its own political leaders. Utilizing all these as a basis for prevailing attitudes, I am able to offer in my close readings strategies for reaching out to these extraordinary women across the centuries to understand something of how they lived and thought and

---

Oxford: Princeton University Press, 2005); Allyson M. Poska, *Women and Authority in Early Modern Spain: The Peasants of Galicia* (Oxford: Oxford University Press, 2005); and Lisa Vollendorf, *The Lives of Women: A New History of Inquisitional Spain* (Nashville: Vanderbilt University Press, 2005).

16. See Julián Olivares and Elizabeth Sievert Boyce, *Tras el espejo la musa escribe: lírica femenina de los Siglos de Oro,* 1st ed. (Madrid: Siglo Veintiuno, 1993), 447. The Sobrino Morillas sisters also enjoyed considerable success in these competitions. For further detail on their writings, see Arenal and Schlau, *Untold Sisters,* 131–89.

the ideas against which they contended. While sincerity may not be expected in poetic works, there is no doubt that many of the sonnets presented in this book come directly from experience or are directed toward specific friends and family members. Hence, these women write both personal and abstract poetry; they utilize an existing system and fashion it to their own ends. For example, when Leonor de la Cueva writes a sonnet praising her brother's military exploits, it serves more than one function, being abstract in that it pertains to a certain form of sonnet writing, but also personal in that the brother is a living being who is related to her. At the same time her sonnet promotes the status of her family, always an important consideration in seventeenth-century Spanish upper-class society.

There are a number of examples in these women's works, especially those by Sor Violante del Cielo, where the sonnet is employed in praise of other women with whom the poet has enjoyed a lengthy personal relationship. In the case of Sor Violante this is not a matter of supposition, since there has been some historical exploration of her life and work. Ramírez's poetry to her family is entirely personal. Given that sonnets in the early modern period are the preeminent poetic form (even though in earlier times Dante may have regarded them as somewhat inferior to the *canzone* [song]), when women show themselves capable of writing intelligent, well-formed, and witty sonnets they are doing more than merely writing poetry; they are inscribing themselves into their society in a way that is not considered possible or desirable for women, lest the effort strain their supposedly limited intellects.

Spain was both politically immensely powerful and also fervently Catholic; the precepts of Catholicism permeated every aspect of life both at home and in the growing colonies, and they were zealously guarded by the Inquisition. Analysis of divine verse therefore appears throughout the book, in the chapters dealing with patronage and friendship poetry, as well as that of the family. The Virgin Mary, as author of the Magnificat, could give comfort to religious women instructed to write by confessors and terrified of inadvertently exposing ideas and feelings that might be construed by the Inquisition as heretical. Clearly, the Virgin Mary played a prominent role as an example to women in their thought and writing. However, the highly erotic, mystical poetry of Luisa de Carvajal y Mendoza is unusual among seventeenth-century female poets' divine verse and is therefore treated separately in Chapter 6. None of the other poets writes mystical sonnets; their religious fervor is that of their contemporaries, lacking the fiercely militant qualities of Carvajal y Mendoza's vocation.

Carvajal y Mendoza's radical and independent life could only be sanctioned on the grounds of her professed vocation from God. As studies of Renaissance and early modern women's history and literature in the last twenty years have indicated, women actively worked against the social restrictions within which they lived and this struggle can be seen in the works of literate women of the period. Studies cite such notable figures as Teresa de Ávila, María de Zayas, Ana Caro, and Sor Juana Inés de la Cruz in the Hispanic world; Aemilia Lanyer and Katherine Philips in England; Louise Labé in France; and Gaspara Stampa and Moderata Fonte in Italy. They show the tragedy of female oppression but also celebrate the triumphs of those who rose above the system and who must have been writing on behalf of a much wider and like-minded group. In general, however, learned women were single, often cloistered, or widowed. Lerner notes a general pattern of intellectual precociousness, encouraged early but discouraged later in life. Those forced into wedlock could not continue their intellectual life after their marriage (Consciousness 30).

The majority of women are absent from the record altogether since most of them were not permitted education or the possibility of participating in the public sphere. While all this is well proven, however, it is not the full story. These works have survived, in spite of a general view of women's intellectual efforts as inferior. A tendency of those in power to observe of writing women that they were *varonil* (manly) ensured that they were seen as exceeding their sex; they could thus be admired for their masculine qualities while making no difference to the prevailing views of feminine inferiority.[17] Nevertheless, as will be seen in the following chapters, the sonnets of these women demonstrate a particu-

---

17. Two studies dealing with women who go beyond what were considered the limits of their sex are Patricia H. Labalme, *Beyond Their Sex: Learned Women of the European Past* (New York: New York University Press, 1980), and Melveena McKendrick, *Woman and Society in the Spanish Drama of the Golden Age: A Study of the Mujer Varonil* (London and New York: Cambridge University Press, 1974).

larly feminine strength and independence. They do not hesitate to burlesque male pretensions and to criticize them. These criticisms tend to be at the personal level rather than being aimed at the governing systems that determined their lives. They certainly support women as intelligent and rational beings, but their works are not radical statements of independence—indeed the poetry frequently suggests that they found life both enjoyable and fulfilling. I therefore tend to support Constance Jordan's "safer and less controversial" terminology, to describe their writing as "pro-woman" (2). As women of the upper classes they could have expected a considerably better quality of life than that of their poorer sisters. However, it is notable that, given the prevalent notions of women's fatally flawed humors, all of these women show their poetic heroines as having a powerful capacity for reason.

Chapter 1 focuses on the poetry of patronage, and particularly on the works of Sor Violante del Cielo and Leonor de la Cueva y Silva. Patronage was of singular importance in securing advantageous positions at court or in provincial government. Sor Violante employs the language of the love sonnet, in the manner of male courtiers, as a means of courting and flattering those higher up the chain of patronage. She does not restrict her flattery to her male superiors, for women too had opportunities to dispense patronage among a female coterie. Sor Violante's closeness to the royal family is evident in her sonnets celebrating royal events, while Cueva's works celebrate the honor accruing to her family through their successful patronage operations.

Chapter 2 will examine the roles of parents in early modern Spain as seen by these women. The family was of great importance as the only means of financial and physical support available in times made uncertain by economic and subsistence crises, and by regular outbreaks of plague. In addition, the domestic and the maternal were the only realms in which women were permitted to operate with a modicum of freedom, though such liberty did not extend to control of the purse or even access to the doors and windows of the home. Carmen Martín Gaite has observed that it was always assumed that women approached the window for erotic purposes; "no se le ocurría a nadie pensar que tal vez no fuera su cuerpo, sino su alma la que tuviera sed de ventana" (36; it never occurred to anybody to think that perhaps it was not her body but her soul that thirsted to see out of the window). Similarly, in her spiritual auto-biography Carvajal y Mendoza notes: "Imitaba mucho a mi madre en aborrecer liviandades y poco recato de puertas y ventanas" (Rhodes "Bi-ography" 42; I was just like my mother in hating fripperies and with little desire to go near doors and windows).

The value placed on family status can be seen in the passionate inter-est of contemporary society in the nature of their bloodlines. This chap-ter draws principally on the works of Sor Violante del Cielo. It does, however, incorporate one work by Ramírez, the only poem by any of these women that celebrates a wedding, a celebration that is decidedly lukewarm. My readings of Sor Violante's sonnets will show that while she seeks to cement Counter-Reformation views on the importance of the father as head of the family unit, she also celebrates a particularly hu-man Virgin Mary, who is both simple mother and champion of women.

Chapter 3 involves poetry that explores the attitudes of children to their parents and siblings. Here I focus on the works of Ramírez, and al-though many of her poems are not sonnets, the fresh information they bring to our perceptions of relationships between family members merits the inclusion of some of them here. Ramírez mocks and cajoles, praises and expresses love for all members of her family with equal facility. There is no sense in her works of a woman cowed by the authoritarian father figure, but much evidence of a daughter who knew how effective per-suasive language could be in attaining her own ends. They promote an alternate view to the traditional picture of relationships between fathers and daughters. In addition, sonnets by Sor Violante about the nature of Christ's relationship with his mother promote the entirely human and caring tenderness that can exist between son and mother, irrespective of their status in the hierarchies of Church and state.

The importance of family relationships to the individual was close-ly seconded by alliances of friendship. The sonnets that celebrate female solidarity and friendship form my discussion in Chapter 4. Whether or not women were as incarcerated in the home as moralists and preach-ers would have liked, the fact remains that men were freer to act as they chose, albeit within class norms; were better educated; and had legal con-trol over the assets of their womenfolk. They were also, at the upper lev-els of society, away from home on business, at court, in the colonies of the New World, or in the armies in the Low Countries.[18] Companionship among women in the domestic sphere was important to personal well-being, as well as to community and moral support, especially during the absence of fathers, husbands, and brothers. Friendship also served a purpose in securing a place in the social scale, in a class-based society dependent, to a large extent, on patronage.

The convents, as well as being sites of patronage, were often the centers of social entertainment both among the nuns and between nuns and visitors from outside. The degree of vocation and strictness of rule varied between convents but, regardless of rule, the exchange of letters, the performance of plays, and readings of poetry strengthened the social bond and provided respite from an arduous daily routine. In the parlors of the more relaxed orders, as Defourneaux points out, there were numerous visitors of both sexes. There were also amateur dramatics and poetico-theological "jousts" modeled on the literary tournaments popular across Spain (110). This competitive, poetic activity is clearly to be seen in Marcia Belisarda's work where many of her sonnets begin with the title "Dándome el asunto . . ." (Giving me the topic . . .), indicating the intellectual poetic play indulged in by nuns in their periods of leisure. These habits of writing and participating may also have altered the way in which women thought about their compositions. As Electa Arenal and Stacey Schlau have argued, works written by nuns reclaim the vernacular and hence the language of birthplace and family, that is, the language of women (2). Furthermore, religious women's writing involves a personal and conversational tone where the Virgin Mary, as author of the Magnificat, is both poet and divine mother-in-law (Arenal and Schlau 15–16). The value of friendship to women is reflected in the fact that all five poets write sonnets about its nature and compose works to or about their friends.

Attempts by these poets to enter the debate about women via their own love sonnets will form the basis of Chapter 5. They take a fascinating approach to writing of love. In male-authored love sonnets women are portrayed as silent objects of desire and as signifiers of divine perfection. This is in line with the Petrarchan mode, where praise of the lady

18. As will be seen in Chapter 3, Cueva and Ramírez write sonnets to male family members away on military service.

and enumeration of her beauties are its principal subject matter. While the blazon did not begin with Petrarch, having its origins in classical antiquity, the Petrarchan beauty rapidly became a codified figure of golden hair, ebony brows, ivory hands, and a snowy bosom. It is a system that readily lends itself to parody and contra-blazon, as is apparent in the love sonnets in this chapter. Aside from parody, nowhere do these women indulge in the blazon for the objects of their love poetry. Furthermore, although poets are still influenced by Petrarchism in the seventeenth century, the *desengaño* (disenchantment) of the Baroque colors the poetic subject matter.

The chapter first discusses women in relation to Petrarchism, both in terms of their objectification under this system and their own appropriation of the Petrarchan mode. The female poets featured show their capacity to write in this masculine manner, while subverting and ridiculing its pretensions, sometimes utilizing a male speaking voice to hold up to scrutiny current notions of masculine honor. Through the problematic process of writing both as subject and object of love poetry, they also write poetry where the love experience becomes an educative process, leading to disillusionment and the discarding of the male lover. Finally, four sonnets in Cueva's play *La firmeza en la ausencia* critique masculine power and its abuse at the highest levels of society. Furthermore, the sonnet vows, which are addressed to each other by the two couples at the center of the action, demonstrate Cueva's determination that genuine love and respect supersede the requirements and expectations of gender and class.

The sixth and final chapter is reserved for Luisa de Carvajal y Mendoza's erotic poetry, addressed to her *amado* (beloved), Christ, and by association, the Host. Carvajal y Mendoza's mysticism is unique among these poets. In her verse she draws heavily on the Song of Songs, as well as on St. John of the Cross and St. Teresa of Ávila, whose works she is known to have owned. Her sonnets are discussed against a background of the Counter-Reformation religious fervor that gripped Spain at the end of the sixteenth century and the beginning of the seventeenth, and the mysticism that was particularly prevalent in Spain in this period. I also draw on the medieval antecedents to Spain's early modern mysticism in my analysis of her works.

All six chapters therefore focus on different aspects of love and friend-ship, viewed from the secular and the sacred, the higher and the lower classes. Most important, however, is that these aspects are the views of contemporary women. I read these women's sonnets as cultural expres-sions of their own sociohistorical context that include the attitudes of the female "other" and show that there was more to the Baroque period than *desengaño,* however prevalent that state of mind may have been in soci-ety. In the course of my analysis I propose that literature and art cannot simply be separated from other kinds of social practice, notwithstanding the fictive nature of poetic production in the early modern period. While the speaking subject of early modern poetry does not necessarily repre-sent either the poet or an appeal to a post-Romantic sincerity, neverthe-less the activities that surround the artist clearly exert an influence on the words they produce.

I contend that the intellectual and social influences that impinged upon the lives of these five women can be discerned in their literary pro-duction and can shed light on their activities and their intentions. In seventeenth-century Spain there was a powerful requirement for order that flowed from both Church and state. As privileged members of the elite and educated class, the women in this study were able to find a means to express their creativity, within the confines of their contempo-rary society, that suited their intellectual and artistic capacities.

CHAPTER I

POLITICS, PATRONAGE, PARENTAGE

AN IMPORTANT PART of the funtioning of upper-class society in early modern Spain was the acquisition of suitable patronage. Class was fundamental to the client's chances of success in the patronage systems that obtained in the greater and lesser courts of the Iberian nobility. The stratification of class was complex, including strands of nobility as well as an upwardly mobile merchant class. For example, in her study of the role of honor and class in the works of María de Zayas, Nieves Romero Díaz identifies in Zayas's *La burlada Aminta* the blending of the *antigua nobleza* (old nobility) with the urban nobility of Segovia. Romero Díaz observes that when Aminta seeks to avenge an offense against her personal honor she is doing far more than avenging herself, since the offense, in ideological terms, has been committed against an entire class, "la nobleza tradicional, que se quería preservar de la amenaza de otros grupos sociales que con el 'negocio' y apoyados en el dinero atentan con desmitificar una pureza ideal nobiliaria" (120; the traditional nobility, which sought to preserve itself from the menace of other social groups who, through commerce and supported by their money, attempt to demystify a pure, nobiliary ideal). Class and family status were intertwined; family name, renown, and proof of *limpieza de sangre* (blood purity) were of the utmost importance in acquiring the appropriate introductions that could set the patronage process moving. Allied to that were the subtle methods of making oneself visible in what was a highly competitive atmosphere.

In this chapter I examine sonnets written specifically to further personal and family status. These are principally the poems of Sor Violante del Cielo, who was unusually close to the sources of power in Portugal, in spite of her monastic status, and the works of Leonor de la Cueva y Silva that promote her family, written from a provincial center. Although they approach their compositions from different viewpoints, they seek to achieve a similar result: an increase in status, rewards, and political protection for the client. In writing to flatter a highly placed patron, to incorporate themselves into the courtly milieu, or to advance the cause of the family as a whole, they engage with a specifically masculine discourse, to which, in most instances, they accommodate their own writing.

A formal definition of the patron-client relationship in early modern Europe describes it as a set of social practices that conditioned all areas of nobiliary and ecclesiastical existence (Baker 106). The system was frequently the butt of criticism from humanists such as Thomas More, whose *Utopia* proposed the abolition of the property relations upon which patronage rested. Within the prevailing model of governance, framed on the hierarchical ideal, where government of the state and the family alike were supposed to mirror the government of heaven, the patronage system operated in a revolving system of debt and favor, carried up the social scale on a tide of flattery. The importance of political patronage that obtained in all the Western European courts is exemplified in the following description:

[P]ower and prestige must always be expressed through a large and impressive entourage . . . met partly by periodic attendance of peers and leading gentry at court. . . . Kings also appointed provincial magnates to ceremonial posts within their households, . . . such appointments served as an important form of patronage, helping to cement allegiance to the crown. More was always involved, however, than a simple exchange of material rewards for political service. Gentlemen coveted court positions not only for the salaries they carried, but for the honor that membership in the king's household conferred. Conversely a crowded court manifested the king's own honor. (Smuts 88)

The value placed upon honor is clearly to be seen in the poetry of Leonor de la Cueva y Silva, who proclaims the aura of *hombría* (overt masculinity) that clings to her male relatives and, through this, the honor that accrues to herself and her family.

Providing a wider definition of the nature of the patronage that structured early modern society, Linda Levy Peck describes a symbiotic and symbolic relationship: private, dependent, and deferential alliances intended both to reward the client and to provide proof of the power and standing of the patron. Patron-client relationships were established through mutual friends, kinship ties, and local bonds, and transactions were often brokered through courtiers and important officials. Patronage employed a specific language, based on a theory of mutual benefits and gift giving, that determined political and social behavior (3).[1] In this respect, Sor Violante del Cielo's patronage sonnets exploit bonds of friendship, giving in return graceful flattery that magnifies the worth and splendor of the subjects. Women both benefited from and were objectified by patronage, which oiled the wheels of state and kept legions of courtiers in a constant state of fawning anxiety. Young women were pawns in the bartering system that saw marriages arranged according to the social benefit accruing to the brides' and grooms' families. As Romero Díaz has pointed out, Zayas critiques the commodification of women in *La burlada Aminta,* where Aminta becomes the focus of conquest for her wealth and nobility, converting the business of commerce into a social enterprise (119). Nevertheless, women submitted to the system. Although they often had little or no choice in the matter, they too enjoyed the social advancement afforded by a suitable marriage or by family connections that enabled them to assert their place above those of their female contemporaries.

At the highest levels, royal marriages were based entirely on dynastic lines, designed to foster the interests of a royal house through marriage and the provision of sons and heirs. Empress María of Austria, for example, was the daughter of Charles V, the daughter-in-law of Ferdinand I, and the wife of her cousin Maximilian II. When she retired to the convent of the Descalzas Reales (Royal Discalced Order) in Madrid, she retained a considerable court, as well as her political interests, confer-

1. Pablo Jauralde Pou details the high levels of corruption at the court of Philip III, which prompted Francisco de Quevedo both to partake of rewards through his association with the Duke of Osuna and other notables and later to criticize the system through his political writings. See Pablo Jauralde Pou, *Francisco de Quevedo (1580–1645),* 2nd ed. (Madrid: Castalia, 1999), 362–83.

ring regularly with both Philip II and Philip III. She provided support
to Margaret of Austria, her niece and the latter's wife, and her perceived
interference was not appreciated by Philip III's favorite, the Duke of Lerma (Sánchez 68, 92). Magdalena Sánchez notes that the empress pursued
personal and familial agendas during her time in Madrid, considering it
her duty to petition for pensions and other types of financial assistance
on behalf of her attendants (94). The system functioned as long as everybody had something to gain from it; each participant knew how to play
his or her part, as the empress's sense of duty reveals. Similarly, Helen
Nader, writing of the powerful women of the Mendoza family, has argued that at the highest levels of society a matriarchy existed alongside
the patriarchal norm where it filled a need. Furthermore, Nader argues
that noblewomen engaged in maintaining and increasing the influence
of various families both locally and nationally (1–25).[2]

For upper-class female religious, profession in a royal convent ensured
continued access to the powerful elites with whom they identified. When
Sor Violante del Cielo withdrew into the convent attached to the Royal Palace in Lisbon in 1630, she remained within the social milieu into
which she had been born, as can be seen in her many poetic compliments
to court notables and the royal family. This flow of praise, in gongoristic
style, ensured that she remained connected firmly to those who held control over Church and state. As such, she was of great benefit to the social
and financial security of her convent. Sor Violante's close connection with
both Church and state hierarchies is made clear in the *Parnaso lusitano*
in a number of sonnets. For example, she dedicates two sonnets to Padre
Mestre Fr. João de Vasconcellos, provincial de Sao Domingos. She marks
the death of General Andrè de Albuquerque at the Battle of Elvas in 1659,
where the Portuguese defeated the Spanish; she congratulates Don Pedro,
regent of Portugal, for his decision to elevate Don Pedro de Lencastre,
duke of Aveiro, to be inquisitor general and cardinal of Portugal in 1672;
and she praises the Duke of Aveiro for his exceptional nature. By using
verse she is able to participate in the important matters of Church and
state in a socially acceptable manner, and by writing in the sonnet form,

2. Nader's collection provides a number of examples of female patronage in the
founding of convents, of the arts and of charities. See *Power and Gender in Renaissance
Spain* (Urbana and Chicago: University of Chicago Press, 2004).

a higher form of poetry, she shows her exceptional poetic skills and enters the realm of the courtier who writes sycophantic sonnets to his lord.

The founding of convents also provided opportunities for female patronage, especially after the Council of Trent, when there was a strong movement toward scrupulous observance of female claustration, codification of religious rites, and greater control of the activities of *beaterio* (religious houses of laywomen).[3] In a study of the convents of Valladolid, Elizabeth Lehfeldt notes that one of the benefits of patronage was the right of the patron to name women who could enter the convent without providing a dowry. Pious charity could thus allow marginalized or impoverished women to avoid a questionable existence outside. However, since the provision of dowries allowed the donors to exercise their personal preferences in the choice of recipients, it also demonstrates the almost ritualistic observance of patronage that existed among the nobility and at court (*Cloister* 15–46). Maureen Flynn goes further in regarding the provision of dowries by wealthy patrons as "the patronage system of old regime society most grievously manipulating with private prejudices the fate of the poor" (59).

Redemption could also be sought through endowing chapels in the convent church, further supporting female monasticism. When patrons sought to be buried in these chapels, as did, for example, Doña Luisa de Zarraga and Doña Ana Paredes Aldrete in Valladolid, they provided substantial sums for masses, chaplains' salaries, and adornments for the chapels (Lehfeldt "Discipline" 1023–24). Similarly, in provincial Llerena, the four daughters of Antonio Núñez Ramírez, grandfather of Catalina Clara Ramírez de Guzmán, all entered convents in the town. When he died in 1619, he left instructions to his wife to found a family chapel in the Iglesia Mayor de Nuestra Señora Santa María de la Granada (The Greater Church of Our Lady St. Mary of the Pomegranate), in Llerena (Carrasco García 101).[4]

---

3. See Elizabeth A. Lehfeldt, *Religious Women in Golden Age Spain: The Permeable Cloister* (Aldershot: Ashgate, 2005), 175–215, for a detailed discussion of the effects of rigid claustration after Trent and the Spanish state's rapid adoption of its precepts.

4. Antonio's widow carried out his instructions, for the will of their last surviving grandchild, Antonia Manuela, commands that she be buried "en el entierro y tumba de los Sres. Maestres de la Orden de Santiago que está dentro de la Capilla Mr. de la Yglesia Mor. de Nra. Sra. Sta Maria de la Granada de esta ciud. que es de mi casa y donde estan

Family considerations extended beyond the founding of chapels. The importance of kinship networks in securing patronage, particularly political patronage, should not be underestimated. When Leonor de la Cueva y Silva wrote sonnets that praised her famous uncle and the feats of her brother in the royal armies, she also recorded her own blood association, linking it with their prestige, as is evident in her verse. Social status and kinship served Violante del Cielo well in providing her with a comfortable and secure convent life, while for Luisa de Carvajal y Mendoza exalted family connections proved to be vitally important to her London mission. The aura that clung to her lineage is revealed in that family trees are still included in recent biographies (Pinillos Iglesias n. pag.; Rees, Appendix 1). Pinillos Iglesias includes information detailing noble and religious titles, showing the importance for a seventeenth-century noble family of their claim to honorable fame. Meritorious service appropriate to, and demanded of, their social status could not only secure advantageous marriages, but also royal favor. Bartolomé Bennassar confirms that the role of the aristocrat was more than mere parasitism at court. He describes an *aristocracia de servicio* (aristocracy of service), a service that often cost dearly in financial terms, in exchange for titles and fame (Historia 378ff.).

Luisa de Carvajal y Mendoza's English mission could not have survived without the assistance she received from her kin and friendship networks, for in Protestant London she was in no position to beg alms from a Catholic community under pressure. This assistance was not merely familial and financial, for the high status of her contacts silenced the criticism at home occasioned by her secret journey to London. Even before her departure, Carvajal y Mendoza's letter to her friend, Inés de la Asunción, from Valladolid, in January 1605, suggests that she was already meeting resistance: "Yo me he resuelto en ir sin aguardar a nadie, que es nunca acabar, y sin coche por la misma causa" (Abad *Epistolario* 145; I have resolved to go without warning anybody, which becomes a never ending story, and not with a coach, for the same reason).

By far Carvajal y Mendoza's most powerful ally was the Marqués de

---

enterrados mis ascendientes" (in the tomb of the Masters of the Order of Santiago within the main chapel of the Greater Church of Our Lady St. Mary of the Pomegranate, of this city, that belongs to my household and where my ancestors are buried); see Gazul, "Familia Ramírez," 541.

Siete Iglesias, Rodrigo de Calderón, husband of her cousin and at that time favorite of the Duke of Lerma. Through this relationship Carvajal y Mendoza was able to secure royal support for her enterprise, to the extent that Philip III ordered that she be provided with a monthly stipend of 300 *reales*.[5] Carvajal y Mendoza wrote to Calderón in August 1611, acknowledging the gesture: "Suplico a vuestra merced se acuerde de sinificar al rey nuestro señor mi gran reconocimiento a la merced que ha hecho a nuestra pobre casita, con la cédula de los 300 reales, que vuestra merced aumentó con real ánimo también" (Epistolario 326; I beg Your Grace to convey to the king, our lord, my great gratitude for the honor that he has done to our poor house, in the granting of the 300 *reales* that Your Grace has also augmented with great willingness).[6]

The sonnets that will be discussed in this chapter reveal these women's ability to work within and to secure benefits from a patronage system more political than literary. They were not seeking to become professional writers in the style of Ana Caro, María de Zayas, or, outside Spain, the French Louise Labé and the English Aphra Behn; such a position would have demeaned their status; rather, they demonstrate their familiarity and facility with the system that ensured their social and economic preeminence. For the purposes of this discussion, the sonnets are divided into four principal sections. In the first, the patron lover, the sonnets of Sor Violante del Cielo in particular appropriate the language of codified seduction to attract the attention of the ladies of the court. The second section explores the encomiastic sonnets of political patronage. These works do not lie within the genre of love poetry, but are written specifically to praise those who themselves functioned within the system, and whose deaths are marked by Sor Violante's verse: these include Bernarda Ferreira de la Cerda, herself a renowned poet, and María de Ataide, a

5. The king's pension of 300 *reales* per month was later increased to 500 *reales*. Among other kin who assisted her mission were D. Juan de Mendoza, one-time ambassador to London; Carvajal y Mendoza's uncle, the cardinal archbishop of Toledo, Bernardo Sandoval y Rojas; her cousins, the Marquess and Marchioness de Caracena, viceroys of Valencia, and Doña Beatriz Ramírez de Mendoza. See Abad, *Misionera*, 241–43. Elizabeth Rhodes notes that bureaucratic incompetence meant that no pension reached her until three months before her death; see Carvajal y Mendoza, *Tight Embrace*, 20.

6. Carvajal y Mendoza did not live to see Calderón's fall from grace after the death of Felipe III, which culminated in his execution in 1622.

lady of the Portuguese court. This leads to a third section, which discusses sonnets directed to the ultimate founts of patronage, the king and, later, the regent of Portugal, by Sor Violante del Cielo, and a poem to the
cardinal-prince of Spain, by Leonor de la Cueva y Silva. Finally, Cueva
provides several examples illustrative of her pride in the honor accruing
to her family through the feats of her soldier brother, Antonio, and her
statesman uncle, Francisco, thus demonstrating the importance to the
family of a successful patronage enterprise

WOOING THE PATRON

Love sonnets to one's patron were common currency among court society across Western Europe. Male courtiers appropriated the language
of Petrarchan courtly love to woo favor in verse that kept the composer's
name in front of a would-be patron.[7] Writing in a typically masculine field
of endeavor, these sonnet writers pursued both political patronage and literary fame. Sor Violante del Cielo, an accomplished poet and intellectual,
had much to gain in drawing herself to the attention of highborn ladies
who had access to the throne. Several of her sonnets to female friends may
be seen as more than just conventional rhetoric, since such women enjoyed a degree of reflected power through their husbands. Indeed, it was
probably through the influence of one such friend, Inés de Noronha, that
Sor Violante's *Rimas varias* were published in 1646 in France, where the
Count de Vidigueira, Inés's husband, was Portuguese ambassador.

Ann Rosalind Jones has observed that the female poet resorts to three
postures in relation to masculine amorous writings: she either accepts
the discourse, accommodates her own discourse to that of the male writer, or subverts the masculine. Jones regards feminine discourse not as

---

7. In England, for example, Ben Jonson and John Donne strove with varying degrees
of success to assert themselves. Donne used literature as a means to secure the social prestige and preferment that successful exploitation of the patronage system provided. He did
not consider himself a professional man of letters. See Arthur Marotti, "John Donne and
the Rewards of Patronage," in *Patronage in the Renaissance,* ed. Guy Fitch Lytle and Stephen Orgel (Princeton: Princeton University Press, 1981), 208. On Jonson, see Robert C.
Evans, *Ben Jonson and the Poetics of Patronage* (Lewisburg and London: Bucknell University Press, 1989). Such behavior was a commonplace among ambitious suitors in the patronage system, as much in Italy, France, and Spain as in England.

a battle for supremacy but as a process in which the female attempts a negotiation and accommodation of her texts within the male rhetorical and symbolic discourse (Currency 3–9). Sor Violante del Cielo's poetry, at least that poetry dedicated to specific members of the court, accommodates itself unapologetically within the prevailing masculine mode familiar to her. This was of social benefit to her and no doubt of financial benefit to her convent, as well as showing off her poetic skills and her superior education. While overt subversion of the masculine would not serve Sor Violante's purpose in these sonnets aimed at self-promotion, her feminine speaker subtly undermines masculine humoral theories and the assumptions of biological determinism.

Two sonnets by Sor Violante not only demonstrate her verbal skill but also her means of remaining visible and relevant to her powerful patrons. One of these poems was clearly intended to be read at two levels, both entertaining the recipient and inspiring admiration for the poet's wit. Sor Violante's love sonnet "Yo tomaré la pluma" (I shall take up the pen) is the opening poem in the *Rimas varias*. It is addressed to "Elisa," possibly the same person who figures in Sor Violante's sonnet "Belisa el amistad es un tesoro" (Belisa, friendship is a treasure), namely, Isabel de Castro:

> Yo tomaré la pluma, y de tus glorias
> coronista seré, dichosa Elisa,
> porque quien tus memorias eterniza
> la tenga de mi amor en tus memorias.
>
> 5 Dulces serán por ti, por mí notorias
> las ansias que Silvano inmortaliza,
> si tus mismas victorias solemniza
> quien debe su dolor a tus victorias.
>
> Yo cantaré, señora, lo que lloro
> 10 pues ordena el amor, quiere la suerte
> que sea, al fin, mi pluma, mi homicida.
>
> ¡Ay decreto cruel del bien que adoro,
> que poseyendo tú, me des la muerte,
> y que escribiendo yo, te de la vida!
>
> (*Rimas varias* 1)

> I shall take up the pen, to be the one
> who crowns your glories, gracious Elisa,
> for she who eternalizes your memories
> shall keep my love in your thoughts.
>
> Sweet for you, but notorious for me,
> the anxieties that Silvano immortalizes,
> if the one who your very victories solemnizes,
> is she whose misery is due to your victories.
>
> I shall sing, lady, that which I weep, since
> Love orders it; he desires that fate should
> decree my pen, finally, to be my homicide.
>
> Oh cruel decree of the beloved whom I adore,
> that you, in possessing, give me death,
> and that I, in writing, give you life!

Like Petrarch, and the legions of poets and courtiers who followed him, Sor Violante seeks to immortalize the beloved through her verse and at the same time to elevate herself as a poet. The specific intention of this apparent determination to praise Elisa is to mark herself as a writer of poetry that will outlive time. She achieves this aim in the opening lines. Elisa becomes the tool that serves her purpose, but benefits through her own chaste fame, enshrined in verse on the page. Elisa and the poet/speaker are closely allied to each other through the sonnet, although always in opposition. One rises as the other falls, one's pleasure is the other's pain, as Sor Violante adopts the pose of the suffering Petrarchan lover, casting the beautiful and elusive Elisa as its cause. Sor Violante also introduces a personal tone when she alludes to the anxieties immortalized by "Silvano": "Dulces serán por ti, por mí notorias / las ansias que Silvano inmortaliza" (5–6). "Silvano" was the name given to Paulo Gonçalves de Andrade in the poetic exchanges between him and Sor Violante. If "Silvano" indeed immortalizes the sufferings of love in verse, then in writing like "Silvano" Sor Violante reveals her willingness to engage in the prevailing masculine discourse. She therefore expresses her love for Elisa as a victory for her subject, but an agony for the speaker, "quien debe su dolor a tus victorias" (8).

Paradoxically, it is in writing within this discourse that Sor Violante shows her originality. She does not attempt to subvert the traditional message of courtly love poetry. Rather, she accommodates her own writing to it. Although she does not shrink from revealing that this love sonnet is penned from one woman to another, Sor Violante must write as a man, since in the Neoplatonic schema that she employs it is impossible for a woman, traditionally the beautiful object that inspires the love sonnet, to pen such a sonnet herself.

The very nature of Neoplatonic thought requires intellectual elevation and superiority, but under humoral theory this is physiologically impossible for a woman, due to her cold, moist humors. As Ian Maclean describes it, the Neoplatonic lover loves not only the woman, but also God and himself as well: "The perfection of love is in reciprocity; but its origin lies in beauty, which women possess in greater store than men." This is the single opportunity provided in Neoplatonic love for a woman to rise above her supposed incompleteness, since her external beauty represents a beautiful soul, and this greater beauty indicates that she is endowed with spiritual gifts above those of men (24). When Sor Violante openly displays the speaking subject as a woman, then, she subtly alters the Neoplatonic and courtly masculine tradition within which she is writing. She frankly challenges humoral theory, yet appears to obey the rules of poetic decorum, as she extols the beauty of the beloved and proclaims her speaker to be painfully possessed by love.

The greater paradox is reserved for the tercets. Rather than the beloved's beauty being her homicide, the speaker claims that the proclamation of love makes a sword of her pen and will procure her death: "[P]ues ordena el amor, quiere la suerte / que sea, al fin, mi pluma, mi homicida" (10–11). In composing this lyric of seduction Sor Violante rehearses the lot of the client of patronage. Freely expressing love of the patron is essential to earning the patron's goodwill, but freedom to act and think in this system is reserved to the person at the top of the chain. In writing love poetry to a patron, the poet seeks to live, both in the poetry and at the hand of the patron, but in order to do so, she or he must sacrifice self in that patron's interests. The poet both creates and dies in subsuming creativity to service, and even then this willing martyrdom might be wasted in the face of magnificent disdain and disparagement. It is for this reason that the pen that openly proclaims the client's love is potentially the weapon that will "kill" her in social and patronage terms.

By obeying love's decree, by falling on her sword and publishing her love for Elisa, life and death become one. However, they are also banished in the eternity of that love, now inscribed on the page: "que poseyendo tú, me des la muerte / y que escribiendo yo, te dé la vida" (14–15). The poet as maker gives birth to her own poetic version of Elisa and of herself, offered and now "possessed" by Elisa. As she proposes, the sonnet to Elisa will outlast both poet/subject and patron/object, giving both Elisa and the poet acceptable eternal fame. Sor Violante's open expression of female love for another woman, although constructed within rhetorical conventions of the period, led nineteenth-century scholars to entertain the possibility of lesbian relationships between Sor Violante and her women friends. For example, Costa e Silva writes of her work:

> [O]ra como me parece que uma amisade simples e pure nunca usou de semilhante linguagem, presumo, que sem escrupulo, poderei inferir desta, e d'outras poesías, que a moderna Sapho ardeo nas chammas daquelle amore inatural, de que foi accusada a antiga Sapho, e que tão frequente se desenvolve nas mulheres, e com especialidade nas Freiras. . . . [P]óde como tudo ser que me engane, nem pretendo que os Leitores adoptem a minha opinião como certa, mas que examinem, e decidam como entenderem. (Costa e Silva 68)[8]

> Since it seems to me that simple, pure friendships never used language like this, I presume that I need not scruple to infer from this and other poems that a modern Sappho burned in the flames of that unnatural love of which the ancient Sappho was accused, and that so frequently entangles women, especially nuns. . . . It could be that I am deluding myself, and I do not intend that other readers should take my views as certain; they should examine these works and decide how to interpret them.

While she may well have been a "modern Sappho" and her poetic desire homoerotic, it is worth noting that she addresses these works to women

---

8. Costa e Silva here refers to a poem not discussed in this study, the first verse of which reads: "Si vivo en ti transformada / Menandra, bien lo averiguas, Pues quando me tiras flechas / Hallas en ti las heridas" (If I am transformed in you, Menandra, well you know that when you fire arrows at me, you find you wound yourself). Closer attention has also been given to this particular poem, and the question of Sor Violante's suspect sexuality, by Julián Olivares and Elizabeth Sievert Boyce, in "Sor Violante del Cielo (y de la Tierra): The Subversion of Amorous Lyrical Discourse," in *A Ricardo Gullón: sus discípulos,* ed. Adelaida López de Martínez (Erie.: Aldeeu, 1995), 189–201.

in powerful positions outside the convent and not to her fellow nuns. The language Costa e Silva found so suspect needs to be read in the context of the period. Overflowing rhetoric and baroque excess were the norms, particularly in addressing those who could benefit the client in the well-established system by which favors were exchanged in a fluid market of flattery and aggrandizement. Sor Violante's baroque love/patronage sonnets show her awareness and utilization of the dynamics of such a system. Her friends were the court ladies and her convent was relaxed in its rule and close to the court.[9]

The sonnet to Elisa shows the clear distinction between the defiance of time in female-authored poetry and the carpe diem sonnets of Petrarch, Shakespeare, Quevedo, and many other poets and courtiers that were fashionable in the early modern period. These were intended to encourage the beloved to make the most of her fleeting beauty by bestowing herself on the lover before that beauty should fade. Like the other women in this study, Sor Violante does not write carpe diem poetry of the masculine type, but adapts the familiar process to her own use. Hence, there are no blazons in these women's poetry, with the single exception of Ramírez's self-portraits, which, in any event, subvert and mock the blazon mode. What is foregrounded in their poetry instead is the sum of all the excellent qualities of the patron/beloved taken together, and it is these that prompt the poetic attempt to defy time. The solidarity of shared experience among a sisterhood of upper-class women, in which everybody knew the role they were expected to play, ensured that pleas to patronage could be more subtly made.

Sor Violante's friendship with Inés de Noronha, countess de Vidigueira, was long-lasting and beneficial, and Sor Violante addresses more than one sonnet to her.[10] Sor Violante's sonnet to her absent friend, "Prendas de aquella diosa soberana" (Tokens of that sovereign goddess), is one

<hr>

9. See also Amanda Powell's fascinating forthcoming work on women's love poetry to women, which considers women's love lyrics from a number of angles, including the homoerotic possibilities inherent in such works. Her discussion includes an interesting reading of this sonnet. See "'Oh qué diversas estamos, / dulce prenda, vos y yo!': Multiple Voicings in Love Poems to Women by Marcia Belisarda, Catalina Clara Ramírez de Guzmán, and Sor Violante del Cielo," in Julian Olivares and Elizabeth Boyce, eds., *En desagravio de las damas: Women's Poetry of the Golden Age* (Asheville, NC: Pegasus, forthcoming).

10. Another sonnet is discussed in Chapter 4, "Feminine Friendship."

of the most gongoristic of her collection, resorting as it does to classical
themes and high-flown language:

> Prendas de aquella Diosa soberana
> que Sol abrasa, cuando estrella inclina,
> reliquias de una mano, que por digna
> divina da temor, y aliento humana.
>
> 5 Qué gusto, qué placer, qué gloria vana
> tuviera yo, si Nise la divina
> a las mismas acciones de benigna
> no vinculara indicios de tirana.
>
> Letras me niega ¡ay Dios! porque de avaros
> 10 no acuse solamente sus luceros
> sino también sus pensamientos raros.
>
> ¡Ay qué importa que en fe de castigaros
> la gloria me conceda de teneros,
> si vida no me da para lograros!
>
> (*Rimas varias* 6)

> Tokens of that sovereign goddess
> burned by the sun as her star rises,
> relics of a divinely human hand that
> offers both fear and inspiration.
>
> What joy, what pleasure, what transient glory
> I might enjoy if the divine Nise
> were not to link signs of tyranny
> to her gracious actions!
>
> She denies me letters, oh God, so that
> I accuse not only her shining gaze
> of avarice, but also her rare thoughts.
>
> Oh, what is served by chastening you, in hope
> that you'll grant me the glory of possessing you,
> if I am denied the life with which to reach you!

It is clearly important to Sor Violante that the absent countess should not forget her, so, in seeking to prompt her friend by means of a cleverly written sonnet, she both maintains the thread of communication and entertains her patroness, concealing her anxiety for recognition in clever and flattering terminology. This is a sustained display of wit, for Sor Violante misappropriates this language, not only to glorify love, but also to complain of the lack of correspondence. Fear of being forgotten was a powerful motivator for the client to bring him- or herself to the attention of the patron.

In the course of this sonnet Sor Violante links Nise "la divina" with Venus: "Prendas de aquella diosa soberana / que Sol abrasa, cuando estrella inclina" (1–2). In ancient times, Venus was thought to be both Eosphorus, the morning star, and Hesperus, the evening star. Sor Violante, in the guise of unrequited lover, calls on the goddess of both love and beauty, linking her to the divine "Nise," while through these hidden references to dawn and dusk she suggests Nise's enduring presence in her thoughts. Through this doubled figure, however, Sor Violante's speaker also accuses Nise of being a Janus, for she is both benign and tyrannical, she promises but also withholds, and what she withholds is herself, showing "indicios de tirana" (8). The speaker despairs that so much potential pleasure in Nise's company is lost to her through the tyranny of distance and the consequent inability to share their thoughts, made worse by the patron/friend's epistolary silence. There is an intimacy in this second quartet that celebrates the likeness of the two in thought, and also their shared class, literacy, and education that suggests genuine friendship apart from an interest in maintaining relations that may be beneficial in patronage terms: "Qué gusto, qué placer, qué gloria vana / tuviera yo, si Nise la divina . . ." (7–8).

The Janus nature of Nise is rediscovered in the tercets, harking back to the duplicitous goddess of the first quartet. The speaker accuses Nise, body and soul, of being miserly in denying the lover/Sor Violante her "pensamientos raros" and her "luceros." This latter word is a delightful pun, for "lucero" represents both Lucifer and the *stella veneris*, Venus. The painful absence and silence of the beloved is summed up in the final tercet: Sor Violante's survival depends on Nise's letters. They not only provide her with news of her friend's life in France, but they also renew the life of their friendship and strengthen the bonds of patronage. All of these aspects are important to Sor Violante in maintaining her position as courtly poet and in enlivening the enclosed life of the nun. Furthermore, the desire to conserve and extend patronage networks points again to Nader's affirmation that women had more power and agency in their hands than has until recently been acknowledged.

Sor Violante, in writing love poetry to her friends, provides a showcase of her talents and reminds them that although she is nominally enclosed in the convent, she is still part of their social circle. As she praises the excellence of the aristocratic court ladies, she works within an established, masculine, amorous discourse. However, she appropriates it to her own ends, creating a tie that binds her to them through female fellowship, unbridled admiration, and a display of her own intelligence and verbal skill. In doing so she defies prevailing physiological theories and permits the recipients of her works to participate in a celebration of feminine excellence. As will be seen in the following section, however, she does not confine her patronage works to the courtly love style. Sor Violante, Cueva y Silva, and Marcia Belisarda all write encomiastic verse, inscribing themselves into a more direct, masculine political discourse, and showing that women can be more than secondary recipients of the male family members' patronage rewards.

POLITICAL PATRONAGE

The kind of political friendships that male courtiers of the early modern period cultivated, those that promised gains in the social and economic scales of the patronage system, were principally available only to those women active in the courts of the highest ladies of the land, such as those of the Portuguese court discussed above.[11] A family's kin and friendship networks could provide opportunities for women to obtain employment suitable to their social class at court, where they could also achieve a measure of financial independence, escape from burdensome marriag-

11. For a detailed account of the roles, rewards, and responsibilities of the seventeenth-century nobility, see Bartolomé Bennassar, *Historia de los Españoles,* trans. Bernat Hervàs (Barcelona: Crítica, 1989), 1: 379–90.

es, or find suitable marriage partners. Noblewomen's service in a noble or royal household, either as a means to a degree of financial independence or to an advantageous marriage, has also been explored in a study of patronage in early modern France. Sharon Kettering notes the intense competition between noblewomen for the few available places in great households. These posts offered advancement opportunities and "a way to secure a dowry and marry or to escape an unhappy marriage" (56).

Existing patronage poems by women both in Spain and elsewhere point to the value to women of these connections, while the sonnets of Sor Juana Inés de la Cruz indicate that the system of reward and favor in return for service also prevailed in Spain's colonies.[12] Her poems to two of Mexico's vicereines, the Marchionesses de Mancera and de la Laguna, suggest not only that Sor Juana relished their friendship at a personal level, but also that these relationships offered her political protection and unique opportunities to further her studies without censure from her superiors in the Church. It was through the Marchioness de la Laguna that her first volume of poems was published under the title of *Inundación Castálida de la única poetisa, musa décima, Soror Juana Inés de la Cruz* (Castalian inundation of the unique poet, tenth muse, Sor Juana Inés de la Cruz) in Madrid, in 1689. Sor Juana's sudden retirement from writing and study came when the ties and protection of vice-regal patronage were less powerful.

Among the many examples of patronage poetry, often single poems, published in Serrano y Sanz's *Apuntes,* is a sonnet by Antonia de Nevares, sister of Lope de Vega's lover Marta de Nevares, to the Countess de Olivares.[13] The sonnet is exceedingly sycophantic, as the opening lines indicate: "Símbolo de la paz te cupo en suerte / ave de Venus, celestial, no humana" (1–2; Symbol of the peace that was your destiny, / dove of Venus, more celestial than human). With the count-duke at the height of his powers, his wife too was a magnet for women seeking favor, a post for themselves or their husbands, or just an acknowledged acquaintanceship

---

12. Similarly, in England, the work of Aemilia Lanyer, *Salve Deus Rex Judeorum,* opened with a series of prefatory poems designed to attract the attention of Queen Anne, Princess Elizabeth, and a number of influential court ladies.

13. Antonia de Nevares' sonnet is mentioned in Serrano y Sanz and published in Clara Janés, *Las Primeras poetisas en lengua castellana* (Madrid: Ayuso, 1986).

that would enable a noblewoman to establish her own clientage. While it is not known whether Antonia de Nevares was personally acquainted with the countess, when Ana Caro writes a sonnet to "Doña Inés Jacinta Manrique de Lara, estando enferma" (Lady Inés Jacinta Manrique de Lara, being ill), the tone of the sonnet, a graceful compliment to a lady of the principal nobility, conveys the impression of a connection that was both personally enriching and socially beneficial:

> Si pensara, señora, que al terrible
> mal que molesta vuestra hermosura
> de alivio le sirviera la pintura,
> que al pincel de los versos es factible,
>
> 5   Bien sin lisonja puede ser creíble
> que a fin de mejorar tal criatura
> en la salud, pues nada a esa hechura
> faltó en lo raro, bello y apacible,
>
> Que anduviera buscando los mayores
> 10   asuntos que ayudaran a mi intento:
> Ea, que hago agravio a los mejores
>
> Si de vos, bella Nise, el pensamiento
> aparto donde hay tantos superiores
> que obfuscan todo humano entendimiento.
>
> (Apuntes 534)

> Should you think, lady, that painting
> might serve as a relief from the terrible
> misfortune that assails your beauty,
> that the paintbrush of poetry is feasible,
>
> then it is possible to say without flattery,
> in seeking to raise the spirits of that figure,
> that since this creation lacked nothing
> in her rarity, beauty, and tranquility,
>
> though I were to search for the best
> subjects that might aid my intent:
> Well, I shall only aggrieve the better ones

if I divert my thoughts, beautiful Nise,
from where such manifold glories
defy all human understanding.

Caro's sonnet is couched in terms of sincerity and truth, and begins by reassuring Inés, under the pastoral name of Nise, that her beauty is ineradicable, as the poet attempts to dispel the patient's fears: "Si pensara, señora, que al terrible / mal que molesta vuestra hermosura / de alivio le sirviera la pintura" (1–3). Caro further emphasizes that this is not the mere flattery of a client. She hence claims a closer, more privileged relationship, while acknowledging the sycophancy of client discourse: "Bien sin lisonja puede ser creíble . . . pues nada a esta hechura / faltó en lo raro, bello y apacible" (5–8). The poet/speaker declares that her attempt to divert the patient from her illness by painting a lovely picture in verse is confounded by the natural beauty of the subject. She finally abandons the search for appropriate superlatives, asserting that such creative endeavor serves only to divert her attention from its rightful place: the captivating presence of the object of the poetic compliment herself. Caro disposes of the illness and its ravaging potential, while complimenting the marquesa's excellence. She thereby projects herself as worthy of attention: "Si de vos, bella Nise, el pensamiento / aparto donde hay tantos superiores" (12–13). Poetry of this type functioned as an advertisement in the patronage and friendship networks of noble poetic subjects, as well as offering the advice and moral support so necessary amid the factionalism of court existence.

Living far from the capital, in Medina del Campo, did not keep Leonor de la Cueva y Silva from full awareness of the pitfalls and benefits of patronage. This is demonstrated through her sonnets that praise her family members and the honor they bring to the family name, as detailed below. Another sonnet offering a more general observation and criticism of the workings of patronage and its precarious nature is entitled: "Introduce un pretendiente, desesperado de salir con su pretensión, que con el favor de un poderoso la consiguió muy presto" (Introducing a suitor, desperate to succeed in his aims, who, winning the favor of a powerful man, achieved his intent very quickly):

Sin esperanza en su tormenta esquiva
un navegante por el mar perdido,
de mil olas furiosas combatido,
rota la nave, al agua se derriba;

5　　y aunque su furia del sentir le priva,
se anima contra el mar embravecido
y sale al puerto de una tabla asido,
muerta su pena ya, su gloria viva.

¡Ay debil pretensión, que ansina eres
10　　navegante en un mar de mil temores!
Rota la nave, muerta la esperanza,

al agua del olvido echarte quieres,
donde, asiendo la tabla de favores,
sales triunfante al puerto de bonanza.

　　　　　　　　　　　(BN ms. 4127 238)

Bereft of hope in a storm of disdain
a sailor lost at sea, his ship destroyed,
is flung into the water, and battered
by a thousand furious waves.

And though its fury deprives him of his senses,
he fights back against that wild sea
and comes into harbor, clinging to a plank,
his suffering now dead, his glory enlivened.

Oh feeble pretension! There you are,
a navigator in a sea of a thousand fears,
your ship broken, your hopes dead,

and you seek to throw yourself into the Lethe,
where, clutching the flotsam of favors
you arrive, triumphant, at a bounteous harbor.

The fall from grace of the powerful, such as the Dukes of Osuna and of Lerma or, even more notably, the Count-Duke Olivares himself, signaled the end of their clientage networks. A well-known example of the calamity that could befall the inferior in the chain of patronage is that of

Francisco de Quevedo, whose brilliance did not save him when he was implicated in Osuna's downfall. As a result it would be some years before he was again able to acquire any kind of traction at court.[14] The patronage client's precarious career is also lampooned by Juan de Zabaleta, who utilizes similar maritime imagery to that employed by Cueva, in observing of the plight of the suitor at court: "La nave que está sólo sobre un áncora no está segura; la que está sobre dos está más firme" (210; The ship that drops only one anchor is not secure; that which puts out two is much firmer). He describes the court as "la fuente que distribuye los premios" (the fount that supplies the prizes) and observes that the *pretendiente* looks for new ways to acquire a post not so that he can perform a service, "sino cómo alcanzará el cargo, y hágalo como lo hiciere" (213; but to see how to acquire the post and do with it what he wishes).

In Cueva's sonnet, the whole tale of the young man's fall and rise is summed up in the quartets, the first of which locates him, devoid of hope, adrift in a storm of disfavor: "Sin esperanza en su tormenta esquiva / un navegante por el mar perdido" (1–2). With the ship of his patron sunk, he is alone and adrift on a sea of indifference unless he can rapidly acquire another. However, although in danger of sinking into social oblivion, he does not yet abandon hope: "y aunque su furia del sentir le priva / se anima contra el mar embravecido" (5–6). It is suggested that the client in a patronage relationship has to be adaptable, and ready for the change of circumstances that will result also in a change of allegiances, if she or he is successful in finding another patron. The effect of the *pretendiente*'s renewed courage is immediate, as the final lines of the quartets reveals: "y sale al puerto de una tabla asido / muerta su pena ya, su gloria viva" (7–8).

Cueva employs a significant metaphor in her conceit that brings the *pretendiente* into port "de una tabla asido." The polysemous "tabla" is both a plank and a table. A plank is an appropriate piece of flotsam to have come from a shipwreck. However, as a table the word offers a feast of meaning, since God furnishes a table for his people in Psalm 23.

---

14. This patronage system existed throughout Western Europe. Samuel Pepys, the famous English diarist of the same period, for example, performed great service to the English navy through his intelligence and industry, but he would never have had the opportunity to achieve the wealth and status that he did without the constant support of the Earl of Sandwich. He was also sufficiently adroit to distance himself from Sandwich as his patron fell from favor.

The table also represents the comforts of home, food, sustenance, solidity, and security, all of which are derived from the patron. The octet closes with a fine balance of life and death; rather than social death, it is his "pena" that dies away. The *pretendiente*'s glory is a living, earthly one of personal gratification, ironically represented in Cueva's portrayal. Here he is an unprepossessing figure, on the brink of ruin, and clutching the "tabla" that will transport him from disaster to success, but only, of course, for as long as the patron wills it.

Cueva's specific use of the term *pretendiente* removes it from the realm of conventional love poetry, as does her title's inclusion of the "favor de un poderoso." In spite of the suggestive "esquiva" of the first quartet that may imply a lovelorn figure, Cueva's love poetry invariably describes the variously disappointed lover as a *galán* (a young gallant). Her maritime imagery also hints strongly that this sonnet is a critique of the patronage system to which, elsewhere, she also aspires, since there are many established literary antecedents for the ship as a metaphor for the state, with all its connotations of control and of navigation by reference to the stars. The stars that Cueva's *navegante* must look to are both the highly placed patron and astrological guidance for his fortunes. Cueva reinforces her point that patronage could make or break an individual by simply summarizing the little story of the quartets in the tercets. Here, she mocks the "débil pretensión" of her subject, who tries to sail his affairs in a "mar de mil temores," becoming a would-be suicide in a Lethe of patronal indifference that leaves him without hope. Cueva's critique of the *pretendiente* accords well with her views of the valor and honor she sees as accruing to her own family through the courage and daring of her family members. Cueva subscribes to the idea that success as a client requires a considerable degree of *sprezzatura* (dash and spirit) and stamina, coupled with a Machiavellian capacity to build metaphorical hedges and ditches against the torrents and outrages of fortune.

The powerful effect that can be achieved by attachment to a patron able to advance the pretensions of even the most feeble fop is achieved by the sudden triumphant ending in the "puerto de bonanza," a particularly apt metaphor that refers both to arrival in safe harbor from the storm and to times of plenty and prosperity. The little journey begins without hope and ends in success, in patronage terms. Throughout, however, the client is not the architect of his own destiny, but is portrayed as an insignificant and unworthy piece of flotsam on the ebbing and flowing tide of political favor. As the anonymous writer of *Lazarillo de Tormes* tells us, the system of patronage was not limited to the upper classes, but existed at all levels of society. When Lazarillo tells his story it is from the safe "buen puerto" (good harbor) of his less than honorable relationship with his wife's employer.

When Sor Violante writes an admiring sonnet to a Portuguese aristocrat, the Countess de Penaguião, she employs similar maritime imagery in groping for superlatives:

> Si como admiro en vos, lo que en vos miro,
> explicará de mí lo que en mí siento,
> no hallara en el abono detrimiento
> lo que en mí siento, y lo que in vos admiro.
>
> 5   Mas ¡ay! que a tanto bien en vano aspiro,
> o rara suspensión del pensamiento,
> explique admiración, y sentimiento,
> el exceso feliz con que deliro.
>
> Que quien en tal objeto contemplando
> 10 como en inmenso mar se va perdiendo
> callando significa, acierta errando:
>
> Pues admirando al paso que sintiendo,
> si ofende la cordura delirando,
> acredita el ingenio conociendo.
>
>   (*Rimas varias* 8)

> If as I admire in you what I see in you,
> I explain of me what I feel in me,
> there is nothing detrimental in the bond
> that I feel in me and that I admire in you.
>
> Oh, that I aspire in vain to such perfection,
> or rare suspension of thought may explain
> my admiration and sentiment,
> the happy excess that makes me delirious.

For whoever contemplates such an object,
feels lost in an immense sea, signifies
in silence, becomes sure by wandering:

Since I'm admiring while I'm feeling,
if my delirium offends your intelligence,
credit my wit with knowing.

Having observed the splendor and intelligence of the countess in
the octet, Sor Violante moves in the tercets to express the effects on her
speaker of such deliriant excellence: "Que quien en tal objeto contem-
plando / como en inmenso mar se va perdiendo / callando significa, aci-
erta errando" (9–11). The language revolves repeatedly around seeing, admiring, and being seen, with linked alternations of "mirar / admirar"
that fix the speaker's besotted gaze on the countess, causing both joy and
mental disturbance. As in the sonnet to Elisa, all this glory is celebrated
without any reference to the woman's body; the countess is presented as
a glowing entirety. Although the fixed gaze of the bewitched lover is present, there is no atomizing of physical features, no golden hair, sapphire
eyes, or ruby lips; rather, the speaker is totally absorbed by the countess's
all-encompassing splendor. There is more to this relationship than mere
beauty. The patron dispenses favor, position, and gifts, but never herself,
and is always just out of reach, so that the petitioning client is always
reaching out, striving for the smallest attention.[15]

Leonor de la Cueva not only writes about the pretensions of others,
she also writes sonnets that locate her in a superior position in the social
hierarchy of her own region. For example, she heaps sonnet praise on the
poetry of the local *regidor* (councillor), don Juan Fernández de Ledesma, and acknowledges a young man's success at *toros y cañas* (bullfighting and jousting).[16] This dangerous game, reserved for the wealthy up-

15. The 1750 Lisbon earthquake destroyed the fabric of Sor Violante's convent and
its records, making it impossible to know whether such blandishments as these brought
any direct financial benefit to the convent institution or whether the countess was in-
duced to provide dowries of the type mentioned by Elizabeth Lehfeldt in *The Permeable
Cloister.*

16. For a detailed description of the aristocratic entertainments of the *juegos de cañas*
(tourneys) and the *corrida* (bullfighting), see Marcelin Defourneaux, *Daily Life in Golden
Age Spain,* trans. Newton Branch (Stanford: Stanford University Press, 1970), 133–34.

per classes, provided opportunities for display and advancement for the successful contestants. In writing of such events, Cueva inscribes herself into this privileged provincial circle and shows that she is knowledgeable about and participates in the lives, interests, and pastimes of the important men of her region.[17] Her knowledge of the activities of her town is most clearly to be seen in a sonnet *con estrambote* (with an extra, short verse) to "Gerardo amigo" about the decline of Medina. It provides historically relevant details about the deteriorating fortunes of the landed gentry in seventeenth-century Spain, and the impact of these changes upon her own life, as the opportunities for social advancement diminish with the town. She joins in a practice begun by Petrarch and continued into her own day, not least by Quevedo, in his famous sonnet "Miré los muros de la patria mía" (I looked at the walls of my native land), when she writes of the ruin of her town as a means to meditate on the passage of time, decay, and the inevitability of death:

A el miserable estado y desdichas de Medina

Quiéroos pintar el miserable estado
en que Medina está, Gerardo amigo;
yo, que de sus desgracias soy testigo,
puedo contar mejor a qué ha llegado.

5   Ya sus juegos y fiestas se han dejado,
sus damas acabó el tiempo enemigo;
de sus galanes solamente os digo
que aun rastro de su gala no ha quedado.

---

17. Cueva's sonnets are entitled "A unas ingeniosas liras que compuso Juan Fernández de Ledesma, Regidor de esta villa, refiriendo el trágico suceso de S. Agustín" (To the witty lyrics composed by Juan Fernández de Ledesma, Councillor of this town, referring to the tragic event of St Augustine) and "A D. Juan Francisco de Peralta y Velasco, habiendo salido aventajado en todo en unas fiestas de toros y cañas en Valladolid" (To Don Juan Francisco de Peralta y Velasco, having come out victorious in everything in the fiestas of *toros y cañas* in Valladolid). The games of *toros y cañas* involved fighting wild bulls from horseback with lances. Juan Fernández de Ledesma appears to have enjoyed a long-term friendship with Cueva. Toward the end of her manuscript, pages 251–53, it is carefully noted that two or three poems are the work of Juan Fernández de Ledesma, while her own name appears again above the works that follow.

No hay caballos, no hay fiestas, no hay carreras,
10   no hay contento, no hay gusto ni alegría:
todo es penas, trabajos, males, muertes.

No se celebran ya las primaveras,
disminúyese todo cada día.
¡Oh triste villa entre contrarios fuertes

15   que hacen en ti mil suertes
el tiempo vario y la cruel fortuna,
pues no tienes en ti buena ninguna!

(Ms. 4127, 232v)

On the miserable state and misfortunes of Medina

I want to paint for you, Gerard my friend,
the miserable state in which Medina finds itself;
I, who of its misfortunes am witness,
can best recount what has come to pass.

Its games and fiestas have gone now,
Time, the enemy, did away with her young ladies,
Of her young men, I can only tell you
that not a trace of their swagger remains.

There are no horses, no festivity, no races,
There's no contentment, pleasure, nor happiness:
All is misery, travail, ills, and deaths.

There's no celebration of Spring's arrival;
it shrivels a little more every day.
Oh sad town, caught up in harsh reversals,

Where vacillating time and cruel fortune
create in you a thousand impediments,
There's not a shred of good left in you!

In a litany of negativity, Cueva joins Spain's economic decline to her own immediate environs, seen in the light of a more illustrious past. She opens in epic style: "Quiéroos pintar el miserable estado / en que Medina está, Gerardo amigo" (1–2), and justifies her own unique position as both witness and victim of the change: "yo, que de sus desgracias soy testigo, / puedo contar mejor a qué ha llegado" (3–4). Expressing a feminine and baroque *desengaño*, Cueva employs the failing town and the withered "damas" as metaphors for the state and its social and economic decline. The powerful symbol of female fecundity and fertility as the seedbed for growth, ripeness, and harvest is converted, in the shriveling of the femininity of the "damas," into a representation of Spain's bankruptcy and lost potency. Gone with the images of ripe beauty are the men who paid court to them and, with them, the social engagements that enlivened the domestic boredom. Also lost are the opportunities for preferment that political friendship once made possible: "de sus galanes solamente os digo / que aún rastro de su gala no ha quedado" (5–6). There is irony too in the fact that Cueva appears to address this sonnet to a friend who has escaped Medina long enough before to be unaware of the decline of the city.

The repeated "no hay . . . no hay . . . no hay" of the second quartet creates a sobbing, wailing note of dissatisfaction, augmented by a catalogue of the town's new problems: "penas," "trabajos," "males," and "muertes" (8). Significantly, there is no shift of argument at the turn, as the grieving negativity fills the sonnet. The wintering of the town's economic glory is reflected in her observation that spring is no longer celebrated; every day the town is reduced still more, with only the old and infirm left; the young have gone to the wars, to find work, or to the colonies to seek their fortune. The fact that Cueva appears never to have married gives an autobiographical twist to this sonnet. As a well-placed and wealthy heiress, she should have been a highly desirable match. It can only be a matter of speculation as to whether she chose single autonomy, or whether it was chosen for her by the shrinking possibilities occasioned by Medina's decline.

Cueva is not alone in celebrating the influential members of her immediate environment. Marcia Belisarda's manuscript includes sonnets of praise to local writers in Toledo and a *romance* written to be sung in the convent chapel for the visit of the provincial Fray Baltasar Fernández that would surely have brought her to the notice of the local church hierarchy (ms 7469 24r).[18] Encomiastic verse provided a legitimate avenue

---

18. The *romance* is a form of ballad, usually of octosyllabic lines, not divided into strophes, rhyming on alternate lines. Belisarda's encomiastic poems to her social circle

through which women poets could express themselves. These works were likely to be read by a wider audience, but, more importantly, in such poetry women could write as the equals of their male counterparts, both in reason and in their ability to judge the worth of the works and words they praise.

As can be deduced from the above examples, the value attached to close relationships with powerful figures is not limited to the centers of power. It can be seen in the rivalries that occurred among the principal families of Catalina Clara Ramírez de Guzmán's own town. Llerena was a relatively important town in the period, as it lay on the road to Seville and was a military base that saw all the principal generals of Philip IV's army pass through it during Spain's war with Portugal. The army's important role in the town, and the facility with which they could requisition war materiel, are revealed in another of Ramírez's works: "Pidiendo a un caballero que tomaba caballos para el ejercito que reservase uno del coche" (Pleading with a gentleman who was taking horses for the army that he leave us one for the coach), complaining "que parece tiranía / dejarnos el coche cojo" (it seems a tyranny to leave us with a lame coach) and puns that "en un potro nos ponéis / si nos quitáis un caballo" (you will leave us in torment if you take away our horse; ms. 240v). *Potro* can signify an instrument of torture (the rack), a stall for securing the head of a restless horse during treatment, or a young colt.

Gazul describes Llerena as a city of "alta burocracia, la de la Inquisición y la de sus órganos administrativos. Sus gobernadores fueron segundones de aristocráticas familias e hidalgos con más pergaminos que fortuna" (517; upper bureaucracy of both the Inquisition and its administrative organs. Its governors were the second sons of aristocratic families and landed gentry with more rank than fortune). This portrayal points to the importance of class and place over mere wealth. Entrambasaguas claims that the activities of Ramírez's father earned him many enemies among the important citizens of the town, including Captain

---

include one to Juan Pérez Roldán, praising his skill as a composer (ms. 7469, 9r). The Biblioteca Nacional, in Spain, contains a small collection of music by Juan Pérez Roldán (1610–1671), "Música para los ministrales de El Pilar de Zaragoza" (Music for the minstrels of El Pilar, of Saragossa), the dates of which suggest that he could be the composer praised by Belisarda.

Lorenzo de Figueroa, whose son-in-law was *alférez* (second lieutenant) in don Francisco Ramírez's company, and who was deprived of "la bandera porque no acudía a las cosas de su capitán" (the banner because he disagreed with his captain's decisions). Such disparagement apparently caused Figueroa to leave the country with the expulsion of the Moriscos in 1609 (15). However, the greatest enmity derived from a family of equal rank and status, the Almezquita.[19] The struggle for supremacy created a rivalry that developed into a lasting feud over questions of protocol and hierarchy, "uno de tantos incidentes que en aquella época provocaba el puesto a ocupar en cualquier sitio público y aun privado" (Gazul 520; one of many incidents that in that era were provoked by the importance of pride of place, both public and private). From these enmities may have developed some of Ramírez's more acid poetry.

Perhaps mindful of the high status to which her family pretended in the community, Ramírez writes no sycophantic poetry to other notables, with the single exception of the *décima* (a poem of ten octosyllabic lines) "a la ausencia de los Condes de la Puebla" (On the absence of the Count and Countess de la Puebla):

> De los condes el ausencia
> siente el lugar a porfía,
> pues consiste su alegría
> en que dure su asistencia.
> 5 Bien se ve con evidencia
> lo que llega a aventurar,
> pues si se quiere apurar,
> ninguno negarle puede
> que es fuerza que solo quede,
> 10 si se despuebla el lugar.
>
> (BN Ms. 3884, 241r)

> The place wants to resist
> the absence of the counts,
> since its contentment consists

19. The family are denominated thus in Entrambasaguas. Gazul refers to them as the "Almerquita."

in their enduring presence.
It is easy to see
what will come to pass
if one considers it deeply;
what is obvious cannot be denied:
that if the place is desolated
its sorrows will be countless.

The poem ends in wordplay punning on the noble title that stresses the loneliness that will be occasioned should they indeed leave. Here she was clearly outranked in nobility, although the light tone of the poem also implies a relationship bordering on equality.

For Sor Violante del Cielo, it may have been the restoration of the Portuguese monarchy in 1640 that made her encomiastic poetry so optimistic and laudatory. She wrote several sonnets to the new Braganza king, Don João IV, who took the Portuguese throne in 1640, and several more to courtier friends. She also commemorates the deaths of highly placed friends, including the Duchess of Aveiro, Juliana de Lencastre, wife of the third duke, and writes laudatory sonnets to other writers, as well as to friends at court.[20] When Sor Violante celebrates her highborn friends in verse, it is their character and their intelligence that she celebrates most. Therefore, although she accommodates herself to male discourse in her sonnets, she adapts it to a form more acceptable to women by focusing her attention on women's capacity for wit and intelligence, which she praises equally with their physical beauty. When Sor Violante writes a sonnet epitaph to the *dama de corte* (lady in waiting) Dona Maria de Ataide, that formed part of the recorded funeral obsequies, she again looks to the imagery of brilliant light and extraordinary intelligence with which she praised the Countess de Penagiuão, to whom the *Memorias funebres* (Funeral memorials) are addressed:

20. These friends include the aforementioned Condesa de Penaguião and dona Mariana de Luna. A further sonnet to Inés de Noronha will be discussed in detail in the chapter on friendship. For details regarding Sor Violante's social position, education, and the friends of both sexes with whom she exchanged verse, see Margarida Vieira Mendes, "Apresentação," in *Violante do Céu: Rimas varias,* ed. introdução notas e fixação do texto: Margarida Vieira Mendes (Lisboa: Editorial Presença, 1993), 13.

Epitafio

Yace en este sepulcro venturoso
que miras suspendido, o caminante,
una luz, que excedió lo mas brillante,
una flor, que venció lo mas hermoso.

5   Yace un entendimiento portentoso,
un objeto mayor de afecto amante,
un exemplar de todo lo elegante
una ocasión de todo lo envidioso.

Yace una suspensión del pensamiento,
10   un asunto capaz de heroica pluma,
un exceso que en todo excesos pide.

Yace un motivo eterno al sentimiento,
mas para que lo diga todo en suma,
yace Doña Maria de Ataide.

(Vieira, *Memorias funebres* n. pag.)

Epitaph

Oh passer-by, there lies in this fortunate
tomb that you see before you
a light that exceeded all brilliance,
a flower that defeated all beauty.

Here lies a wondrous intelligence,
the greatest object of loving affection,
an example of all that is most elegant,
such as to inspire the greatest envy.

Here lies a suspension of thought,
a subject worthy of heroic praise,
an excellence that all excellence would seek.

Here lies an eternal motif of sentiment,
but to sum up all that I have said,
Here lies Donna María de Ataide.

The epitaph is written to arrest the attention of the passer-by. It is not the conventional warning to prepare for death that is the end of all living things, but extends the beauty and intelligence of her subject beyond the grave. The reiteration of "yace," "yace," "yace" acknowledges the *dama*'s death but is juxtaposed with a celebration of her specific qualities, enumerated throughout the sonnet, to be summed up in the final line with the name of the deceased: "yace Dona Maria de Ataide." Donna María is a light, a flower, an object of affection and envy, and an example of perfect elegance. The first line of the tercets suggests the temporary nature of this earthly death: "Yace una suspensión del pensamiento," as if Dona Maria has merely paused for a moment before continuing her brilliant career in the heavenly court. This line was used also by Sor Violante in her sonnet praising the Countess de Penagiuão, discussed earlier, where the countess's magnificence gave pause for contemplation.

The sentiment which likens the earthly court to that of heaven, is picked up and embellished in the second of Sor Violante's sonnets published in the funeral obsequies:

> Pasó de firmamento a firmamento
> Maria, presunción del ser humano,
> pues pasó del palacio Lusitano
> a la esfera mayor del lucimiento.
>
> 5   En vano procuró su detrimento
> de la Parca cruel la injusta mano,
> pues subir al Palacio soberano,
> fue conseguir en todo eterno aumento.
>
> Pero si con Deidades asistía
> 10   en la esfera de un Jove sin segundo,
> (que es la mayor Deidad en mortal velo),
>
> ¡Qué aumento superior conseguiría
> la que asistía a lo mejor del mundo,
> sino pasando a lo mejor del Cielo!
>
> (*Memorias funebres* n. pag.)

She passed from one firmament to another,
Maria, a perfect example of humanity,
for she passed from the Lusitanian palace
to the greatest sphere of light.

In vain did the unjust hand of the cruel Parca
attempt to procure her detriment,
since to rise to the sovereign palace
was to achieve the greatest eternity of all.

But she had attended upon deities
in the sphere of a Jove without peer
(who is the greatest deity in mortal guise).

What greater achievement could there be,
for she who attended on the greatest of the world,
than to pass to the greatest of heaven!

Here Sor Violante writes of Dona Maria's passage from the earthly to the heavenly court in almost identical terms to those in her sonnet, in the *Parnaso lusitano,* on the fourth glorious mystery, the Assumption of the Virgin Mary into heaven.[21] In these sonnets Sor Violante seizes the opportunity of a great public funeral to praise both her apparent subject, María, and her king, the ultimate fount of benefits. This is not the only sonnet in which Sor Violante employs extravagant language in praise of her king, as will be revealed in the following section.

The sonnets discussed above show these women poets' awareness of the nature of patronage, its benefits and rewards, as well as their consciousness of the pitfalls and traps inherent in such an imperfect system. Nevertheless, as women who benefited socially and financially from the system, they subscribed to it as a normal part of their social environment. Though it was engaged in principally by male courtiers, the potential for social advancement and independence that the system provided for women ensured that they seized any opportunities to display their intellectual and social gifts.

---

21. This sonnet is discussed in detail in Chapter 2.

ROMANCING ROYALTY

Celebrating the royal rites of passage in verse offered a variety of opportunities to the poet: to create the propaganda that reinforced the desired social norm of the state as a family, under the benevolent paternity of its king; to stand out from among the other suitors for patronage by an elegant display of wit and flattery; and to inscribe oneself into the literary heritage of the nation since public celebrations of royal events were likely to result in the circulation of verse and song that could become part of the national literature. The publication of the funeral rites of María de Ataide is one example of such writing; it was partially by this means that Sor Violante was able to straddle the line between retired and public life. The honorable status accrued through her family connections secured her entry into the royal convent, while the combination of her own skills and this royal connection ensured her literary fame within her own society, a fame that probably saved her and her work from the censure and censorship endured by other notable religious, such as Sor Juana Inés de la Cruz or the Sobrino Morillas sisters.[22]

Celebrating the revolution of 1640 that saw João IV take the throne by popular acclaim, Sor Violante's sonnet in the *Rimas varias,* "A el Rei Dom João IV de Portugal, Soneto em dialogo" (To the King Don João IV of Portugal, a sonnet in dialogue), recites a catechism:

> Que logras Portugal? um Rei perfeito,
> quem o constituyo? sacra piedade,
> que alcançaste com ele? a liberdade,
> que liberdade tens? ser-lhe sujeito.
>
> 5   Que tens na sujeição? honra, e proveito,
> que é o novo Rei'? quasi Deidade,
> que ostenta nas acções? felicidade,
> e que tem de feliz? ser por Deus feito.

22. From a talented family, the Sobrino Morillas sisters both entered St. Teresa's convent of the Discalced Carmelites in Valladolid, taking the names of María de San Alberto and Cecilia del Nacimiento. Their manuscripts reveal details of the censorship to which they were subjected. For a more detailed analysis of their work, see Arenal and Schlau, *Untold Sisters;* or Stacey Schlau, *Viva al siglo, muerta al mundo: Selected Works/Obras escogidas de/by María de San Alberto (1568–1640)* (New Orleans: University Press of the South, 1998).

Que eras antes dele? um laberinto,
10   que te julgas agora? um firmamento,
temes alguém? não temo a mesma Parca.

Sentes alguma pena? a só sinto,
qual é? não ser um mundo, ou não ser cento,
para ser mais capaz de tal Monarca.

(Rimas varias 10)

What does Portugal achieve? A perfect king,
Who made him so? Holy grace.
What does she attain with him? Liberty.
Of what does this liberty consist? To be his subject.

What does this subjection give her? Honor and profit.
What is the new king? A near deity.
What does he show in his deeds? Joy.
And why is he joyful? He is made by God.

What was she before this? A labyrinth.
How do you see her now? A firmament.
Do you fear anything? Not even death itself.

Do you feel any sadness? Only one thing I feel.
What is it? Not to be a whole world, not to be complete,
so as to be more worthy of such a monarch.

Where almost half of Sor Violante's sonnets in the *Rimas varias* are rendered in Spanish, when she writes on the important matter of succession within Portugal and the return of her own king, she reverts to Portuguese. She also lays down the appropriate service to one's king in an oxymoron that converts service into liberty: "que liberdade tens? ser-lhe sujeito" (4). Entwined with this liberating and noble service is the honor and profit to be gained from patronage, emphasized by the express view that with the transition to Portuguese rule the country has been transformed from a labyrinth to a firmament of political stars: "Que eras antes dele? um laberinto, / que te julgas agora? um firmamento" (9–10). With the royal government based in Madrid for sixty years, opportunities for patronage were considerably reduced; expectations of the new king must have been prodigious among the aristocracy. In another sonnet, addressed directly to the king, Sor Violante's second quartet describes the benefits that accrue to those in royal service, concluding that dying in the king's service ensures redemption, thus further imprinting the idea of a king as a representative of God:

> Quem se vos rende, alcança liberdade,
> quem vos adora, ostenta sutileza,
> servir-vos muito, é denotar grandeza,
> morrer por vós, buscar eternidade.
>
> (5–8) (*Rimas varias,* 16)

> Who submits to you, achieves freedom,
> Who adores you, displays their ingenuity.
> To serve you wholly, is to denote greatness,
> To die for you, is to seek eternity.

The fervent nature of these sonnets was surely connected to the state of war that existed between Spain and Portugal following the revolution; the throne was not securely in Portuguese hands until 1668, twelve years after João IV's death. Irrespective of this supposition, the notion that service to one's superiors ensured reward is firmly entrenched in the sonnet's terminology as a natural part of aristocratic existence.

Sor Violante's long life, most of which was spent beside the court, and her literary fame during her own lifetime ensured a flow of sonnets marking the royal rites of passage. In 1669 she wrote in praise of the birth of a daughter to the regent, Dom Pedro; in 1687 she marked the second marriage of the king, now Pedro II, to Maria Sofia Isabel. She offers moral support and praises the strength of her "Monarca generoso" (generous monarch) when his first child, D. João, dies within a few days of his birth and, in 1689, she celebrates the birth of the new heir, concluding that the Portuguese throne is now secured in succession, while hastening to wish the present incumbent a long life: "Nasce para depois de eternidades, / suceder a hum Monarca sem segundo / nos meritos, no cetro, e na coroa" (*Parnaso lusitano,* 74: 12–14; He is born so that after eternities / he shall succeed a monarch without peer / in his merit, in his scepter, and in his crown).

The above sonnet is immediately followed by another, which concludes the first volume of the *Parnaso lusitano,* addressed to "El Rey nosso Senhor em agradecimento de hua mercè, que fez à Autora em o dia do nascimento do Principe D. João, que Deos guarde" (To the King, our lord, in gratitude for a favor he granted the author on the day Prince Don João was born, may God preserve him). Sor Violante abases herself appropriately in the opening line: "A Vossos pès, Monarca generoso" (At your feet, generous monarch), and from this humble position offers thanks:

> A Vossos pès, Monarca generoso,
> graças vos sacrifico agradecida,
> por conceder soccorros a huma vida
> contra o poder do fado rigoroso.
>
> 5   Remunère o Senhor mais poderoso
> huma acção tanto às suas parecida,
> pois quanto tem de menos merecida,
> tanto mais vos abona de piedoso.
>
> 10   Oh vivey, Alexandre Lusitano,
> idades tão sem conto, que divino
> Vos presuma tal vez o ser humano:
>
> Vivey para alcançardes de contino
> Jà victorias do perfido othomano,
> Jà triunfos tambem de meu destino.
>
>   (*Parnaso lusitano* 75)

> At your feet, oh generous monarch,
> I make an offering of gratitude and thanks,
> for your granting of succor to a life
> beset by the power of stern fate.
>
> Most powerful sovereign, you endow,
> an action so typical of you,
> since however little may be merited,
> so much more you offer out of your grace.

Oh Lusitanian Alexander, may you live
through such countless ages, that
you will be thought more divine than human:

May you live to achieve continuous
victories, now against the perfidious Ottoman,
now also triumphs of my own destiny.

The tercets liken the king to Alexander the Great and wish him a life long enough that humankind will regard him as essentially divine, and long enough to triumph over the perfidious Turks. Skillfully, Sor Violante converts her king into a Christian hero, a Portuguese Santiago Matamoros (St. James the Moorslayer), who, through his God-given power, will defeat the infidel. It is an extraordinarily martial end to a sonnet of thanks for benefits received from the ultimate fount of patronage. It thus suggests that Sor Violante took the opportunity as a favored and faithful old retainer, now nearly ninety years old, to apprise the king of her own desire for a Christian victory by force of arms. The regular flow of adulation that reached the royal family from her pen was no doubt aided in its progress by the relationships she had carefully established with other members of the court and as an unofficial poet laureate; marking rites of passage as if by right, she would have expected her works to reach her royal benefactors, further cementing her preeminent position.

As Sor Violante seeks to aggrandize the nobility, honor, and martial prowess of the Portuguese king, she also demonstrates the importance attached to family honor and prowess. In this she is not alone among these poets. The opportunities for patronage afforded by being part of an honorable and honored family are celebrated in the poetry written in praise of her family members by Leonor de la Cueva y Silva.

PATRONAGE AND THE FAMILY

Awareness of the value of well-managed patronage and the importance of being associated with the right families can be seen in several sonnets by Leonor de la Cueva y Silva. These also reveal the importance that she places on family honor as a conduit to appropriate family renown. In a funeral sonnet she celebrates the life of her famous poet/lawyer uncle, Francisco de la Cueva y Silva;[23] in two others she celebrates her brother's military prowess, which saw him singularly favored by the cardinal-prince Ferdinand, brother of Philip IV. These sonnets emphasize the benefits that accrue through association with the favored kin, rather than on affectionate familial relationships. They bear no relationship to the love sonnets of the type already discussed, those intended to flatter and impress the patron. Rather, they establish the importance of bloodlines in determining social status. It is social status that has so much bearing on the success or failure of patronage negotiations.

In the funeral sonnet, Cueva immediately asserts her relationship to the dead man in the title: "Al sepulcro de el Sr. Don Francisco de la Cueva y Silva, mi tío" (At the tomb of the gentleman Don Francisco de la Cueva y Silva, my uncle). The sonnet is filled with admiration for the man's accomplishments as Cueva extols his intellectual brilliance, linking it to the great names of antiquity. In the process, she associates herself with his fame and name and locates herself at his side, sharing his classical learning:

> Este que ves que cubre blanca losa,
> aunque la dura tierra le consuma,
> fue en el saber otro segundo Numa,
> y otro Catón en ciencia milagrosa.
>
> 5   De su ingenio, la fama numerosa
> triunfos publica, y de su rara pluma,
> mil grandezas aclama en breve suma,
> con que hace su memoria más gloriosa.
>
> Callen los siete sabios de la Grecia
> 10   y humille Atenas su laurel sagrado,
> pues éste de Minerva el triunfo lleva.

23. Among Francisco de la Cueva y Silva's extant works in the Biblioteca Nacional in Madrid are legal treatises on the election of Saint Teresa as Patron of Spain, 1615, and on the Immaculate Conception, a work coauthored with Philip III's favorite, the Duke of Lerma. Some of his sonnets are included in Leonor de la Cueva y Silva's manuscript in the Biblioteca Nacional, Madrid. Quevedo also dedicated a funeral sonnet to him. He appears also in a lengthy entry in Lope de Vega's *Laurel de Apolo*, Silva III; see Lope Felix de Vega Carpio, *Colección escogida de obras no dramáticas de Frey Lope Felix de Vega Carpio, por don Cayetano Rosell*, Biblioteca de Autores Españoles, vol. 38 (Madrid: Atlas, 1950), 199.

¿A quién con más razón el mundo precia?
que de uno a otro polo es ya llamado
el grande Silva y el insigne Cueva.

(Serrano y Sanz 337)

He whom you see beneath this white stone,
though the hard soil may consume him,
was in wisdom a second Numa,
in miraculous knowledge another Cato.

Fame publishes the numerous triumphs
of his genius, and of his rare pen a
thousandfold greatness is hailed in brief sum.
And all these make his memory more glorious.

May he silence the Seven Sages of Greece,
and humble Athens with his sacred crown of bays,
for he steals even Minerva's triumph.

Whom could the world more fairly prize,
than one who is renowned from one pole to the other
as the great Silva and the outstanding Cueva?

The man is known by and praised for his literary and social feats, trumpeted in the quartets with a series of statements that cover his wisdom and statesmanship, revealed in his favorable comparison with Numa and Cato.[24] Cueva also reiterates her uncle's literary genius: "fama," "triunfos publica," "rara pluma," "aclama," all of which will ensure that he remains unfaded in memory.

In the tercets Cueva turns to broader themes still. Reflecting the Renaissance interest in classical thinkers as the epitome of intellectual en-

---

24. The reference to Numa is probably to Numa Pompilius, in legendary Roman history the successor of Romulus as second king of Rome. His long and peaceful reign was regarded in later times as a sort of golden age. The reference to Cato is either to Dionysius Cato (fourth century A.D., the author of a volume of 164 moral precepts in Latin hexameters, or to Marcus Porcius Cato the elder (234–149 B.C.), also known as the Censor (a distinguished soldier, lawyer, and moralist who crushed an insurrection in Spain and advocated the simple, strict social life of ancient Roman tradition). See M. C. Howatson and Ian Chilvers, eds., *The Concise Oxford Companion to Classical Literature* (Oxford and New York: Oxford University Press, 1993).

deavor, she claims that the famous *tío*'s accomplishments are superior to those of the Seven Sages of Athens, and to the Roman goddess of war, Minerva.[25] But Minerva is a multitasking goddess, honored also as goddess of crafts and of reason. Significantly, Cueva insists that pure reason demands this appreciation of her uncle. Conventional wisdom of the period, steeped in humoral theory that portrays women as hapless victims of their own physiology, has it that reason is not the province of women. However, Cueva, in drawing the goddess to the reader's attention, affirms that women too are capable of education and reason. Indeed, Minerva's mythical skills are also associated with those of *hombría,* as she is surpassingly excellent in both reason and in war. In asserting that her uncle is even greater than Minerva, Cueva praises his statesmanship and reason, as well as his warrior and leadership qualities. At the same time she reminds the reader that she shares her uncle's blood, and therefore potentially his outstanding qualities. Furthermore, Cueva inherits the honor associated with his famous name as she aggrandizes both sides of her family, separating the two names that represent her lineage with laudatory adjectives: "que de uno a otro polo es ya llamado / el grande Silva y el insigne Cueva" (13–14). Name is clearly of great importance to Cueva, as is her own value within the family. She is punctilious in putting her name to each of her poems in the Biblioteca Nacional's manuscript, inscribing herself into the record as the creator of intellectual works.

There is a striking difference between this sonnet and the *liras* (stanzas of five eleven-syllable and seven-syllable lines) written on the death of her father, which exhibit love and sadness:

> *Liras en la muerte de mi querido padre y señor*
> Dejad cansados ojos
> el justo llanto que os convierte en fuentes.
> Cesen ya los enojos
> y enjugad vuestros líquidos corrientes,

---

25. The Seven Sages, known in Greek tradition as statesmen, lawgivers, and philosophers of the seventh and sixth centuries B.C., are generally acknowledged to be Solon of Athens, Thales of Miletus, Pittacus of Mitylene, Cleobulus of Rhodes, Chilon of Sparta, Bias of Priene, and Periander of Corinth; see Howatson and Chilvers, eds., *Classical Literature.*

5   que al mal que oprime el pecho
el alma y corazón le viene estrecho,
y en tan terrible pena
ni hallo descanso gusto ni alegría.
De todo estoy ajena

10   y solo tengo la desdicha mía
por alivio y consuelo.
Que de todo lo más me priva el cielo,
quitóme en breves días
airado y riguroso un bien amado,

15   a las fortunas mías
añadiendo este golpe desdichado.
¡O suerte fiera y dura!
Llorad ojos llorad mi desventura.
Contenta el alma estaba

20   en sus trabajos, penas y dolores,
con el bien que gozaba.
Mas la parca cruel con mil rigores,
fiera y embravecida,
cortó el hilo al estambre de su vida.

25   ¡Musa detente un poco!
Que si de tantos males hago suma
y en el presente toco,
no es suficiente mi grosera pluma,
que pues estoy penando,
cuanto puedo decir digo callando.

                (BN ms. 4127 189r)

Lyrics on the death of my beloved father

Leave, tired eyes, the rightful weeping
that converts you into springs.
Cease now your sorrows
and your liquid torrents,

5   for the ills that oppress my body
constrict my heart and soul,
and I suffer so terribly that

I find no rest, pleasure, or joy.
All is strange, alien, and I have
10   only my sad tribulations
as comfort and consolation,
for proud and arrogant heaven
deprives me of all else.
In the space of a few days
15   it quit me of my most beloved, adding
this dreadful blow to my misfortunes.
Oh wild and cruel fate!
Weep, eyes! Weep my sad adversity;
my soul finds contentment in its
20   travail, pain, and suffering,
recalling the love that I enjoyed.
But cruel Atropos, wild, fierce,
and a thousand times harsh,
cut the thread that joined him to life.
25   Oh Muse, pause a moment!
For my vulgar pen is insufficient
to enumerate so many ills
and touch on them now;
I am in so much pain that all
30   I care to say I pronounce in silence.

Here there is no mistaking the personal tone that expresses an affectionate relationship within the private family sphere. There is no attempt to
locate her father within his social group, nor to celebrate family honor.
Where she reserves the sonnet for the formal praise of a dead statesman,
she chooses a more homely style to write of her father. It is significant
that women like Cueva participate in the honor process through sonnets
such as that which lauds her uncle.[26] She pursues this line further in sonnets written for her brother, don Antonio, praising his military prowess
in the train of Cardinal-Prince Ferdinand, brother of Philip IV.

26. Cueva, like Sor Violante del Cielo, also wrote verse to royalty. Two elegiac sonnets were published, marking the deaths of Isabel de Borbón in 1645 and, in 1689, of
Queen María Luisa de Borbón; see Olivares and Boyce, *Espejo,* 105.

Women's access to the important concept of honor in the seventeenth century was theoretically circumscribed. Until recently, anthropologists and historians have considered that women were unable to partake in family honor except as the conduit through which honor passed. For example, in discussing the masculine notion of honor, Donald Larson observes that under the banner of *hombría,* or "overt masculinity," honor was described as the greatest value apart from religion. For the Old Christian, "the only way for a man to be truly a man was to exercise to the fullest the masculine attributes of fortitude, bravery, and domination." Added to this was the importance of blood purity and the subordinate relationship of women to men, since honor "depends on the ability to impress one's will on others" (7–10). Under this schema, sexually deviant behavior by the women of any man's family, whether father, son, or brother, deprives male kin of their honor. Women themselves may theoretically possess honor through their chastity, but this is also a possession of their menfolk; women do not possess it but merely pass honor on to their sons.

While there is little doubt that women could find themselves at risk from male relatives who assumed their personal and family honor to have been besmirched, recent scholarship has contested the purely masculinist view of honor as being circumscribed for women. Though it was an important concept in early modern Spain, as the plays and conduct manuals of the period indicate, attitudes to honor were not universal across Spain. Allyson Poska, for example, in discussing attitudes to honor in early modern Galicia notes that "honour was not a rigid social and sexual code. Recent research has forced scholars to contextualize closely the multivalent meanings and uses of honour in Spanish society . . . a person's honour was constituted . . . by a combination of one's own articulation of one's behaviour and one's interaction with the community" (107). It should be noted, however, that in general Poska is not discussing the social interactions of the higher classes of society, for whom honor must have continued to be a large determinant in their social comportment.[27]

27. For further relevant discussion of honor in Spanish society, see Yvonne Yarbro-Bejarano, *Feminism and the Honor Plays of Lope de Vega,* Purdue Studies in Romance Literatures 4 (West Lafayette: Purdue University Press, 1994). See also Mary Elizabeth Perry, *Gender and Disorder in Early Modern Seville* (Princeton: Princeton University Press,

In spite of the moralists' obsession with female honor, it seems they did not so overtly censure noblewomen. Helen Nader, in her introduction to a collection of essays on the Mendoza family, women of the highest Spanish nobility, observes that "the authors in this work found no cases in which honor was even mentioned" (4). However, honor appears to be an important component in the few extant plays written by upper-class women as, for example, Ana Caro's *Valor, Agravio, Mujer* (Valor, outrage, women) and Leonor de la Cueva y Silva's *La firmeza en la ausencia* (Constancy in absence). In the first, the female protagonist seeks personal revenge on the man who has stolen her honor; in the second, the sonnets of which will be discussed in Chapter 5, it is the protagonist's fierce and intelligent defense of her honor that achieves the desired felicitous ending.[28]

In his observations about *hombría,* Larson does not consider the beneficial effects that the masculine honor accruing to its male members has on the entire family. A blood association with the principal families of the realm can only have enhanced the futures of all the extended family members, including their women, whose commodification in the matter of marriage and honor could at least secure them a step up the social ladder, even if it granted them no greater independence. At the beginning of Philip III's reign, for example, the king distributed considerable sums among his courtiers and these favors extended to the women of the court: "Las mercedes que se concedían a las damas de honor de las reinas e infantas—siempre escogidas entre los linajes más distinguidos—eran ya tradicionales, y acostumbraban a ascender a millares de ducados" (Bennassar, Historia 380; The rewards conceded to the ladies in waiting of the queens and princesses—always chosen from among the most distinguished rank—were by now traditional and usually amounted to thousands of ducats).[29]

1990). Nieves Romero Díaz discusses the strong defense of women's honor proposed in the works of María de Zayas in *Nueva nobleza, nueva novela: reescribiendo la cultura urbana del barroco* (Newark: Juan de la Cuesta, 2002).

28. For a fuller discussion of the works of seventeenth-century female playwrights, see Lisa Vollendorf, *The Lives of Women: A New History of Inquisitional Spain* (Nashville: Vanderbilt University Press, 2005), 74–89.

29. For a social portrait of Castilian nobility in the period, see Bartolomé Bennassar, *La España del Siglo de Oro* (Barcelona: Crítica, 2001), 187–88.

Cueva's sonnets to her brother reflect the *hombría* detailed by Larson, for her brother finds royal favor through his military feats. She incorporates into them both the affection she feels for her brother and praise of the honor he brings to the family. Cueva also inserts herself and her family into Spanish history, for it is clear from the content of the sonnets that Antonio de la Cueva y Silva was an officer in the cardinal-prince's army, en route to the decisive battle of Nördlingen, which took place in 1634. The first sonnet is preceded in her manuscript by adulatory *octavas*[30] addressed to Cardinal-Prince Ferdinand, entitled "Al Serenísimo Infante Cardenal don Fernando de Austria cuando dio la capitanía de caballos e hizo su gentilhombre de la boca a mi hermano don Antonio de la Cueva y Silva el día que entró en Milán con el guión" (To the Most Serene Prince-Cardinal Don Fernando of Austria when he granted my brother, Don Antonio de la Cueva y Silva, the captaincy of horse and made him his gentleman of the mouth, on the day he entered Milan with the standard):

> Segundo Apolo de el mayor de el mundo,
> Hijo de Marte, nieto de Felipe,
> Fenix raro divino y sin segundo
> que no hay valor que al tuyo se anticipe.
> 5 Lauro te rinda tierra y mar profundo,
> y cuanto adora tronco el de Aganipe,
> Divino príncipe y protector luciente,
> corona te ha de ser no suficiente.
> Gallardo Atlante de el Iberio suelo,
> 10 en cuyos hombros penden las Españas,
> Hermosa afrenta de el Señor de Delo,
> que en luz mas clara todo el orbe bañas.
> La fama escriba en el celeste velo
> con pluma de diamante tus hazañas,
> 15 y el sol y luna alfombra de tus huellas
> tus plantas besen en lugar de estrellas.
> ¡Goze insignes victorias de tu mano

---

30. An eight-line stanza of hendecasyllabic verse.

nuestro Rey! y pasando a tus mayores,
más que el aurora aljofar da a verano,
20   fe de la suerte, triunfos superiores
de el príncipe de Roma soberano.
La silla alcances gracias y sabores
y siempre de tu nombre, en paz y en guerra,
al cielo admiración—yugo a la tierra.
25   Pues premios dignos das a tus criados,
Cesar piadoso y Romulo valiente,
como el Magno Alejandro adelantados
para hacerte inmortal de gente en gente.
Con tan grandes mercedes animados
30   quien no te ha de ofrecer su sangre ardiente,
poniendo en tu servicio espada y vida,
dichosa suerte si por ti perdida.
A nuevo empeño tal favor nos llama,
joven dichoso, invicto Ferdinando,
35   pues asido—mi hermano de tal rama
la desbocada envidia va pisando.
Mi indigna pluma tu grandeza aclama
con que humilde doy fin tus pies besando.
Perdona mi atrevida rustiqueza
pues soy esclava de tu Real alteza.

(BN ms 4127 248v–250v)

Second Apollo of the world's best,
Son of Mars, grandson of Philip,
Rare, divine Phoenix without peer,
of whom we could not expect greater valor.
5   May earth and deep sea render you laurels,
and greater adoration from Aganippe's spring,
divine prince and shining protector,
for whom a crown will not suffice.
Gracious Atlas of the Iberian soil
10   on whose shoulders rests all of Spain;
beautiful affront to the Lord of Delos

for you bathe all the earth in a clearer light.
Fame shall write your feats on the celestial veil
with a pen of diamonds, and the sun and
15   moon shall form a carpet for your tread,
kissing your soles in place of the stars.
May our king enjoy great victories
by your hand, and passing to your greatest,
more than the pearly dawn of summer,
20   fate's truth, superior triumphs
of the sovereign prince of Rome.
May you achieve the throne of grace and favor,
and may your name, in peace and war, bring
heaven's admiration, and earth to the yoke,
25   for you bring great honors to your servants,
merciful Caesar and valiant Romulus.
Like the great Alexander, your excellence
makes you immortal in the mouths of men.
Those who offer you their ardent blood
30   put their lives and swords in your service,
counting it a great favor and
fortunate fate to lose them in your service.
To greater effort such favor calls us,
gracious youth, victorious Ferdinand.
35   Now my brother, seizing such a noble branch
treads down the meanest envy.
My unworthy pen acclaims your greatness
as I end in humbly kissing your feet.
Pardon my audacious rusticity,
40   for I am your Royal Highness's slave.

It is conceivable that Cueva sent this poem with the sonnet to her brother in the hope that it would pass through the hands of the cardinal-prince himself. The sonnet bears a similar title: "Parabien a mi hermano don Antonio de esta MI [¿merced insigne?] que su Alteza le hizo el día que tomó el guión" (Congratulating my brother, Don Antonio, for this significant favor granted him by His Highness on the day he took the standard). Cueva's knowledge of classical practice creates an appropriately high tone, in crowning her brother with laurels of congratulation. She further elevates him by juxtaposing the young man and the king's brother, Ferdinand, in the opening lines:

> Goza joven gallardo la dichosa
> merced insigne de su Real alteza;
> de el árbol se corone tu cabeza,
> en que fue convertida Dafne hermosa.
>
> 5   Muestre, muestre tu diestra valerosa,
> conforme al cargo heroica fortaleza,
> y en las empresas de mayor grandeza,
> salga siempre tu espada vitoriosa.
>
> Guarde el cielo a tu divino soberano,
> 10   amparo de caídos generoso,
> y a ti gozar te deje en larga vida.
>
> A tanto bien y favor querido hermano,
> y en todo trance seas tan dichoso
> que ganes nombre y fama esclarecida.
>
> (ms. 4127 250v–251r)

Take pleasure, privileged young gallant,
in the notable favor of his Royal Highness;
He crowns your head from the tree
into which the beauteous Daphne was changed.

Show, show your brave skills, that conform
to that heroic charge and cardinal virtue,
and in the greatest enterprises
may your sword always emerge victorious.

May heaven keep your divine sovereign,
generous shelter of the fallen,
and may it leave you to enjoy long life.

Beloved brother, may you enjoy reward and favor
and in all troubles be so favored
that you gain renown and shining fame.

In the tercets, the prince and her brother are again linked, as she asks heaven's protection for the fount of her brother's future success and for Antonio himself. The concluding tercet acknowledges the bonds of affection between Cueva and her brother, as it once more links honorable fame with the family's name. Similarly, the sonnet addressed to Antonio before the army's march into the Low Countries expresses love for her brother as well as pride in the family's rank and achievements. She begins by wishing her brother a long life in the most affectionate terms: "Goza felices años dichosos, / querido y dulce hermano" (1–2; May you enjoy fortunate and happy years / sweet, beloved brother). However, once again the second quartet is dominated by ancestral *hombría,* now carried, through her brother, into the period of her own generation:

> *A d. Antonio de la Cueva y Silva mi hermano estando*
> *muy favorecido de su alteza cuando partió a Flandes*
>
> Goza felices años dichosos,
> querido y dulce hermano, la ventura
> que de tantos pesares asegura
> por tu medio los fines más gloriosos.
>
> 5   De tus antecesores generosos
> la gran fama que eternamente dura,
> la tuya aumente, pues que ya procura
> cantar de tu valor hechos famosos.
>
> El mundo espero los viva tan grandes
> 10 que las hazañas del valiente Aquiles
> junto a las tuyas deslucidas veas.
>
> De el invicto Ferdinando en Flandes
> a los pies pongas los rebeldes viles,
> mostrando bienes del gran Silvio Eneas.
>
> (ms. 4127 269r–269v)

> *To don Antonio de la Cueva y Silva, my brother, being*
> *highly favored by His Highness when he left for Flanders*
>
> May you enjoy fortunate and happy years
> sweet, beloved brother, in the venture

that through you shall ensure the most
glorious end to so many afflictions.

The great, eternally enduring fame
of your generous ancestors
augmented now by your own, seeks
to sing the famous deeds of your valor.

The world hopes you may achieve such great
feats that the deeds of valiant Achilles,
beside yours, will lose their brilliance.

May you place the vile rebels of Flanders
at the feet of the matchless Ferdinando,
and reveal the grandeur of the great Aeneas.

As in the sonnet to her dead uncle, Cueva measures Antonio against the
perfect classical examples, anticipating that his feats will eclipse those of
the Greek hero of Troy, Achilles. Although, as a woman, she does not
take part in warfare, she seeks to enhance her own status through the
aura of honor and fame that she creates around her brother's participation in the king's forces.

Given that the poetry by seventeenth-century women still surviving
in the present day can only be a sample of a much larger body of work,
Cueva's sonnets celebrating her uncle, her brother, and his master stand as
a representative indicator of the value placed by noblewomen on family
honor and fame. The opportunities to write and to place themselves on
the record alongside successful men were few, but women took advantage
of the chances that came their way, articulating their intellectual equality
in poems composed for *certámenes* (poetry competitions) and in elegiac
verse. These provided opportunities to add personally to family honor,
rather than to be viewed merely as the channel for masculine *hombría*,
achieved through socially sanctioned marriage and motherhood.

CONCLUSION

These sonnets to patrons demonstrate a wider range of possibilities
for women than may previously have been conceded. They also reveal

that women were fully aware of the benefits available to them, their families, and their convents through the workings of patronage, and that women did not pass up the opportunities to participate when they were presented to them. These poets did not simply wait, passively, for any benefit that might accrue to them as a reflection of masculine endeavor. Instead, they knowingly engaged in a masculine field, negotiating benefits in the patronage marketplace, seeking to elevate their own status and to show their intellectual excellence in the written word. Women's language was seen by moralists and preachers as excessive, a symptom of moral laxity and sexual availability. Hence, the writing of sycophantic poetry to those who could offer them political protection may be another strategy by which women bypassed the restrictions that nominally governed their lives. These restrictions were not only enjoined by moralists, but were enshrined in the patriarchal family structure that represented a microcosmic model of the governing system of the Church and the state. Women's own views of their familial role in this schema can be discerned in their poetry pertaining to the family and its divine model, the Holy Family.

CHAPTER 2

MARRIAGE, MOTHERHOOD, PATRIARCHY

꓿ꙮꙷ

T HE FAMILY IN EARLY MODERN SPAIN was the smallest element through which social control was exerted by the patriarchal establishments of Church and state. Seventeenth-century notions of
the family stemmed partially from the Church Fathers and from post-
Tridentine Church doctrine. These notions were supported by the many
moralists who went into print in didactic literature, of whom the most
widely known and respected were probably Juan Luis Vives, Luis de
León, and Juan de Zabaleta. Also still current and a valuable source of
education, in spite of their relative antiquity, were the precepts of Alfonso X el Sabio (Alfonso the Wise) and his *Siete partidas* (seven divisions
of the law). The post-Trent urge for order as a means to present a united
front to growing Protestantism reinforced the paradigm. As head of the
household, the father was responsible for all under his roof, and with absolute power over every aspect of their lives he held a power reinforced
by law. The family, however, stood for more than this. At the upper levels of society, the importance attached to *limpieza de sangre* and *hombría*
established the family as a social statement and a ladder to preferment
in the patronage system. The value of these connections to social success
can be discerned in the sonnets written by Leonor de la Cueva y Silva to
her uncle and to her brother, already discussed.

Family and home were the approved, indeed the only, life paths for secular women that the Church, the state, and the moralists who went into print would countenance. In her poems to St. Joseph, Sor Violante del Cielo demonstrates her adherence to Counter-Reformation orthodoxy in promoting the nuclear family, with the pater familias at its head, as the epitome of Christian organization. However, within the family, Sor Violante's sonnets on the motherhood of the Virgin Mary present an entirely different view of maternal empowerment from that promulgated by the Church. Her view proposes Mary as an example to other women, not of meek submission, but of strength and independence.

The poems these women write about the family virtually ignore the institution of marriage, but find much to say about the role and responsibilities of the father as head of the family. They also demonstrate the empowering role that motherhood could provide for women. These poems cover both religious and secular matters, but at the base of almost all of them is a determination to express independent thought, clearly held views that reveal a great deal about the authors' intentions and concerns with regard to their own families and an awareness of their own importance within the family structure. Through them can be gained a glimpse into the hidden world of women's experience of family life in seventeenth-century Spain. Even bearing in mind Anne Cruz's warnings about the danger of misreading the writing in search of its authors, I shall contend, as she does, that, "we may still glean significant aspects of women's subjectivity through the self-referential traces left in their literary production" ("Challenging Lives" 104).

THE YOKE OF MARRIAGE

Family links provided opportunities for an advantageous marriage organized between the respective fathers without any requirement to consult the wishes of their daughters. Marriage was an important rite of passage, not only for its class significance, but also because it marked the beginning of a new, legally and theologically sanctioned, socially recognized unit in the patriarchal system. Though marriage is often portrayed as the silent enslavement of women to their husbands' control, where women were able to secure socially advantageous marriages they also gained in prestige. There are no poems, even among Ramírez's often acid verse, that denounce the institution of marriage or want of affective support. It is nevertheless significant, in the terms of this study, that, with one solitary exception, these poets do not celebrate the marriages of family members and friends in verse. As always when reading early modern works by women, it is as important to study their silences as the words they inscribe on the page.

Marriage in this period meant more than the advantageous linking of families and the production of children. It also included marriage to Christ through enclosure in the convent or, less formally and with greater difficulty, a semienclosed life with a group of like-minded women in a *beaterio*.[1] For many women, marriage to Christ provided them with security and a measure of independence, as well as with strong bonds of community and friendship. For others, the daughters of impoverished members of the middling and upper classes unable to marry them off for want of a dowry, it meant incarceration for life, with or without the necessary vocation. Nevertheless, the optimistic verse of Marcia Belisarda shows that, for her, to welcome a new bride of Christ into the convent was a cause for celebration.

The Church and the Spanish state were united in their views on social control and had common objectives with regard to the secular world, such as the protection of the family nucleus, one of the principal axes of social control. There were ample scriptural and patristic sources to bolster this approach. Augustine, for example, regarded marriage as a truly good institution because it was created by God before sin existed in the world.[2] For Augustine, the principal goods of marriage were the procreation of children, spousal fidelity, and the sacred commitment of husband and wife to each other until death. After the Council of Trent made a sacrament of marriage and the Protestant faith cultivated family sentiment, the authority of the husband over his wife became even stronger. Even in a loving marriage there were inherent contradictions and ten-

---

1. For a detailed study of women's lives both in convents and *beaterios,* see Elizabeth A. Lehfeldt, *Religious Women in Golden Age Spain: The Permeable Cloister* (Aldershot: Ashgate, 2005).

2. Augustine's view of marriage as a divine institution can be found in a number of texts, notably *The Good of Marriage* 1.1, *The City of God* 14.22, *Marriage and Concupiscence* 1.1, and the *Commentary on the Gospel of John* 10.2.2.

sions. The wife was excluded from economic activity that did not accord with the biological unit of mother, father, and children. As the Church supported a stable, domestic union, it also undermined it and interfered in its structure, enhancing the role of the father (King 38). The prevailing ideal of marriage in early modern Spain was that of the dominant husband, lord in his own domain, and of the subservient and obedient wife, who managed hearth and home under his protection and domination. The husband administered all his wife's affairs and only with his permission could she could sign legal documents. He had a concomitant duty to provide for his family and to bestow dowries. He also had the absolute power to punish and to authorize marriage until the child reached the age of twenty-five years (Alcalá Zamora 170).

Well-intentioned and influential works by moralists such as Juan Luis Vives and Luis de León endorsed prevailing views of women's basic inferiority and their appropriate role in the home. The humanist Vives wrote *Education of a Christian Woman*, originally in Latin, in 1523, for Catherine of Aragón, to assist in the education of her daughter, Mary Tudor, the future queen of England. He portrayed himself as a defender of women and was considered to be so in his time, yet, although he advocated women's education, it was only within the tight parameters of learning for moral self-improvement and to deter idleness. However, as Valerie Wayne has proposed, in spite of the derivative nature of his preoccupation with women's chastity and mental weakness, he was an innovator in the early years of the Northern Renaissance: "The rigid life he prescribes for women . . . was not the worst alternative for them then: it was one of the best available" (28). Vives, after all, considered companionship to be essential to the correct functioning of a marriage, although such companionship and mutual concern would always be subsumed under the husband's overall control.

Like his contemporaries, Vives is particularly preoccupied with female chastity, expressed in marriage through a woman's continence, and made evident in her silent, meek, and obedient deportment; a chaste woman did not provoke lust in her husband. With regard to speech, he subscribes to humoral theory; his concern is that it is the weakness of women's minds that prevents them from being able to bridle their tongues and "as a result there is no limit to their quarreling and no logic in their abusiveness, since there is no room for reason or judgment" (219). Because of this perceived lack of temperance and reason he urges women not to disagree with their husbands or to hurl insults, for once provoked, "it will be difficult for him to make reconciliation, and even if he does become reconciled, every time he remembers that humiliation, he will not be able to look at his wife with a favorable eye. In the eyes of God too what displeasure it brings!" (219). His advice is based on the assumption that since women cannot avoid their natural weakness, it is important to provide them with the tools of passive acceptance necessary to endure their God-assigned deferential role.

Writing at about the same time, the highly influential Fray Luis de León does not share Vives's comparatively enlightened opinions on female education. He endorses the long-held Aristotelian view of women's mental incapacity and inferiority. In his widely circulated treatise *La perfecta casada* (The perfect wife) he also proclaims the absolute necessity for the wife's obedience to the husband in every aspect of life. Bolstered by Scripture, Greek philosophy, and the Church Fathers, León's rationale is that only by accepting her naturally inferior status to the male can a woman truly fulfill her divinely ordered role as center of the household and helpmeet to her husband, whose goods she is able to augment by her zeal and care.

However, invective poetry by prominent poets like Francisco de Quevedo, the absence or generally negative portrayal of wives in *comedias* (plays) and the critical writings of seventeenth-century moralists suggest that the ideal was not always achieved.[3] Women found ways to circumvent the irksome restriction of household enclosure. It was difficult for a devout husband to prevent his wife from going to church, for example, and this created problems concerning unsanctioned social contact with men, despite the presence of *dueñas* (older female chaperones) or *escuderos* (male servants). Wives also attended processions, *romerías* (pilgrimages), and religious fiestas. For the more daring, the *tapado* (concealment under a voluminous cape that completely covered the head and body) also allowed

---

3. There are always exceptions, such as Lope de Vega's Casilda in *Peribañez,* but it is commonly noted that wives and mothers are not well represented. Quevedo's satirical sonnets provide a rich vein of misogyny directed principally at the old, those who use cosmetics, and the presumed infidelity of married women. Quevedo's own late failed marriage to the widowed Doña Esperanza de Mendoza is, of course, well documented. See, for example, Jauralde Pou, *Francisco de Quevedo (1580–1645),* 632–33, 70–75.

illicit outings, while some tolerant husbands permitted visits to friends, though these were frowned upon by the Church (Alcalá Zamora 174).

A century before Vives, Alfonso X "El Sabio," who enshrined the importance of marriage as a social pacifier and regulator in the fourth of his *Siete partidas,* and hence as a social rather than a private good, shared Augustine's view of marriage as the holiest of the sacraments because it was ordained by God: "Por aquellas palabras creed y multiplicad y fenchid la tierra" (qtd. in M. Stone 63; Through these words you grow and multiply and fill the earth).[4] The fourth Partida also stressed the importance of mutual consent between partners to the marriage. Yet it was not until the Council of Trent that the Church grudgingly accepted the idea that couples could marry without also obtaining parental consent. Even then, such marriages were regarded as indecorous or illicit (38).

The Church's doctrine on marriage and the paternal role in partner choice did not, however, always accord with popular practice.[5] Marilyn Stone records that illegitimate births were common in the thirteenth and fourteenth centuries in all social classes and that clandestine marriages were common from the thirteenth to the sixteenth centuries (61). The Church experienced difficulty in formalizing marriage patterns at all levels of society in Catholic Europe, and it was only after Trent that the Church was able to impose its authority by invalidating marriages that had not been performed in public before the parish priest (Goody 148). These facts suggest that there was no lack of affection and desire between couples, but that they simply wished to have the freedom to choose their partners.

An important conduit and outlet for social comment was the *comedia,* where married women were largely invisible. However, while wives may be ignored in seventeenth-century *comedias,* the path to marriage frequently forms the core of the action. Melveena McKendrick has argued that in the seventeenth century it was only the dramatists who continued the Erasmian liberalism of the sixteenth century, albeit within

4. The *Siete Partidas* were compiled during the reign of Alfonso X (1252–1284). The Church did not officially recognize marriage as one of the sacraments until Session 24 of the Council of Trent in 1563.

5. See R. H. Helmholz, *Marriage Litigation in Medieval England* (London and New York: Cambridge University Press, 1974), 25ff. Studying medieval English marriage practices and examining court records, Helmholz asserts that people resented Church interference and preferred to regulate their own marriage practices.

the circumscribing attitudes of their day. She notes the playwrights' concern that women should be free to follow their inclinations in the choice of a husband and that parents who try to force their daughter to marry against her will must be responsible for the consequences (327–28). When marriages were arranged along dynastic or economic lines, however, mutuality was not a concern. The writings of the moralist Juan de Zabaleta nevertheless suggest that many married women did their best to please their husbands. In his popular *El día de la fiesta por la mañana y por la tarde* (The holy day in the morning and in the evening), Zabaleta, in inveighing against women's use of cosmetics, observes that all that is required of a wife is that she perform her office. He encapsulates the inequity of female enclosure and male freedom in his refutation of the idea that women paint themselves to "rehacer el cariño del matrimonio" (recreate marital affection):

Pienso que se engañan. El amor entre los casados bien puede ser que le empiece la hermosura, pero quien le prosigue en la condición, los hijos y los buenos oficios. La palabra esposa lo más que significa es comodidad, lo menos es deleite. La mujer que trata blanda y atentamente a su marido con cualquier cara es hermosa. (115)

I think that they fool themselves. Love between married couples may well begin with physical beauty but it is prolonged by children and good offices. The word "wife" means more comfort than delight. The woman who treats her husband attentively and with mildness is beautiful with any face.

It is at least to Zabaleta's credit that in the same paragraph he censures husbands who mistreat the wives who meekly conform to the approved model: "Muy inicuo, muy ingrato es menester que sea el hombre que no quiere bien a la mujer propia *que cumple con las obligaciones de mujer*" (my italics; Very iniquitous, very ungrateful is the husband who does not dearly love his wife *if she complies with the obligations of a wife*). However, in the case of those regarded as transgressive women—for example, those accused of adultery—the important matters of male honor, pride, and *limpieza de sangre* supersede any other consideration:

[L]os jueces, para castigarla, no preguntan la causa, sino averiguan el delito; convencida, la condenan a muerte, aunque su marido la hubiese dado mucha causa. ¿Con qué ojos mirará el mundo, con qué ojos mirarán las leyes, a la mujer que, porque su marido la hace alguna vez mal pasaje, se vuelve contra la honra de su marido? (133)

To punish her the judges do not ask the reason but prove the crime; convinced, they condemn her to death, even though the husband may have given her much cause. With what eyes does the world, with what eyes do the laws look upon the wife who, because her husband sometimes treats her badly, acts against her husband's honor?

Women's lack of a real role to play in the matter of matrimony, other than that allowed them by masculine expectation and control, is strongly suggested by the paucity of poetry by women to mark this important event. Those who went along with the system were officially and legally imprisoned by it, regardless of the small freedoms they could secure for themselves. Those who resisted and sought greater independence found themselves at variance with societal norms. Writing of Catalonia in this period, for example, Isabel Pérez Molina states that masculine control and tutelage were channeled through matrimony that was always a contract between men permitting the circulation of women among the various families. The purpose of this circulation, requiring control of female sexuality, was the continuation of patrilineal descent and reproduction of the existing social structure ("Mujeres y matrimonio" 27).

As commodities in a marriage market controlled by fathers, and bearing both economic and social rewards and consequences, it is not surprising that these women do not write epithalamia or sonnets in praise of marriage. The survival of the patriarchal ideas underlying the commodification and exchange of women into the modern period has been criticized by prominent feminist philosophers such as Luce Irigaray: "The society we know, our own culture, is based upon the exchange of women. . . . The passage into the social order, into the symbolic order, . . . is assured by the fact that men, or groups of men, circulate women among themselves" (170). Irigaray harnesses Marxist theories of commodities as the elementary form of capitalist wealth to the status of women in so-called patriarchal societies. In this schema women's reproductive capacity and exchange value contribute, without compensation, to the symbolic patriarchal order. Women are exchanged, not as women, but as women reduced to a common feature: "their current price in gold, or phalluses" (174–75). Romero Díaz also observes Zayas's critique of women as an object of exchange in her story "La burlada Aminta," adding that this is more than just an exchange of status and lineage and ancestors, it is also a transfer of wealth (119).

It is, then, significant that none of the poets in this study married, and that among all their poetry, only one *romance* by Catalina Clara Ramírez de Guzmán concerns a marriage: that of her youngest sister, Ana Rosalea, ten years her junior, to whom Ramírez gives the pastoral name of Anarda in her verse. Ana married don García Alonso de Villalobos, a lawyer of the Reales Consejos, who took Ana with him to Úbeda, leaving behind a trail of debt (Carrasco García 114):

> *A el desposorio de una dama*
>
> Para las bodas de Anarda
> convidado estuvo el sol,
> y habiendo de competirla
> vergonzoso se aumentó.
> 5 Quiere negar que el huir
> no ha sido poco valor,
> alegando que él es uno
> y que sus ojos son dos.
> La esperanza acreditada
> 10 se halla con el garzón,
> pues ha puesto sus deseos
> en tan dulce posesión.
> Sin duda que con Anarda
> la dicha se equivocó,
> 15 que iba en casa de una fea
> y por yerro le tocó.
> Vivan a pesar de el tiempo
> en tan apacible unión,
> que juzguen horas los siglos
> 20 dándole envidia al amor.
> Dilátese su progenie
> en tan bella sucesión
> que eternice su memoria
> que es la fortuna mayor.
> (BN ms. 3884 237v)

On the marriage of a lady

The sun was invited to
the marriage of Anarda,
and having to compete with her
he grew more and more ashamed.
He tried to deny that to flee
showed his lack of valor,
alleging he is only one,
while her eyes are two.
Accredited hope is to
be found in the young man,
for he has placed his desires
on such a sweet possession.
There's no doubt that in Anarda
Dame Fortune made an error,
while going to an ugly woman's house,
she touched on Anarda instead.
May you both outlive time
in such peaceful union
that centuries will seem like hours,
provoking Love's envy.
May your progeny increase
in such beautiful succession
as to eternalize your memory,
for that is the greatest fortune.

Half of the *romance* is taken up in acknowledging the beauty of the bride, who outrivals the sun. It ends in conventional wishes for a peaceful and enduring marriage (18–19) and the hope that the marriage may be fruitful. Children, Ramírez reveals in the final line, perpetuate your line, which is the greater fortune.[6] Don García barely appears in the

6. The marriage of Ramírez's youngest sister was not fruitful, nor were those of her other siblings. The last surviving sibling, Antonia Manuela (Antandra in Ramírez's poetry), notes this in her testament of 1697, also affirming that she herself did not marry: "Nunca tomado estado ni dejado hijos ni descendientes mis hermanos" (I never married, nor did my brothers and sisters leave any children or descendants). See Carrasco García,

poem at all, except as the "garzón" whose hopes have been realized, and in the same stanza Anarda is described as "tan dulce posesión" (12). For Ramírez, marriage makes Anarda one item in the husband's catalogue of assets; there is no suggestion that she also possesses him.

Ramírez is exceptional among these poets in writing many poems to and about identifiable members of her own family that celebrate rites of passage as well as everyday family events. It is not so much surprising that she wrote a poem about a sibling's marriage as that she wrote only one, given that six of the ten siblings of the family survived to adulthood and that three, Beatriz, Lorenzo, and Ana, subsequently married. Given her propensity to write on all manner of family events, this surprising lack of epithalamic verse may well indicate Ramírez's disdain for, or disapproval of, the marriages finally settled upon by her family. Beatriz's ill-fated marriage, when she was past fifty, lasted only two days, when her husband, don Álvaro de Henestrosa y Cabrera, died (Gazul 524).

Marriage to Christ via enclosure in the convent brought its own restrictions, although it also provided opportunities denied to secular wives. Nevertheless, it must have been particularly irksome for those young women incarcerated against their will by their families. Whatever the circumstances of young women's enclosure, when Marcia Belisarda celebrates a number of nuns' professions in her poems, she expresses joy that these women have joined with Christ in marriage and proclaims their enduring purity. For example, in a *romance* she writes: "sabed que el supremo Rey / sus desposorios se letra / con hija del gran Bernardo" (5–7; know that the supreme king pronounces his nuptials / with a daughter of the great Bernard), and a *villancico* (a Spanish song and verse form with rustic origins) opens with "Tierna esposa del cordero" (1; Sweet bride of the lamb).[7] Many women entered the convent as a means of avoiding

---

La Plaza Mayor de Llerena y otros estudios, 113. The illegitimate son of her brother Lorenzo clearly did not rate a mention.

7. Three poems, a sonnet, a *romance,* and a *villancico,* dealing with the profession of nuns and celebrating their *desposorios* (marriages) with Christ are entitled *A la profesión de una monja bernarda que la hizo en día de la degollación del baptista estando el santísimo sacramento descubierto y su nombre Paula* (ms. 7469: 19r); *Villancico a doña María de la Puebla profesando en la Concepción franciscana de Toledo estando el santísimo sacramento descubierto* (ms. 7469: 56r); and *A la profesión de doña Petronila de la Palma en la Concepción Real de Toledo siguiendo la metáfora de la palma* (ms. 7469: 7v). This last sonnet will be discussed fully in the chapter on friendship.

the pressures of marriage and, in the cases of women like Sor Violante del Cielo or the Mexican Sor Juana Inés de la Cruz, to be able to pursue their spiritual or intellectual interests. Spiritual marriage to Christ is expressed in much poetry by religious women, often with strong bodily overtones, as the physical consummation of the marriage is deferred until the day of their resurrection.

This desire to fuse her own body with that of Christ is a common feature of Luisa de Carvajal y Mendoza's poetry. She transgressed the norms of society and achieved remarkable independence by neither marrying nor entering a convent; her high social status probably gave her the latitude she desired, but also made her behavior all the more shocking to her peers. Although Carvajal y Mendoza rejected marriage and shrank from male contact, her poetry abounds with images of reciprocal love between her persona, Silva, an anagram of Luisa, and Christ. In a funeral sermon preached in her honor at the Jesuit English College of St. Gregory in Seville, Father Juan de Pineda, while never missing an opportunity to describe the manly qualities without which, in his view, her mission would have been impossible, speaks of Carvajal y Mendoza's perfect marriage to Christ:

Pregunto, ¿cuál es la más perfecta casada, la que lo es con un hombre mortal, y tiene el corazón partido como dice el Apóstol, o la que desposada con el celestial desposo con voto de fe y lealtad (que es aquello, desponsabo te mihi in fide) está dedicada al único servicio y amor de su criador, que no se muere, ni se acaba? Casad una flaqueza y delicadeza mujeril, con un corazón de varón, una flaca naturaleza con un espíritu fuerte, intrépido, acometedor de grandes y heróicas empresas, y haréis una perfecta casada, aunque sea una perpetua y perfeta virgen. (7)

And I ask you, which is the most perfect wife, she who is wife of a mortal man and has her heart divided, as the Apostle says, or she who, married with a celestial spouse with vows of faith and loyalty (which is that *desponsabo te mihi in fide*), is dedicated uniquely to the service and adoration of her creator, who never dies and never ends? Marry feminine weakness and delicacy with the heart of a man, a natural frailty with a strong, intrepid spirit, capable of great and heroic enterprise, and you will have a perfect wife, though she be a perfect and perpetual virgin.

Father Pineda here persists in the medieval ideal in which virginity was always superior to marriage and the most perfect *casada* was she who pledged herself to Christ, pursuing a life of blameless sanctity freed from the pull of the flesh. However, Carvajal y Mendoza's sonnets are remarkably erotic, as will be seen in Chapter 6.

Leaving aside her personal preferences on the matter, Carvajal y Mendoza does not reject marriage for the women of her own extended family; a number of her letters are addressed to her married cousin Isabel de Velasco, and she writes in affectionate terms about the concerns of that family.[8] Her considerable correspondence to Rodrigo de Calderón (favorite of the Duke of Lerma, who in turn was a favorite of King Philip III) originated in the family connection through his marriage to another cousin. Furthermore, her own vow of obedience indicates that hers was not a rebellious position toward the norms of Spanish society; it was simply that, for Carvajal y Mendoza, those norms could not supersede those of God, from whom she believed her vocation for martyrdom to derive. Paradoxically, she couched her rebellion in a discourse of obedience both to God and to those she regarded as her religious superiors. By citing God as her authority, she could pursue the independent course that she had determined to follow while still displaying obedience, albeit to a higher power. Experience had taught her the importance of obedience to powerful men and to Catholic protocol, which she claimed to have practiced since childhood (Rhodes, "Tight Embrace" 5).

This requirement for obedience to a superior male figure obtained at all levels of society, as well as the spiritual arm of the state. Hence, women were answerable to a paternalistic chain of command, whether their marriages were ordained by the Church or by their fathers. The control and power exercised by the father figure as head of his family is nowhere more clearly seen than in the sonnets of Sor Violante del Cielo. However, even as she promotes the Counter-Reformation ideal, she also inserts her own preference for a gentle tolerant exercise of power that incorporates feminine aspirations.

8. Isabel de Velasco was married to Luis Carrillo de Toledo, marquis de Caracena, viceroy of Valencia. In a letter to her on 15 September 1598, Carvajal y Mendoza includes an affectionate family detail: "[L]e puedo juntamente dar a v.sría la enhorabuena de un sobrino que me dicen le ha nacido a vra sría, de su hermana" (I should at the same time like to congratulate your honor on the new nephew born to your honor by your sister). See Carvajal y Mendoza, 98.

THE PATERFAMILIAS

Unlike Juan Luis Vives or Luis de León, Augustine's view of masculine dominance in marriage rested not on women's supposed mental weakness and propensity to sin, but on the type of wisdom of which they were capable. While he saw men and women as having both speculative and practical wisdom, both being essential to managing one's life, he believed that women excelled in the practical and men in the speculative, in accordance with the opposition between *scientia* and *sapientia*. Donald Burt encapsulates Augustine's views on the matter of subordination in the family as the superiority of speculative wisdom over the practical, a dominance necessary for a normal society (107). This dominance, for Augustine, bore considerable responsibility:

> In homes dominated by love, those who command are those charged to have regard for the interests of the others. In such families those who command are actually at the service of those whom they seem to order about. They rule out of duty to those they care for and compassion for those for whom they must provide. (City 19: 14)

Augustine's benevolent dictatorship discusses a subtle and effective ideal that achieves its objectives without brutality: the home dominated by love. Such a home conceals the paternalistic inflexibility that still inscribes the norm. In the early modern upper-class household, the pater familias reflected the kingly role and represented God the father at a microcosmic level; he was a controlling agent responsible for all people under his roof, from family members to servants. As it was his responsibility to discipline and order his household, he was also answerable for any transgressions that took place within it, and this made him a jealous guardian of family honor (Alcalá Zamora 171).

This strong, honorable, and authoritative father figure became harnessed to Church propaganda following the Council of Trent when serious attempts were made to normalize sacramental marriage in the face of the increasing number of liaisons devoid of official sanction (Ibero 108). The Church turned to art as widely accessible visual propaganda, using idealized images of the Holy Family to strengthen its message of benign paternalism. Indeed, Baroque Spanish artists' depictions of the Holy

Family differ widely from those of the Renaissance. These early paintings that put Joseph in the background accord with the very minor role he played in the religious thought of earlier Christians. The Scriptures provide little information about him or his life. Apocryphal stories of Joseph record him as a widower with five children, married at the age of forty, who lived with his wife for forty-nine years. He was therefore ninety at the time of his betrothal to Mary. Alba Ibero notes that until the Baroque period he was not only a secondary figure but frequently an object of derision among the popular classes (106). In her study of Baroque art as a tool of the Church, Ibero records that the Church, as art patron, procured paintings of the Virgin and Child that had a didactic function since these representations "ilustran perfectamente el pensamiento cristiano basado en la sujeción de la mujer a la maternidad, considerada como la culminación máxima de su vida" (102–3; perfectly illustrate Christian thought based on the subjection of woman to maternity, considered to be the highest culmination of her life). Ibero also notes a significant change in pictures of the Holy Family. The figure of Joseph, in Renaissance works an aged figure in the background, becomes progressively younger in Baroque paintings and takes a more dominant position as pater familias. This contrasts with an increasing effacement of the Virgin, whose pictorial dominance in earlier works is replaced by representations of a passive mother, obedient and fulfilled in her role.[9] There is also a process of secularization of the figures, providing exemplary didactic images of the ideal family (106). Particularly illustrative of this change are the paintings by Murillo of the Holy Family. The Virgin is represented only through her role as mother: passive, seated, occasionally engaged in needlework, while a young, virile, and dark-haired Joseph is variously portrayed as busy about his carpentry, protectively guiding his family into Egypt, and even holding the baby himself before the seated Madonna. In moving into the domestic realm, the authoritative father displaces the preeminence of the Virgin mother.

9. See also Marina Warner, *Alone of All Her Sex* (New York: Random House, 1983). Warner notes that in Byzantine nativities Joseph is fast asleep beside a rock, his back to the miracle. With the new domestic idealism after the Renaissance he begins to inspire a cult of his own, even being adopted by St. Teresa of Ávila as her personal patron, "the father of my soul" (189).

This figuring of Joseph as the dominant and controlling figure in the family group can also be seen in two sonnets written by Sor Violante del Cielo celebrating not only Joseph's sanctity and power, but also his humanity. He fulfills the appropriate role as ideal head of the family in caring for his wife and child, which Sor Violante establishes immediately in the first sonnet's title:

Al glorioso Patriarca S. Joseph

Pues en la humanidad de ser Divino,
padre adoptivo al temporal gobierno
fuistes del mismo Dios, que niño tierno
desde su Padre a sujetarse vino.

5   ¡O cómo parecido os imagino
en esta dignidad al Padre Eterno!
Pues aquel, de quien tiembla el mismo infierno,
a daros obediencia se previno:

Y si en defensa de su Madre pura
10   esposo os hizo de su propia Madre,
y en vos su mismo crédito asegura,

¿Qué excelencia hay, Joseph, que a vos no os cuadre:
Si el mismo, a que obedece la ventura,
súbdito es vuestro a título de Padre?

(Parnaso lusitano 25)

To the glorious Patriarch St Joseph

Since, in the humanizing of the Divine,
you were adoptive father and temporal governor
of God himself, who as a tender child
came from his Father to surrender himself,

Oh how similar in this dignity
I imagine you to be to the eternal Father!
For he, before whom the very Hell trembles,
foretold the obedience he would show you.

And to defend his pure Mother
he made you his own Mother's husband,
and in you assured her good reputation.

What greater excellence, Joseph, though you
may not realize, than that he whom fate obeys
is your subject, and calls you Father?

Sor Violante also affirms her adherence to orthodox thinking in making Joseph an authoritarian figure of the highest order in the first quartet. God assumes human form and subjects himself to the household discipline of Joseph, who, in his role as adoptive father, is raised to God-like power and status: "¡O cómo parecido os imagino / en esta dignidad al Padre Eterno!" (5–6). This description of Joseph figures the microcosmic representation of God's greater realm, exactly in line with the received wisdom of the time as to the divinely ordered nature of human society.

Furthermore, Joseph is both spouse and defender of the pregnant Mary: "Y si en defensa de su Madre pura / esposo os hizo de su propia Madre, / y en vos su mismo crédito asegura" (9–11). The protective role is confirmed by Scripture, but only once divine revelation assures him of the child's divinity.[10] The effects of injury to a husband's honor in this period have been studied by Yvonne Yarbro-Bejarano, through the lens of Lope de Vega's plays. These reveal that the degree of violence required to recuperate lost honor depends on the extent to which the husband has lost control: "Wives whose illicit desire remains in the realm of the imagination can be brought back under control through punishment . . . or set at a distance through banishment." Where sexual appropriation has occurred, either by consent or through rape, murder is the most likely outcome. The husband's power and control are mediated through his menacing presence once he becomes aware of his dishonor (132–33). Sor Violante's portrayal sets Joseph apart from the prevailing ideologies of honor and blood purity in seventeenth-century Spain, where husbands could legitimately kill adulterous wives, provided both wife and lover were caught in the act. However, this is not necessarily a divergence from

10. The scriptural authority is Matthew, who records Joseph's revelation at 1: 18–21 that saw him cleave to his wife rather than quietly divorce her.

the orthodox view on Sor Violante's part since Joseph's special status derives from his role as adoptive father of a child of divine origin.

Unusually in Sor Violante's poetry, the Virgin Mary is figured in this sonnet in the same passive manner as the paintings of the period. Such a portrayal faithfully mirrors traditional concepts of maternity. Sor Violante sets out to emphasize the relationship between Joseph, as earthly father and representative of a divine father, and the Christ child, both God and helpless baby, as the sonnet again reverses the social order in the final tercet. Sor Violante affirms that as the Christ child is obedient to his fate, he also becomes Joseph's "súbdito," humbled before him in the household hierarchy. Nevertheless, her concern that Joseph may not fully realize the significant elevation in his status is reflected in "que a vos no os cuadre" (12).

In addressing a sonnet, ostensibly of praise, to Joseph, but suggesting that he does not know his own worth, Sor Violante sets herself as sonnet creator in a position dominant to that of Joseph. In portraying Joseph as unaware of his part in the unfolding drama of the Nativity, Sor Violante inserts herself into the sonnet as a superior figure in reason and knowledge to the person she venerates. Sor Violante subtly reverses the basis of power; she has the benefit of history and faith to support her statement, but she also takes the opportunity to manifest her intelligence as a woman writing in an era when science had determined women to be weaker, both physically and mentally, than their male superiors.

Sor Violante's second sonnet to St. Joseph is a triumph of wordplays and Old Testament typology, as she employs poetic praise to reveal her own worth as a poet versed in the art of the conceit:

Al mismo santo

Previniendo el peligro más contrario,
guarda trigo un Joseph de eterna fama,
con que del mundo salvador le aclama
la varia multitud del vulgo vario.

5   Mas de otro mejor Pan depositario
Otro Joseph, que en Dios de amor se inflama,
Ostentando feliz su ardiente llama,
guardó de cielo y tierra el sacro erario.

Y porque en todo al otro pareciese,
10   siete abriles le tuvo tan guardado,
que al primero excedió Joseph segundo.

¿Qué mucho, pues, que el título adquiriese
de creador del Creador, que le ha creado,
de salvador del Salvador del mundo?

(Parnaso lusitano 26)

To the same saint

Foreseeing great and perverse peril,
a Joseph of eternal fame hoards the corn
and a multitude of many peoples
acclaim him savior of the world.

But another Joseph, inflamed by God's love,
was repository of a better bread.
His burning flame brightly shining, he guarded
the sacred treasure of heaven and earth.

And like the other in every way,
who for seven springs kept his treasure safe,
the second Joseph exceeded the first.

How great, then, is the title he acquires for
himself, of creator of the Creator who created him,
and savior of the Savior of the world?

Again, Joseph is portrayed as the Counter-Reformation ideal of protective, providing fatherhood. Indeed, Sor Violante's choice of the Old Testament Joseph as the prefiguring model serves to reinforce the positive qualities of an even more heroic New Testament Joseph. The comparison of the two Josephs is particularly apt, and not only because they share a name; balanced analogies between the Old and the New Testament provided proof of the truth of Christian revelation. In this sonnet, Sor Violante maintains her two Josephs in perfect equilibrium as she rehearses their separate exploits in the first two quartets, opening with the Old Testament Joseph. This Joseph was sold into slavery in Egypt and rose to prominence for his wisdom, his perspicacity, and his ability to interpret the pharaoh's dreams. The New Testament Joseph fled before Herod into Egypt to keep his little family safe and in so doing saved the souls of humanity from spiritual famine, since his act permitted Christ to achieve his goal of sacrifice on earth. This Joseph too received divine instructions in a series of dreams.[11] As is usual in employing Old Testament typology to reveal Christian "truth," the *pan* (bread) of the new covenant of love is a better bread than that of the old covenant of the law: "Mas de otro mejor Pan depositario" (5). Faith and belief are as essential to spiritual survival as bread is to bodily preservation: the sonnet refers specifically to the perfectibility of the Old Testament types in the New, as the grain in the Old Testament becomes the bread of the Host. The second Joseph also exceeds the first in his length of service: the first Joseph garnered food for seven years, the second Joseph reared Christ to adulthood, as Sor Violante proclaims in the tercets: "Y porque en todo al otro pareciese, / siete abriles le tuvo tan guardado, / que al primero excedió Joseph segundo" (9–11).

Infused by the love of God, Joseph cares for his "sacro erario," as Christ is cradled in the center of the poem. This protective Joseph becomes something of a Janus figure, caring for and protecting the child like a mother, guarding and managing his family like the ideal father. The poet sings Joseph's praises in the final tercet in clever wordplay that weaves a circular path of creation and salvation. In rearing the child Christ to adulthood, Joseph becomes the creator of his own Creator and the savior of his own Savior: "¿Qué mucho pues que el título adquiriese / de Creador del Creador, que le ha creado, / de Salvador del Salvador del mundo?" (12–14).

Sor Violante's positive affirmation of Joseph as head of his household and loving protector of his wife and child accords well with the observations of Electa Arenal and Georgina Sabat de Rivers. They affirm that St. Joseph was a favorite subject for female religious writers as "una figura serena, comprensiva y lejana de las actitudes que se identifican con el hombre intransigente" (71; a serene figure, understanding and far from the attitudes that are identified with the intransigent male). The imagery

---

11. In Matthew 1: 20 he is made aware of the divinity of the Christ child. After the birth of the child in Bethlehem, Joseph receives a second vision warning him to take the family into Egypt (Matthew 2: 13). Finally, as promised, when Herod dies, Joseph is again instructed via a dream.

of Sor Violante's two sonnets of praise is wholly affirming, extolling Joseph's wisdom, warmth, and humility. The social and religious paradigm enabled the Church to enjoin loving warmth on fathers without damaging the natural order. As Joseph comes to the foreground in so many paintings of the same period, so Sor Violante joins in the educative process in works that were available to an influential coterie readership. In two further sonnets she strives both to praise exemplary male figures and to soften the edges of the patriarchal imagery.

Having established St. Joseph as the ideal of fatherhood, Sor Violante moves on to express the warmth of a more gentle father love, relating it to divine revelation and allegory, in sonnets that praise a saint and a priest. In the first, "A S. Antonio de Lisboa, llamado vulgarmente de Padua, con el Niño Jesus en los brazos" (To St. Anthony of Lisbon, commonly called of Padua, with the Child Jesus in his arms), she celebrates St. Anthony's vision of a loving child who affectionately embraces him:

> Quiso representar el Verbo Eterno
> su pasión a Francisco milagroso,
> y vuelto crucifixo el cuerpo hermoso
> diole de su dolor el más interno.
>
> 5 Y queriendo después el Sempiterno
> favorecer a Antonio venturoso,
> su Nacimiento le mostró glorioso
> en forma de un desnudo Niño tierno.
>
> Y por representarlo más al vivo
> 10 púsosele en los brazos soberanos,
> igualándole en esto con su Madre.
>
> Oh favor celestial, raro, excesivo,
> que vuelva Cielo Empíreo vuestras manos
> la summa Idea del Eterno Padre.
>
> (*Parnaso lusitano* 42)

> The Eternal Word wished to portray
> his passion to the miraculous Francis,
> and making his beautiful body a crucifix
> gave of himself his deepest agony.

Then the Eternal One, wanting to
favor the fortunate Anthony,
showed him his glorious nativity
in the form of a tender, naked child.

And to make his representation more real
He put himself into those sovereign arms,
equalling him, in this, to his mother.

O rare, excessive celestial favor,
that makes your hands an Empyrean Heaven
the full Idea of the Eternal Father.

Although the sonnet removes the subject matter from the sublunary
to the divine, in representing the love of God for the human soul, nevertheless the outward manifestation of the miracle is of an affectionate
embrace between man and child. St. Anthony of Padua was Portuguese
and a contemporary of St. Francis, whose order he joined seeking the
martyrdom already achieved in Morocco by a number of St. Francis's fol-
lowers. Sor Violante links them closely through the double miracle of
St. Francis's stigmata, celebrated in the first quartet: "Y vuelto crucifixo el
cuerpo hermoso / Diole de su dolor el más interno" (3–4); and through
the appearance of Christ to St. Anthony as a child in the second: "Su
Nacimiento le mostró glorioso / en forma de un desnudo Niño tierno"
(7–8).

As the child embraces St. Anthony in his vision, Sor Violante pres-
ents the man in the role of mother: "Púsosele en los brazos soberanos /
Igualándose en esto con su Madre" (10–11). In the terminology used by
Sor Violante, this representation in the first tercet is no disparagement of
St. Anthony. Rather, she refocuses the Counter-Reformation representations of the Virgin and Christ child to privilege the female over the male,
while contriving to show the affection between man and child, saint and
God, and mother and child. Sor Violante blurs the distinctions between
the sexes and their roles and duties in the family, even though she rights
the hierarchical imagery in the final tercet. In cradling the child, St. Anthony represents God the Father in Heaven who cradles all humanity:
"Oh favor celestial, raro, excesivo, / Que vuelva Cielo Empíreo vuestras

manos / La summa Idea del Eterno padre" (12–14).[12] The imagery is not only of a miraculous vision of divine favor, but of the same loving relations between parent and child that she presents in the St. Joseph sonnets. The heavenly father is reflected in the specular re-creation of the holy man. As the child is the repeated image of the parent, man is the earthly image of God; this image is doubled as the miraculous child represents both the human and the divine. Sor Violante recurs to this imagery in a sonnet that attempts to elevate the status of Fray Antonio de la Concepción, of Lisbon, a Trinitarian who experienced a vision in which the Host became a child who embraced him. In each sonnet the embrace is mutual, suggesting reciprocity in child-adult relationships, and, in the feminizing of St. Anthony, a potential fluidity in parental roles as well. It also presents her with another opportunity for fascinating wordplay that foregrounds the Trinity and Fray Antonio's order:

Al venerable Padre Fray Antonio de la Concepción,
Religioso del Convento de la Santísima Trinidad
de Lisboa

¡Oh qué premios ganaron los servicios,
que habeis hecho feliz al Rey sagrado!
Pues depuso por vos lo rebozado,
cuando abrazos os dio por sacrificios.

5   Si el amor se conoce en los indicios,
como lo merecido en lo alcanzado,
mucho del mismo Dios fuistes amado.
Pues Dios hizo de amante los oficios,

y tanto os regaló su Omnipotencia,
10   que niño, como Dios de los amores,
Os dio los atributos de divino:

---

12. In her terminology, Sor Violante suggests a knowledge of Plato's theories, described by her contemporary Covarrubias as "Idea, vale tanto como un exemplar eterno, perpetuo e inmutable de cada una cosa de todas las que la naturaleza acá produce [Idea means an eternal, perpetual, and immutable exemplar of every single one of the things that nature produces]."

Pues como es Trino, si Único en la Esencia,
único os hizo a vos en los favores,
y en el hábito (Antonio) os hizo Trino.

(Parnaso lusitano 39)

To the venerable Father Antonio of the Conception, religious of the Convent of the Holy Trinity, Lisbon

Oh what rewards your services have won,
as you have pleased the sacred King!
For he revealed the hidden mystery to you
when he exchanged sacrifices for embraces.

If love is seen in the signs,
like the merited in the achieved,
you were well loved by God himself,
since God made the office into love.

And he gave you so much of his Omnipotence
that as a child, like the little god of lovers,
he gave you divine attributes.

For as he is Triune, though unique in essence,
he made you unique in favors,
and in the habit (Anthony) he made you Triune.

Sor Violante's celebrations of fatherly love, represented by Joseph as an ideal, protective pater familias, together with her location of the Virgin mother in a nurturing role, indicate that she subscribed to the Counter-Reformation ideology of the family. However, her advancement of St. Anthony and Fray Anthony in a more feminized role shows her drive to value the mother figure, and her poetic approach to the Virgin Mary is not at all orthodox. The Virgin Mary, as simple woman, mother, and divine, provides the pivot around which many of Sor Violante's poetic arguments are based; in Sor Violante's works she becomes "Everywoman." As such, she provides a safe, socially acceptable vehicle for Sor Violante's defense of women and mothers that does not work overtly against Church doctrine.

WOMEN'S VIEW OF MOTHERHOOD

As Mariló Vigil has observed in relation to the mother figure, however prescriptive her role may have been in the paintings of the period, she was otherwise almost invisible. The *comedia* gives the impression that society has no mother; when she does appear she is either without maternal sentiment or frankly antimaternal (126). Indeed, Cruz describes the *comedia* as "the most egregious in its absence of maternal roles; when the mother appears on stage it is to fulfill an archetype, never to assume a 'real' subject position" ("Feminism" 38). Cruz and Vigil are amply supported in this view. Ludwig Pfandl, for example, goes further in asserting that "la mujer como madre era algo misterioso, de lo cual no se hablaba fuera de los límites del hogar. La madre . . . no figura nunca como personaje en las comedias, ni es objeto de glorificación en la lírica" (Cultura 125; woman as mother is somewhat mysterious, nothing is said about her outside the limits of the home. The mother . . . never figures as a character in dramas, nor is she an object of glorification in lyric [poetry]). This last may have been true of the production of male poets, who did not hesitate to burlesque women in general and wives in particular, and at the time Pfandl made these comments much of the excellent scholarship on women's writing had yet to occur. However, women poets often take a surprisingly positive view of the family, given women's supposedly subservient place within it.

For a noblewoman, motherhood had other important connotations. Motherhood was often imposed on them by the men on whom they depended or by their obligation to provide an heir. For women of all classes, to raise sons to adulthood was the means to secure their own support in old age (Lerner, Consciousness 122). Since motherhood was of vital importance in securing a noble wife's future, this may account for Sor Violante's choice of the most perfect and noble mother, the Virgin Mary, as her model, over and above the exemplary value she held for the Church. She does not, however, seek to celebrate a meekly submissive Virgin model. So many of Sor Violante's sonnets are devoted to eulogizing and praising women's fortitude, wisdom, and achievements that they manifest a determination to raise women's status and seek recognition for their contribution to society.

The Virgin as mother is exempt from the biological and physical facts of normal childbirth; as Warner has observed, the only function she shares with ordinary womankind is that of suckling an infant (*Alone* 192). Yet Sor Violante does not celebrate this important nutritive activity in any of her poetry, nor does she pray to the Virgin in her more traditional role of intercessor for sinful humankind. Instead, through Sor Violante, the Virgin as human mother becomes a rallying symbol of female agency and independence and, above all, of power and dominance.[13]

As a nun, Sor Violante had opportunities to read the prescriptive works of Luis de León, Juan Luis Vives, and Luis de Granada, among others, but she also had access to saints' lives, such as Pedro de Ribadeneyra's *Flos Sanctorum,* made available to nuns as examples of tolerant suffering. As Armon has argued, the multiple cultural archetypes provided to literate women in Counter-Reformation Spain taught more than mere silent obedience. As martyred saints were by nature rebels, the lives of the saints taught resistance as well as submission, while teachings about the Virgin Mary could both encourage surrender to the Church or a desire to expand book learning (26). Sor Violante is unusual among women writers of poetry in the number of her sonnets that concern or address the Virgin Mary. Scholars of the medieval period, when the cult of the Virgin was at its height, have found that Marian veneration was more the province of male religious. While women's worship of Mary was an important part of their devotional practice, they were far more interested in the humanity of Christ (Bynum, *Jesus as Mother* 269),[14] as is certainly the case in the mystical poetry of Luisa de Carvajal y Mendoza. This attitude appears to have continued in the seventeenth century. Of the more than two hundred seventeenth-century sonnets noted or published in Serrano y Sanz's *Apuntes para una biblioteca de mujeres,* only fifty-five address a specific religious figure, and of these only fifteen are addressed to the Virgin Mary. Although this represents approximate-

13. Conversely, for Elizabeth I of England, it was her virginity and untouchability that gave her power. Marriage may have provided her with a direct heir, but it would also have brought her into conflict with a husband. Her status made her the epitome of dynastic desirability, but by remaining aloof she retained undisputed power in her own hands.

14. On the medieval veneration of the Virgin, see also Marina Warner, *Monuments and Maidens: The Allegory of the Female Form* (London: Picador, 1985).

ly 8 percent of the whole, seven of these are written for one *certamen*, in Zaragoza in 1644, celebrating the Virgen de Cogullada. By contrast, a *certamen* marking the translation of the relics of San Ramón Nonato, also at Zaragoza in 1618, provided eleven sonnets for the record.

The divine motherhood of Mary is accepted by all Christian churches because it appears in Scripture. Nevertheless, as Lerner reveals, her many functions were interpreted by both theologians and Church officials in patriarchal and conservative terms. Not only did her virginity sanctify that choice for ordinary women but her submissiveness to the divine will in the Annunciation was to be the model for female behavior. She also served as a paradigm of silent submission to female destiny through her tragic motherhood (*Consciousness* 127). According to Warner, this model of humility rapidly gained ascendancy through the Franciscans and, later, the Dominicans, through whose example the Virgin "left her starry throne in the heavens and laid aside her robes and insignia and diadem to sit cross-legged on the bare earth like a peasant mother with her child" (*Alone* 182).

Sor Violante's sonnets, however, envision the Virgin Mary from a number of opposing angles, none of which is submissive. Although portrayed as the simple mother concerned for the welfare of her child, she is also a woman who exerts control. This power does not mirror the patriarchal jurisdiction of the divinely ordered hierarchy mediated through the intercessory figure of Mary. Instead, the protagonist appropriates societal expectations of the demure female figure to a subtler form of dominance. In her sonnet on the Annunciation, from her Mysteries cycle, for example, Sor Violante specifically locates the Virgin, a simple, young peasant woman, as the controlling figure in the exchange between herself and the angel. The crux of the sonnet is Mary's silence, which occasions considerable anxiety on the part of the speaker. The angel is at first portrayed as a foreign diplomat seeking a noble or royal bride for a political marriage:[15]

15. Such a practice was common among the kingdoms of Western Europe in securing dynastic marriages. Just one example is the failed attempt in 1623 to secure a political alliance between England and Spain through the betrothal between Henry, heir of Charles I to the throne of England, and the daughter of Philip III of Spain.

Primer misterio del rosario santísimo.
La Anunciación de Nuestra Señora

Dad, Virgen Soberana, el *sí* dichoso
al Nuncio celestial, que veis presente,
Que deste *sí* Divino está pendiente
del mundo todo el general reposo.

5   El Verbo, que le aguarda respetuoso,
(Si bien es de licencia independiente)
obedeciendo anticipadamente,
no ha de bajar sin este *sí* glorioso.

Mirad lo que debeis a su clemencia,
10   pues pudiendo bajar Dios soberano
al claustro puro, que por Dios merece,

No baja, hasta que vos le deis licencia,
porque veáis, qué hará después de humano
quien antes de humanarse os obedece.

(*Parnaso lusitano* 8)

First Mystery of the Blessed Rosary:
The Annunciation of Our Lady

Sovereign Virgin, give that joyous *yes*
to the celestial herald you see before you,
On this divine *yes* depends the general
repose of the entire world.

The Word, who respectfully awaits you,
(even though he can act independently)
obeying you in anticipation,
will not come down without this glorious *yes*.

See what you owe to his clemency,
for, being able to come down as a sovereign God
to the pure cloister, worthy of God himself,

He will not descend until you give your consent,
so that you may see what he will do once human,
for even before becoming human he obeys you.

Sor Violante proposes that Mary achieves power through her silence, as she keeps the divine "nuncio" waiting for her response. The speaker urges Mary's assent, for only thus can Jesus come into the world and reverse the effect of original sin. Her acquiescence will also lead to the vindication of all womankind, as Mary replaces the culpable figure of Eve and creates an entirely different and more favorable model of female agency. This ransoming of Eve by a second Eve was already a popular image; in the medieval mind it "inspired the ingenious imagination of the medieval Christian to pun and riddle. For the greeting of the angel—Ave—neatly reversed the curse of Eve" (Warner, *Monuments* 60). Through the angel and Mary, Sor Violante creates two parallel images of the female: the approved social ideal of the subservient supplicant speaker and the new model of powerful agent for female good:

> El Verbo, que le aguarda respetuoso,
> (si bien es de licencia independiente)
> obedeciendo anticipadamente
> no ha de bajar sin este *sí* glorioso.
>
> (5–8)

In Sor Violante's determination that it is the woman who holds the upper hand, "licencia" represents both Mary's freedom to assent or decline, and God's freedom to act, willingly held in check by his proleptic deference to the woman who will become his mother.

Sor Violante's version of the events of the Annunciation owes nothing to Scripture or to dogma; rather, it seems to come out of her own meditation on the impact of such an apparition on the young woman. She develops the importance of this respectful obedience to a woman on the part of the Messiah by shunning the usual turn after the quartets. Instead, Sor Violante continues to elaborate on Mary's control of the situation right to the last line: "No baja, hasta que vos le deis licencia, / Porque veáis, que hará después de humano / quien antes de humanarse os obedece" (12–14). In the course of the sonnet Mary's role in the drama of the Annunciation changes from that of the bride begged for her hand to that of the mother whom God will obey. Sor Violante may also have been influenced by the preaching of St. Francis de Sales and Cardinal Bellarmine, both of whom discuss the marriage of God and the Virgin. St. Francis affirms the notion that God bestowed the divine kiss that caused Mary to conceive at the moment she acquiesced. Similarly, Bellarmine preaches that God sent the Archangel Gabriel to secure the consent required of a bride before a marriage can occur (Ellington 161). Yet in Counter-Reformation Spain the bride's consent was, at least in official terms, barely a matter for consideration; women were not in a position either to agree to the arrangement or to choose. Pérez Molina, for example, argues that fathers maintained an interest in controlling their daughters' marriages for patrimonial and economic reasons and, in relation to these, the creation of alliances between families that permitted them to rise in the social scale or maintain themselves within a socioeconomic group. Although marriage without parental consent was legal in canon law after Trent, the requirement to celebrate marriage before a priest and two witnesses made marriages without consent more difficult ("Las mujeres y el matrimonio" 31).

Available figures on marriage in the period indicate that one of the reasons for the population crisis of the seventeenth century was the increasingly late age at first marriage of both males and females, with most marrying in their late twenties. Alcalá Zamora shows an average age at marriage of twenty-two to twenty-four in the Middle Ages, which then fell for a period before rising again in the seventeenth century due to emigration (172–73). Similarly, Armon debates women's relative freedom from the travail of wifely duties due to their later age at marriage and a scarcity of eligible men (46). Existing biographical data on Sor Violante suggests that it was at just this age that she entered the convent, when an intention to marry was disastrously interrupted by her family. According to Vieira Mendes, the poet Paulo Gonçalves de Andrade sought to marry Violante de Montesinos but was prevented by her grandfather, Gonçalo Nunes de Ávila. Andrade left the kingdom and never returned. This account, provided by a contemporary, dispels the idea of earlier biographers that Sor Violante entered the convent because her love was not returned ("Apresentação," 11). In Mary's reticence Sor Violante joins the playwrights in affirming that it is women who should be free to make decisions about their lives and about whom they marry. It is symbolic of the patriarchally ordered formation of families that Sor Violante resorts to Mary, the ideal mother and an incontrovertible divine source, to fortify her argument.

Similarly, Sor Violante emphasizes her desire for female agency by figuring no mere mortal father, but the divine *Verbo* (Word) who waits respectfully for Mary's acquiescence. Since God is outside time and all-seeing, he knows that as a human child Christ will have to obey this woman who will be his mother. This divine obedience to a mortal parent emphasizes the moral worth of the mother figure in particular, and women in general, thus contesting the arguments devised to keep women in their position of powerlessness. In this sonnet, the controlling father is nowhere to be seen, either as God or man. This absence is in direct contrast to Sor Violante's idealized Counter-Reformation presentation of Joseph as the ideal pater familias. Furthermore, Sor Violante's privileging of the ideal figure of Mary does not conform to her intercessory role. Such a paradigm, for all its importance, reinforces the hierarchical marginalizing of the female, albeit as an ally in the heavenly court. Sor Violante seeks to champion the limiting domestic and maternal roles permitted to women through the supreme example of the mother of God. It is principally in a number of sonnets to the Virgin Mary that Sor Violante deviates from her religious orthodoxy.

In her sonnet on the Third Mystery of the Rosary, *Del nacimiento de Cristo Señor Nuestro* (On the birth of Christ our Lord), Sor Violante manifests her views on maternal and filial tenderness. She returns to the pictorial imagery of the holy family in a companion work to her sonnet to St. Joseph. Again, Old Testament typology serves to bring forth and amplify the New Testament miracle. Just as she linked the Old and New Testament Josephs in the earlier sonnet, Sor Violante similarly makes clever use of the Old Testament figure of Ruth as a model of female loyalty, moral strength, and daughterly devotion. As the Book of Ruth reveals, in the midst of abject widowed poverty, far from her own land, she was favored (and later married), by Boaz because of the devotion she showed to her mother-in-law, whose family had become hers on marriage.[16] As Boaz's wife she was the ancestor of David, himself a type for Jesus Christ. The language of the sonnet is simple, in contrast with the complex imagery that reveals the peasant life of the Old Testament figures, the holy family, and the humble birth of Christ. This same imagery

16. The relevant scriptural reference source for Sor Violante is Ruth 2: 11.

also projects long-held pagan associations of the female body with the earth that nurtures the seed:[17]

> Este trigo, que en pajas recogido
> anhela Ruth con singular cuidado,
> si le adoráis, por ser de Dios sembrado,
> Dios le sembró, por ser de vos nacido.
>
> 5   Si le queréis (Señora) ver crecido,
> rociadle bien con este llanto amado,
> pues sabéis que le tiene el Rey sagrado
> para pan de las almas escogido.
>
> Rociadle bien, que si en la humana esfera
> 10   vuestra rara pureza no se hallara,
> nunca tan bello trigo el mundo viera.
>
> Porque si Dios tan pura no os formara,
> aunque el género humano pereciera,
> nunca en la humanidad tal pan sembrara.
>
> (*Parnaso lusitano* 9)

> This wheat, collected from the straw,
> for which Ruth yearns with singular concern,
> though you adore him for being sown by God,
> God sowed him to be born of you.
>
> If (Señora) you would see him grow,
> water him well with those loving tears,
> since you know that you hold the sacred King,
> chosen as the bread of souls.
>
> Water him well, for if, in the human sphere
> your rare purity had not been found,
> the world would not have seen such glorious wheat.

17. Regarding the metaphors of the female body and its relation to the plowing and seeding of the earth in early agricultural societies of Greece, see Page DuBois, *Sowing the Body: Psychoanalysis and Ancient Representations of Women* (Chicago: University of Chicago Press, 1988), 39–64.

For if God had not made you so immaculate,
even though the human species were to perish,
he would never have sown such bread in mortal kind.

Whereas Ruth gleaned barley in the fields of Boaz, in this later (and therefore better) version of the event, Christ is both the seed of Christianity and the wheat of the eucharistic bread, even as he is a child lying on straw in a manger. As Ruth gleaned her grains in a time of famine, Mary cradles her "trigo" in a time of spiritual famine, in Christian terms. Not only does Sor Violante portray the mother as the ancient earth, ploughed and seeded to produce the bread of life, she is also the gardener who nurtures the seed into life and tends the growing plant. The importance for Sor Violante of this vision is evident in repeated references to the life-giving process of grain growing, where seeding, watering, and nurturing also express the mother's homely role.

Sor Violante goes on to argue that it is Mary's exceptional nature that makes the bread of the "Rey sagrado" even better: "que si en la humana esfera / vuestra rara pureza no se hallara, / nunca tan bello trigo el mundo viera" (9–11). It is significant that the poet chooses the metaphor of kindly nature as a nurturing mother who sustains all her children. Sor Violante is writing at the dawn of the Scientific Revolution, which, as Western culture became increasingly mechanized, would transform the metaphor of benign nature into a wilderness that could be tamed and exploited. Such a change in paradigm is discussed by Carolyn Merchant, particularly in relation to the mining of the earth, which had been a cause for debate even in the times of Plato, Ovid, and Pliny. Merchant argues that moral restraint and, conversely, greed, avarice, and lust, were associated in the Renaissance with the image of the female earth. However, new positive values connected with mining viewed it as a means to improve the human condition, a position supported by Agrícola and Bacon (40).[18]

As nature could be controlled, so too could women, as the enlightened educational opportunities of a humanist Renaissance fell back un-

---

18. For a more detailed discussion of the increasing exploitation of nature and the earth in the seventeenth and eighteenth centuries, see "Nature as Female," Carolyn Merchant, *The Death of Nature* (San Francisco: Harper & Row, 1990), 1–41.

der the pressures of the Counter-Reformation's dominion. Sor Violante, however, creates positive, dual feminine images: Mary was chosen by God, as the child-king of the Jews is chosen to be sacrificed: "si le adoráis, por ser de Dios sembrado, / Dios le sembró, por ser de vos nacido" (3–4). As both seedbed and gardener, Mary is urged to care for the child so that he may fulfill his destiny and become the "pan de las almas escogido" (8). The Virgin Mary is proposed as an exemplary mother rather than as the passive, powerless woman of the sonnets to Joseph. Furthermore, she is firmly allied to the ordinary peasant women who work in the fields and tend the plants rather than to an impossible ideal of purity and parthenogenesis.

Mary's foreknowledge of Christ's sacrifice is revealed in the second quartet where Sor Violante's scriptural knowledge evokes the first of the Seven Sorrows of the Virgin:[19]

> Si le queréis (Señora) ver crecido,
> rociadle bien con este llanto amado
> pues sabéis, que le tiene el Rey sagrado
> para pan de las almas escogido.

The first sorrow is related to the prophecy of Simeon at the time of the presentation in the Temple: "Behold, this child is set for the fall and rising again of many in Israel; and for a sign which shall be spoken against; (Yea, a sword shall pierce through thy own soul also,) that the thoughts of many hearts may be revealed" (Luke 2: 34–35). Hence the mother's tears are symbolic of both emotional nourishment and maternal grief at the loss of a child, a frequent occurrence in the period. In spite of this proleptic sorrow, the tears also convey ideas of abundance, fecundity, and plenty associated with the life-giving qualities of water, and this is emphasized in the repetition at the turn: "Rociadle bien . . ." (9). Tears, as Warner has observed, flow from the body without the implications of

---

19. The sorrows of the Virgin, which in medieval liturgies varied between five and fifteen, were officially fixed at seven in the seventeenth century by Pope Paul V (Warner, *Alone* 218). They are the prophecy of Simeon, the flight into Egypt, the loss of Jesus in the temple, the meeting with Jesus on the road to Calvary, the Crucifixion, the Deposition, and the Entombment. All of these are celebrated in sonnets from Sor Violante's sequence on the rosary, in the *Parnaso lusitano*.

pollution that accompany other bodily fluids. They are thought of as pure, like water, used by the Christian Church as a symbol of life and purification (*Alone* 222).

The tercets, however, are given over to supposition; the frailty and uncertainty of human survival, and perhaps of perinatal survival, is reflected in the imperfect subjunctive: ". . . si Dios tan pura no os formara, / aunque el género humano pereciera, / nunca en la humanidad tal pan sembrara" (12–14). In the chain of events unfolding around the birth of Christ, one missing element, Mary's perfection, would have prevented its occurrence and damned the world for eternity. There would have been no promise of salvation enshrined in the Eucharist and no celebration of Christmas, the feast for which the sonnet is written. As the sonnet progresses, Sor Violante moves away from the simple, flawed humanity of the peasant mother to the divine example that the Virgin Mary represents for her and that she wishes to hold up as an example to other women. However, in privileging Mary's exceptional nature and linking it to her role as loving mother, she also advances the cause of women as valuable responsible members of society, promoting their domestic roles as vitally important to the well-being of the nuclear family.

For Sor Violante, a divinely authoritarian Mary was a model worth emulating and presenting repeatedly to her female readers. The sonnet that marks the end of her sequence on the Mysteries of the Rosary, the Coronation of Mary as Queen of Heaven, is a triumphant celebration of Mary's elevation. Sor Violante repeats the important message of the first mystery of the rosary, the Annunciation, discussed above—that being queen of heaven and earth pales compared with being obeyed by God:

De la Coronación de Nuestra Señora

Recebid la corona merecida
(o Reina de dos mundos adorada)
que aun es poco ser de ellos respetada
quien fue del mismo Dios obedecida.

5   Tan amorosamente introducida
os tiene en sí la Trinidad sagrada,
que, aunque estáis de su mano coronada,
parecéis de su seno procedida.

¡Oh! lograd para siempre la ventura,
10   que el soberano Sol el Uno, y Trino
en su misma Deidad os asegura.

Y pues honrar debéis lo femenino,
dad a musa incapaz, a voz impura,
si no dulce favor, perdón benigno.

(Parnaso lusitano 23)

On the coronation of Our Lady

Receive your merited crown
(oh adored Queen of two worlds)
though it's a minor matter for one who
was obeyed by God to be respected by them.

So lovingly introduced,
you hold in yourself the Holy Trinity,
so that though crowned by his hand
he seems to proceed from your breast.

Oh! May you eternally achieve the prize
that the sovereign Sun, the One and Triune
assures you in your own Divinity.

And since you should honor the feminine,
give this unworthy muse, this impure voice,
if not sweet favor, then benign pardon.

Sor Violante goes even further in the second quartet, where, as she is introduced into the heavenly court, Mary contains the Holy Trinity within her body.[20] It is as though she is in a state of permanent pregnancy that does away with time and mortality, for Mary, as a divine figure, is outside time. The quartet is complex and tortuous as Sor Violante attempts to insert Mary into a state of equality with the Trinity. Each

---

20. Sor Violante's use of the word *introducido* makes clear that this is no ordinary arrival. She enhances the superiority of the Virgin's incorporation into the royal court of heaven, following Covarrubias's definition of the word: "como introduzir a uno en palacio para que hable al rey" (740; meaning to introduce someone into the palace so that they may speak to the king).

gives birth to the other. As she is crowned by the Trinity, held within her body, the Trinity in turn gives birth to her as a divine figure: "Que, aunque estáis de su mano coronada, / parecéis de su seno procedida." This serpentine weaving of images is typical of Sor Violante's style, and here it creates the effect of turning the Trinity into a Quaternity, proposing Mary as equal in power to the three members of the Trinity. Sor Violante affirms again that without Mary Christ could not have come into the world; Mary was therefore as essential to the formation of the Trinity as God was to her creation.

Sor Violante may, in this imagery, be expressing her awareness of the Orthodox rite of the Dormition, which, in a number of iconographic representations, sees Mary become a child in the arms of her son. As Kristeva further explains: "Indeed, *mother* of her son and his *daughter* as well, Mary is also, and besides, his *wife:* she therefore actualizes the threefold metamorphosis of a woman in the tightest parenthood structure" (169). Though this imagery may have informed her writing, Sor Violante does not seek to insert Mary into the inferiority of mother, daughter, or wife. Instead, in negotiating the parameters of women's power and its limitations, she presents Mary as the prime example of feminine empowerment, achieved through the maternal role.

Having magnified Mary to the highest degree, Sor Violante prays to her as to a God, reminding her that she is the champion of women: "Y pues honrar debéis lo femenino" (12). She also hints at a more earthbound court patronage in specifically repudiating the request for court favor from her queen to ask instead for divine pardon: "Dad a musa incapaz, a voz impura, / si no dulce favor, perdón benigno" (13–14). This last tercet confirms Sor Violante's vision of the Virgin Mary as a female deity rather than as an intercessor for humankind whose mortality she has shared. Indeed, a reading of all one hundred sonnets in the *Parnaso lusitano* does not reveal a single instance where the poet appeals to the Virgin Mary as intercessor, though she frequently praises the excellence of the Mother of God.

Warner has argued that the Church harnessed the Assumption of Mary into heaven to promote the honor of queens in earthly hierarchies, to the exclusion of other women. This strategy served to uphold the status quo to the advantage of the powerful elites (*Alone* 104). I contest this view, at least in regard to Sor Violante's poetry, as well as the idea of the Virgin's inaccessibility to women. For Warner, the impossible ideal set up by the Church creates a position of hopeless yearning and inferiority: "The process is self-perpetuating; if the Virgin were not venerated, the dangers of sex, the fear of corruption, the sense of sin would not be woven together in this particular misogynist web, but would be articulated in a different way" (*Alone* 104). I argue that Sor Violante both venerates the Virgin and articulates her sentiments in a different way, by not following the Church's misogynist view. As Sor Violante's sonnet sequence follows the lives of Christ and his mother, and as she moves from Mary's maternal role to her heavenly one, Sor Violante seeks to occlude the problematic status occasioned by Mary's immaculate divinity. For Sor Violante, the Virgin Mary, as a divine queen, remains accessible to women, both as a deity and as a cosharer in female experience. She is also a friend, confidante, and peasant mother, analogous and accessible to human mothers at all levels.

CONCLUSION

As both Church and state attempted to reinforce social control through the exemplary figures of Joseph and the Virgin Mary, Sor Violante both promotes and takes issue with these ideals, raising questions as to how this humane view of parenthood manifested itself in poetry about the family. The role of the father is complex in Sor Violante's idealizing portraits of Joseph; he is a remarkably feminized individual, as is St. Anthony of Padua, far from the militaristic and paternalistic ideal described by the moralists and required by a society almost perpetually at war. Similarly, Sor Violante does not take an orthodox line in portraying the role of the mother, which she shows to be an important and sustaining one for women. In providing a simultaneously humanizing and venerating view of the Virgin Mary, Sor Violante does much to bridge the gap between the impossible ideal of Marian perfection and the lot of mortal womankind, creating of the Virgin an active proponent of feminine worth.

CHAPTER 3

CHILDREN AND SIBLINGS

MORALISTS AND THINKERS, drawing on the Church Fathers, had much to say about the appropriate education for children of both sexes, as well as about the relationship of fear and respect that ideally should exist between children and their parents. In the poetry of Ramírez, however, relationships within the family were not always as austere as the moralists would have us believe. Her poetry shows deep and reciprocal affection between all members of the family, humor, and often a complete lack of the formality prescribed for relations within the familial hierarchy.

A silence on the part of the moralists as to the appropriate relationship that should obtain between siblings is also breached by these poets. This is particularly so for Cueva and Ramírez in their poems, and Carvajal y Mendoza in her letters. Continuing communication between free brothers and enclosed, or semienclosed sisters, brought new ideas and interests into the home. The poetry demonstrates enduring affection and contact, and relaxed and loving relationships, between parents and children and between siblings that provided social and emotional support.

CHILDREN

Although St. Augustine insists on strict discipline as an essential part of childrearing, he permits infants some respite in the earliest stages of their lives. Portrayed as gifts of God, loved equally with their parents by God, they thus create great responsibilities for their parents, given their helplessness compared with other young animals. Burt describes Augustine's thinking on parenthood as the requirement for parents to love their children "not as friends but in order that they might become friends" (93). This creates a disciplinary burden, for although an infant is incapable of personal sin, as it grows its behavior must be disciplined to avoid the possibility of falling into sin:

Our infancy proves how ignorant we humans are when we begin our lives and our adolescence proves how full of folly and concupiscence we become. . . . This is the reason why we use fear in trying to control the wildness of growing children. This is the reason why we have teachers and school-masters with their rulers and straps and canes. In our training of even a beloved child we not infrequently follow the advice of Scripture to "beat his sides lest he grow stubborn." (*City* 22.22)

Augustine's writings were particularly influential in the medieval and early modern periods. His concern for parental love and care for children, even the very young, is at variance with Philippe Ariès's study *Centuries of Childhood*, which claims that medieval and early modern concepts of childhood were very different from those of today. Ariès argues that it was not that parents neglected or despised their children, but simply that the idea of childhood, as we understand it today, did not exist in medieval times. Ariès quotes from Molière in asserting that an infant too fragile to take part in the life of adults simply "did not count."[1] Similarly, Lawrence Stone, writing of the changes taking place in English society between 1500 and 1800, also considers omnipresent death to color relations in society; parents did not invest emotional capital in any single individual and especially not in "such ephemeral creatures as infants." Stone argues that the resultant emotional neglect of infants by their parents actually reduced the former's prospects for survival (651–52).[2]

---

1. Ariès attributes a medieval mind-set to Molière's seventeenth-century character, Argan, in *Le malade imaginaire*. A father of two daughters, one an infant, one of marriageable age, he acknowledges only the elder. The younger is too young to count "because she could disappear." See Philippe Ariès, *Centuries of Childhood*, trans. Robert Baldick (London: Cape, 1962), 128.

2. Lawrence Stone's statements on the ephemeral nature of infants is more than a lit-

Montaigne's essay "Of the Affection of Fathers for Their Children," first published in 1588, appears to agree with the sentiments of Lawrence Stone, Ariès, and Molière:

I cannot entertain that passion which makes people hug infants that are hardly born yet, having neither movement in the soul nor recognizable shape to the body by which they can make themselves lovable. . . . A true and well-regulated affection should be born and increase with the knowledge children give us of themselves; and then, if they are worthy of it, the natural propensity going along with reason, we should cherish them with a truly paternal love. (280)

Montaigne's argument certainly measures affection according to the capacity of the child to earn it. Moreoever, there is naturally no post-Romantic notion that the childrearing practices of the parents have anything to do with the end result. He derides the fascination that childhood games hold for some adults, "as if we had loved them for our pastime, like monkeys, not like men" (281). However, his avowed inability to understand those who coddle their children and delight in their antics suggests that other views than his predominated, while his argument depends on the age of the child. He too sees no reason to waste emotion on a child who may soon die, but he endorses affective relations with older children.

On the care of children, the *Siete Partidas,* particularly *Partida 4,* is seeded with references to the precious nature of children and their need for demonstrative love and care. In *Partida 2,* on the raising of royal children, affection is proposed as an essential ingredient for the child to grow and thrive. Sarcasm and physical harm are considered to inspire fear, which may lead to illness or death (M. Stone 90). According to *Partida* 4.19, both parents have authority over their children and are obliged to care for them through that natural law that moves all things in the world to raise and care for what is born to them (98). The *Parti-*

---

tle offset by the epigrams of Ben Jonson that commemorate his dead children. His sonnet to his seven-year-old son, who died of plague, begins, "Farewell thou child of my right hand, and joy," and includes the line, "Here doth lie Ben Jonson his best piece of poetry." To his daughter he writes, "Here lies, to each her parents' ruth, / Mary, the daughter of their youth." See Hugh Maclean, *Ben Jonson and the Cavalier Poets: Authoritative Texts, Criticism* (New York: Norton, 1974), 7–8. That Jonson should compose a tender poem to a baby of six months to honor her memory indicates that he clearly did not consider her to be "ephemeral."

das differentiate in the matter of parental responsibility, however; before children reach the age of three years, the mothers should nourish and care for their children, but they become the father's responsibility after that age. This ideal was still current in Renaissance thought; while women could exert control over slaves, the pater familias exercised control over his children (I. Maclean 59). The extensive space given in the *Partidas* to the care and rearing of children, even to noting that children are more likely to love and obey a father who takes the trouble to rear them himself, points to affection in the home (4.19.2). Moreover, the inheritance rights pertaining to legitimate children, and the insistence that all children, licit or not, are entitled to be reared with affection, is at odds with Ariès's and Stone's views that parents did not form emotional attachments to their infants.

Like the *Partidas,* the content of women's sonnets regarding the family portrays a love that is intimate and reciprocal. Where Sor Violante del Cielo views familial love through the orthodox, post-Tridentine lens of the Holy Family, she nevertheless uses these exempla to postulate tenderness and enduring love between parents and their children. In the same way, Ramírez's poetry clearly reflects a warm, lively, and loving family relationship that accords with Augustine's views on the household dominated by love, as will be seen below. Similarly, the journal of Lady Ann Fanshawe, wife of a seventeenth-century English ambassador to Madrid, makes clear that her young daughter accompanied her and was warmly welcomed on social visits. Lady Ann's memoirs have particular value as testimonial narrative because they offer, an eyewitness account written by an outsider. Since the upper classes across all the countries of Western Europe had more in common with each other than with their own country's lower classes, Lady Ann's observations provide valuable evidence of Spanish women's comportment compared with the strictures of the moralists. Where Sor Violante's sonnets support tender maternity toward children of all ages, Ramírez's verse focuses on her and her siblings' affection for their parents, expressing the sentiments of older, even adult children.

Advice on the raising of older children differs markedly from that given with regard to the very young. For example, Montaigne's interest in older children bears no relation to his attitude to infants. In the same essay on fatherhood he asserts that a father should make himself worthy, by his virtue and ability, of [his children's] love by his goodness and the kindness of his behavior. . . . No old age can be so decrepit and rancid in a person who has passed his life in honor as not to be venerable, especially to his children, whose souls he ought to have trained to their duty by reason, not by necessity and need nor by harshness and force. (281)

Montaigne is not the only writer of the period to record this degree of paternal tenderness. Francis Bacon, for example, writes that a wife and children are a kind of discipline of humanity, asserting that single men "are more cruel and hard-hearted (good to make severe inquisitors), because their tenderness is not so oft called upon" (82).[3]

On the education of children, Montaigne differs also from Augustine, who expects parental love to be exhibited through command and correction in the early years, using fear as a means to control "the wildness of growing children" (*City* 22.22). In contrast, Montaigne looks forward to the enlightened educational views of Rousseau, and condemns violence in the education "of a tender soul," holding that what cannot be done by reason, wisdom, and tact cannot be effected by force. He affirms that his one surviving daughter, six years old, has never been punished for her childish faults. This is not an all-embracing attitude, however. He goes on to declare that, given the different, more commanding, and disciplined role expected of men, he would have been "much more scrupulous in this respect toward boys, who are less born to serve and of a freer condition: I should have loved to swell their hearts with ingenuousness and frankness" (281–82).

A hundred years after Montaigne, as Sor Violante's long life came to an end, John Locke, the English philosopher, writing after the overthrow of divine right monarchy in England, pitches his advice on education somewhere between Augustine and Montaigne. Although he seeks a friendly and companionable relationship in the adult, he regards the means to acquiring this to be fear and awe instilled in childhood:

---

3. Unfortunately, Bacon's essay goes on to reinsert the wife into the subservient role common to his time but irksome in the twenty-first century: "Wives are young men's mistresses, companions for middle age, and old men's nurses" (82). As mistresses, companions, and nurses, women are never granted the opportunity to be individuals with needs and desires of their own.

Those therefore that intend ever to govern their children should begin it whilst they are very little, and look that they perfectly comply with the will of their parents. Would you have your son obedient to you when past a child; be sure then to establish the authority of a father as soon as he is capable of submission, and can understand in whose power he is. If you would have him stand in awe of you, imprint it in his infancy; and as he approaches more to a man, admit him nearer to your familiarity; so shall you have him your obedient subject (as is fit) whilst he is a child and your affectionate friend when he is a man. (Locke pt. 3 s. 40)

Locke's views on childrearing may have been colored by his role as tutor to the son and heir of the Earl of Shaftesbury, for whose education he was responsible, with none of the bonds of blood.

Sor Violante's sonnets on the family always show strong ties of affection between parent and child. In a sonnet on one of the Sorrows of the Virgin—in this instance the loss of the holy child in Jerusalem—Sor Violante's homely first quartet foregrounds the tears of relief shed by a mother when her child is found safe and well:[4]

Quinto Misterio: Del Niño perdido

Que bien muestra Señora, el justo llanto,
que con exceso tanto habéis vertido,
que quien a Dios presume, que ha perdido,
debe buscarle con exceso tanto.

5   Ni al Cielo, ni a la tierra cause espanto
lo mucho, que tal pena habéis sentido,
pues perder un Infante habéis temido
que aclama el Serafín tres veces santo.

Pero bien el pesar os recompensa,
10   pues la gloria, que os da después de hallarle
es cual la misma pena de no verle.

No queráis vos, ni su Deidad inmensa,
que el alma, que una vez supo buscarle,
llegue nunca por culpas a perderle.

(*Parnaso lusitano* 11)

---

4. For the biblical account, see Luke 2: 42–49.

Fifth Mystery: Of the Lost Child.

Señora, how well you show by the just tears
you have so copiously spilled, that
whoever has lost one presumed a God,
needs to seek him with the greatest urgency.

It could not cause so much horror in heaven
nor on earth, that you have felt such pain,
since you feared to have lost a Prince whom
the Seraphim acclaim three times holy.

But your misery is well repaid, since
the glory that you feel on finding him
is equal to the suffering of not seeing him.

Would not you and the immense God
wish that the soul, once it knew how to find him,
would never come to lose him through error.

Although Sor Violante acknowledges, rather comically, that to lose a god is a good reason to shed tears and conduct an urgent search, Mary's tears are also those of a worried mother, concerned for her missing boy, rather than those of worship for a divine figure. The biblical record of Mary's expostulation when she finds Jesus discoursing with the elders in the temple is typical of a mother's outraged relief at finding a wayward child: "And when they saw him they were astonished; and his mother said to him, 'Son, why have you treated us so? Behold, your father and I have been looking for you anxiously'" (Luke 2: 48). Sor Violante expresses this not in querulous irritation, but in relief and pleasure that balances the misery of the quartets: "pues la gloria, que os da después de hallarle / es cual la misma pena de no verle" (10–11).

In the tercets Sor Violante converts the mother's search to allegory, thus cleverly manipulating and highlighting two concerns: for mothers, epitomized in the figure of Mary, and for consolation of the human soul through faith: "No queráis vos, ni su Deidad inmensa, / que el alma, que una vez supo buscarle, / llegue nunca por culpas a perderle" (12–14). Mary's desperate search for the Christ child becomes an allegorical figuring of the soul's anxious quest for God which, once complete, brings such bliss that disengagement from it is impossible. Since the soul is usually portrayed as female, this may account for the absence of Joseph.

As seen in Chapter 2, the Church used manipulated images of the Holy Family in its determination to show how a Spanish family of the Baroque era should comport itself. Sor Violante uses these images as both exempla for her readers and representations of real and affectionate interest in the welfare of their children. The enduring presence of the *Siete Partidas* suggests that this concern was not a new phenomenon in Spanish society, at least as regards relations between women and children. However, once the children were of an age to be the father's responsibility, moralists take a stronger stand against this tenderness, as is explained by Mariló Vigil:

> Vives y Justiniano . . . tras propugnar una vinculación místico-maternal entre madre e hijo, con objeto de conseguir que las mujeres críen personalmente a sus niños, atacan las manifestaciones de ternura de la madre hacia los hijos que ya no están en edad de lactancia. Vives cree que las mujeres deben mantener una actitud autoritaria y distante con sus hijos y pone como ejemplo a su propia madre. (132)

> Vives and Justinian . . . after proposing a mystico-maternal link between mother and child, with the object of ensuring that women personally raise their children, attack demonstrations of maternal tenderness toward children after breastfeeding age. Vives believes that women should maintain a distant and authoritarian attitude toward their children and uses his own mother as an example.

Confusion in the stand taken by many of the moralists makes it clear that tenderness toward children did not stop at weaning and that considerable cosseting of children continued in spite of injunctions to the contrary. Neither was there any difference between the attitudes of fathers and mothers toward their offspring: "Lo normal, de acuerdo con los testimonios de la mayoría de los moralistas, que también eran partidarios de una educación autoritaria, era que los padres—no sólo la madre—mimaran y consintieran a sus niños" (Vigil 132–34;[5] Normally, in line with the testimonies of the majority of the moralists, who were also in favor

---

5. Such demonstrative affection by both parents is also represented in Montaigne's determination that a son should feel more for his father than fear, though he retains the masculine-centered theories of his era: "It is also wrong and foolish to prohibit children who have come of age from being familiar with their fathers, and to prefer to maintain an

of an authoritarian education, it was the fathers—not just the mothers—
who spoiled and gave in to their children).

For Sor Violante, the bond established at birth between mother and
child is reciprocal, equal, and enduring, as is revealed in several of her
holy sonnets on the Mysteries of the Rosary, specifically those of the Seven Sorrows of the Virgin. They draw startling conclusions at variance
with the biblical record. Once again they privilege the affectionate relationship between Mary and Jesus, mother and son, at the time of his
betrayal and Crucifixion, as Christ contemplates his impending fate. It
seems that in her determination to foreground the human dimension of
maternal/filial love, Sor Violante utilizes the most powerful images of
love and sacrifice available to her, but not by appealing to the divine or
intercessory qualities possessed by Mary and her son.

In her sonnet on the first dolorous mystery, Christ's prayer in the
Garden of Gethsemane, Sor Violante makes it abundantly clear that in
her view Christ loved his mother as a devoted and human son. Thus,
Christ's prayer is not about his ordeal at all; instead, he is concerned with
the suffering his Crucifixion will cause his mother. This is at variance
with the teachings of Augustine, with which Sor Violante would certainly have been familiar. Augustine projects love of the family as right
and proper because they are loved by God, and affirms that Christ loved
Mary not as evidence of the bond between child and mother, but because she was God's faithful daughter (Burt 97). However, Sor Violante
clearly shares Alfonso the Wise's view of familial love and support as a
good, beneficial to society, since she frequently recurs to Christ's humanity, always manifested in its most selfless form:

Al primer misterio doloroso: A la Oración del Huerto

El ruego, que a su Padre soberano
con lágrimas de sangre el Verbo ofrece,
aunque temor de humano al fin parece,
más es temor de amante, que de humano.

---

austere and disdainful gravity toward them, hoping thereby to keep them in fear and obedience. . . . Even if I could make myself feared, I would much rather make myself loved."
See Montaigne, *The Complete Essays of Montaigne,* trans. Donald M. Frame (Stanford:
Stanford University Press, 1965), 284.

5   Porque si bien, Señora, lo tirano
de la muerte su espíritu entristece,
si bien por lo mortal casi enflaquece
quien tiene todo el orbe en una mano,

más teme en vos pesar tan infalible:
10   Y así al Padre suplica tiernamente,
que su muerte le exente, si es posible.

Mirad, si os ama con afecto ardiente
¿quien más, que de su muerte lo terrible,
teme de vuestra pena lo valiente?

(Parnaso lusitano 12)

On the first dolorous mystery: The Prayer in the Garden

The plea that the Word, with tears
of blood, offers to his sovereign Father,
though it seems like human fear of the end,
is more about love than simple fear.

For while, Señora, it is clear to see
that the tyranny of death oppresses his spirit,
and even though he who holds the whole world in
one hand almost fails from human frailty,

he fears more for your undoubted suffering:
he tenderly begs his Father
that, if possible, he exempt him from death.

See, how he loves you with passionate devotion.
Who else could be so valiant as to fear more
your misery than his own terrible death?

The most complete biblical account of the Agony in the Garden is in Matthew 26: 26, where it is recorded that Jesus prayed three times to be spared the forthcoming trial, each time terminating with the subjection of his own desires to the will of his father.[6] Sor Violante expresses

6. See Matthew 26: 37–44.

the agony of Christ's impassioned prayer in the first quartet, but already she lays the ground for her argument: "Aunque temor de humano al fin parece, / Más es temor de amante, que de humano" (3–4). While fearing one's end is a common human preoccupation, Sor Violante places Christ's love for his mother in another category altogether; his love for her is not merely that of a divine figure for his creation, for in his mortal state human self-interest is superseded by his concern to spare her suffering. By emphasizing Christ's filial love, Sor Violante again pursues her determination to portray Christ as a human figure, quite separate from the divinity he will assume after the Crucifixion. By bringing Christ into a more earthly dimension she can also make his sacrifice more accessible to human comprehension. Sor Violante figures the prayer as an Ignatian meditation, in which the octet "composition of place" overflows into the tercets. In this way, she expresses the intensity of Christ's feeling: "Más teme en vos pesar tan infalible" (9). Sor Violante then turns to extol the exceptional virtue of Christ, not in his sacrifice for humankind, nor in his divinity, but in his overriding love for Mary as his human mother: "Mirad, si os ama con afecto ardiente / ¿quien más, que de su muerte lo terrible, / teme de vuestra pena lo valiente?" (12–14).

This expression of filial concern, tenderness, and devotion is no accident on Sor Violante's part. She repeats it even more explicitly in another sonnet, entitled *Quarto Mysterio doloroso de Cristo Señor Nuestro con la cruz al hombro* (Fourth dolorous mystery of Christ Our Lord with the cross on his shoulder). Sor Violante takes her inspiration from John, as the other three gospels detail Simon of Cyrene as the cross bearer.[7] For the remainder of the story she is dependent upon tradition rather than biblical exegesis. Christ's falls on the Via Dolorosa number three, according to some traditions, and more according to others, though none is mentioned in the Bible. Sor Violante appropriates these stories to her own purpose, to emphasize the humanity of Christ and the loving ties that bind children and parents. Rather than use the occasion of Christ stumbling under the weight of the cross as a metaphor for the burdens of human life and sin from which he will both be liberated and be the liber-

7. See John 19: 17.

ating force, Sor Violante uses it to show the strong and self-negating love of a son for his mother. The sonnet opens with a series of negatives that firmly state her fresh look at an old story:

> No del largo camino enflaquecido,
> Ni del peso del leño derribado,
> en la tierra (Señora) está postrado
> el vencedor en acto de vencido.
>
> 5   La causa porque en tierra está caído
> (Dejo del Adán el misero pecado)
> Es peso del pesar, que le ha causado
> verse de vuestros ojos dividido.
>
> Bien lo acredita así su rostro santo,
> 10   que mostrando que busca tal presencia,
> los ojos vuelve atrás con tierno llanto.
>
> ¡O logre tal favor tal diligencia,
> Que para quien (Señora) os ama tanto
> la más pesada Cruz es vuestra ausencia!
>
> (*Parnaso lusitano* 15)

> It is not from the long, exhausting path,
> nor from the weight of that fallen timber
> (Señora) that he lies spreadeagled,
> this victor in the act of the vanquished.
>
> The reason why he is fallen to earth
> (Forget the miserable sin of Adam)
> is the weight of despair, caused by
> seeing himself deprived of your eyes.
>
> Hence it is clear that thus his holy face,
> seeking your presence, turns back his
> gaze, while gently weeping.
>
> Oh, that such care should achieve such favor,
> that for he (Lady) who so dearly loves you,
> the heaviest cross to bear is your absence!

The speaker is in the privileged position of knowing already that Christ is the "vencedor." Hence his fall is not attributed to his apparent defeat, although Sor Violante achieves a nicely balanced wordplay in the juxtaposition of "vencedor/vencido," which suggests Christ's divine majesty even as he lies in the dusty road on the way to his Crucifixion.

While the first two lines of the second quartet begin to develop Sor Violante's new argument regarding the fall to earth, they also constitute a metaphorical statement of the reason for Christ's ministry on earth: "la causa porque en tierra está caido / (Dejo de Adán el misero pecado)" (5–6). Although she parenthetically leaves aside the sin of the Garden, which she attributes to Adam rather than Eve, the location of the statement next to Christ's "fall to earth" serves to strengthen Christ's victorious role, since the reason he "fell" to earth in the first place was to fulfill the fate he now completes, to become conqueror of original sin. This first line of the quartet also looks forward to the remaining two lines, which resort to repetitive wordplay, as Sor Violante insists that Christ's true burden, and the reason for his fall on the road, is the impact of the impending separation from his beloved mother: "Es peso del pesar, que le ha causado / Verse de vuestros ojos dividido" (7–8). As in a love sonnet, Sor Violante privileges the eyes in both quartet and tercet. The first tercet focuses on the face of Christ, and the sight of his mother, coupled with awareness of their impending parting, fills his eyes with tears as they meet hers. In the quartet Christ grieves to be separated from his mother's eyes; in the tercets their eyes are reunited across the road: "Bien lo acredita así su rostro santo, / que mostrando, que busca tal presencia, / Los ojos vuelve atrás con tierno llanto" (9–11).

Sor Violante wrote her sonnets as mothers across the Iberian Peninsula were bidding tearful farewells to sons who, like Cueva's brother, Antonio, were going off to the wars, or like Ramírez's brother, Lorenzo, were sailing away to the New World. By foregrounding such relationships in her verse, Sor Violante makes Christ's message more accessible to her readers and listeners, and his example easier to follow, for however much he may suffer the emotional pain of a human son, Christ does not fail to do his duty.

Finishing where the sonnet began, the inevitability of the Crucifixion sees Christ again shoulder his cross. Now, however, it is a metaphorical burden, bound up in the separation that will break off the mutual gaze. The relationship between the son and the woman who is his mother will be irrevocably changed from this moment: "O logre tal favor tal diligencia, / que para quien (Señora) os ama tanto / la más pesada Cruz es vuestra ausencia" (12–14). The Gospels make it clear that Christ went willingly and obediently, if in dread, to his death. By converting his dread of death into dread of separation from his mother, Sor Violante depicts the enclosed and hidden world of home and family, setting maternal selflessness in a position of equality with Christ's expiatory sacrifice.

Sor Violante's determination to foreground mutual and reciprocal love between mothers and sons is again evident in her treatment of the Ascension. It is clearly important to Sor Violante that motherhood be lifted out of its position of inevitability and be seen as more than the duty and culmination of every wife's experience. Warner has argued that there has been no logical equivalence in any society, pagan or Christian, between exalted female objects of worship and a high position for women, and that veneration of the Virgin brings no corresponding rise in status for women, especially not in the Roman Catholic world (*Alone* 283). However, it may well be for just this reason that Sor Violante so determinedly humanizes the divine. By showing that Christ and his mother share human understanding and emotion, Sor Violante seeks both to use their perfect example and to project it at a level where motherhood and womanhood can be valued in society.

In the sonnet on the Ascension, joy, maternal pride, and sadness are embodied in the figure of the mother:

Segundo Misterio Doloroso: De la Ascensión

Compiten en vos misma juntamente
el placer, y el pesar o Reina amante,
es el placer, porque va Dios triunfante,
es el pesar; porque quedáis ausente.

5   Cada cual de los dos es tan valiente
que a poder más presume, que es bastante,
mas como vuestro amor es tan constante
prefiere lo que estima a lo que siente.

Dais a placer tan justo la victoria;
10 porque como el amaros enajena,
ni del pesar queréis tener memoria:

¡Pasión en fin de admiraciones llena!
Que es de mayor placer la ajena gloria
de lo que os da pesar la propia pena.

(Parnaso lusitano 20)

Second Dolorous Mystery: The Ascension

There simultaneously compete in you,
oh loving Queen, both pleasure and sorrow.
The pleasure is because God is triumphant,
the pain because he is gone from you.

Each of these two is so strong that
it is enough to be thought capable of more.
But because your love is so constant
you prefer what you value to what you feel.

Take just pleasure in the victory;
For as it is through loving you he leaves you,
you will not care to keep that pain's memory.

A passion, then, filled with wonders!
For another's glory is a greater pleasure
than the misery of your own suffering.

Mary's own self-sacrificing nature is expressed in the second quartet: "Mas como vuestro amor es tan constante / Prefiere lo que estima a lo que siente" (7–8). Her personal loss is subsumed under the crescendo of pleasure, victory, and love at the conquest of death. Sor Violante likens the grief of parting to the pain of labor, traditionally forgotten when the mother receives her child into her arms: "Ni del pesar queréis tener memoria" (11). Christ, now occupying a divine realm, is not, as in the previous sonnets, the main focus here. Instead, Sor Violante utilizes the unique moment of the Ascension to privilege the role of the mother as heroic, noble, loving, and self-sacrificing. This exemplary mother is strong enough to favor "lo que estima" over her own sorrow. Women everywhere were putting the needs of the empire before their own, thus giving particular resonance to Sor Violante's repeated message.

In portraying the Virgin in human terms, Sor Violante also gives new dignity to the limiting roles women were officially permitted to play. As she toes the party line in her poetry, she also exalts the female role and claims for it a stamp of divine approval. By promoting women's strength through the figure of the Virgin Mary to an audience accustomed to the propagandistic nature of Baroque religious art, she is also able to enter the *querelle des femmes* (argument about women), protected by the exemplary nature of her subject. Sor Violante reinforces her message in her sonnet to John the Evangelist, where she extols the virtues of the man who was linked indissolubly to Mary by Jesus from the cross:

A San Juan Evangelista

Águila, cuyo vuelo peregrino,
a más alto llegó que al mismo Cielo,
pues al pecho de Dios llegó tu vuelo,
y a la mayor ventura tu destino.

5   Fenix de amor, amante siempre fino,
gloria del mismo Dios, honra del suelo,
soberano exemplar, raro modelo
de todo lo perfecto, y lo divino:

Tú del más alto Rey digno cuidado,
10   iman de su afección tan poderoso,
como de sus secretos dulce archivo.

¿Mas qué mucho, que fuistes tan amado,
si mereciste (O Juan) ser venturoso
de la Madre de Dios hijo adoptivo?

(*Parnaso lusitano* 27)

To St. John the Evangelist

Eagle, whose extraordinary flight
to the most high equalled that of heaven itself,
since your flight took you to God's breast
and to your destiny of greater glory.

Phoenix of love, a perfect beloved,
glory of God himself, honor to the earth,
sovereign example, rare model
of all that is perfect and divine:

You were worthy of the care of the mightiest King
magnet of his so-powerful affections,
and sweet archive of his secrets.

But how much more were you beloved,
(Oh John) since you were worthy to be the
favored adoptive son of the mother of God?

Warner has argued that the Virgin receives the human race in trust when
Christ gives her into John's keeping and John into hers, where he comes
to personify the Church (*Alone* 220). Sor Violante does not pursue this
line in her sonnet to St. John, which is an unabashed paean of praise to
the evangelist. The concluding tercet measures John's merit not by his
deeds, but by Christ's nomination of him as Mary's adoptive son: "¿Mas
qué mucho, que fuiste tan amado, / Si mereciste (o Juan) ser venturoso / de la Madre de Dios hijo adoptivo?" (12–14). Thus Christ's care for
his mother after his death and Resurrection endorses Sor Violante's arguments in the sonnets that precede the Crucifixion: her overwhelming
conviction that Christ was more concerned for the welfare of his mother than his own fate in the hours before his torture and Crucifixion. It is
hardly coincidental that this analogy of John, at Calvary made the adoptive son of Mary, is used by Augustine as his model for loving one's parents:

The good Teacher does what He thereby reminds us ought to be done, and by
His own example instructed His disciples that care for their parents ought to be
a matter of concern to pious children. . . . From this wholesome doctrine it was
that the Apostle Paul had learned what he taught in turn, when he said, "But if
any provide not for his own, and especially for those of his own house, he hath
denied the faith, and is worse than an infidel." And what are so much home concerns to any one, as parents to children, or children to parents? Of this most
wholesome precept, therefore, the very Master of the saints set the example from
Himself, when, not as God for the hand-maid whom He had created and governed, but as a man for the mother, of whom He had been created, and whom

He was now leaving behind, He provided in some measure another son in place of Himself. (Augustine, *Gospel of John* 119.2)

As so often in Augustine's writing, he refutes here his own comment, discussed earlier, that we must love our families not above God but because they are loved by God, and that Christ's love of Mary stemmed not from her role as his mother but because she was a faithful daughter of God. In the Gospel of John, Augustine sees Christ's action as the last act of love by a human son for his mother.

Sor Violante's sonnets demonstrate the earthbound expression of mutual need for love and recognition that exists among family members at all levels of society. It is not that she does not show due reverence for God, but rather that she refuses to diminish the importance of human tenderness as a reflection of God's love. In the same manner, Ramírez's loving, witty, and funny poems to her family indicate a warm tenderness that is not measured against one's love for God, a given for every Christian, but exists in a realm of its own.

Unlike Sor Violante's preoccupation with the Holy Family, Ramírez writes many poems to and about her own family. The majority are barely concealed by pastoral names, both for herself and for her familial subjects.[8] Although few of her works are sonnets, the glimpses that her poetry affords into the lives and pastimes of the Spanish rural elites in the seventeenth century merit a digression to some of her other poems such as, for example, the short poem to her father, in which Ramírez begs him to bring her a modish sheer *manto* (cloak) from Madrid, using her wit to inveigle him into complying:

> *Pidiendo la autora a su padre que la*
> *trujese un manto estando en Madrid.*
>
> Doña Catalina Clara
> un manto pide de gloria,
> y si como la memoria

---

8. Gazul details the baptismal details of ten children born to the family, of whom six survived. Ramírez's pastoral names for her family were Tisbe for Beatriz, born 1617; Lauro for Lorenzo, born 1622; Antandra for Antonia Manuela, born 1625; Anarda, for Ana Rosalea, born 1628; Clori for herself; and Píramo for her older brother Pedro Antonio, born 1619.

la voluntad enviara,
5   no duda que se comprara;
mas sabe sufriros tanto
que no le causará espanto,
si os hallaréis sin dinero,
que le enviéis un no quiero
que sea más claro que el manto.

(BN ms. 3884 240r)

The author pleads with her father to bring her a cloak from Madrid

Lady Catalina Clara
begs a diaphanous cloak,
and if it is so that memory
follows the will, she
does not doubt it will be bought;
but she knows you would suffer terribly,
if you find yourself without money,
and so as not to cause a fright
you should send her an "I don't wish to"
that will be clearer than the cloak.

In another, she pleads for an *almilla*, a form of tunic:

Pidiendo el autor a su padre una almilla

No os causara maravilla
ni es justo que os dé cuidado,
que quien el alma os ha dado
os pida en cambio una almilla
5   de la tela que más brilla,
me la sacad encarnada.
Petición tan ajustada
no debe causaros pena
porque para nada es buena
una mujer desalmada.

(BN ms. 3884 222r)

The author asks her father for a tunic

It should not cause you wonder,
nor is it right that it should worry you,
that she who has given you her soul
should plead a tunic in exchange,
of the most shining fabric:
choose me a red one.
This petition is so fitting
as to cause you no suffering,
because a soulless woman
is no good at all.

Her witty utilization of wordplays about the soul (*alma-almilla*) are designed to ensure that her father will be charmed into complying. The moralist Juan de Zabaleta deplores such garments, writing thus of the *dama:* "Pónele una criada el manto de humo; ella queda como sin manto; tan en cuerpo se está como se estaba, y de aquella manera quiere ir a la calle. . . . El humo, por su naturaleza hace llorar a todos; muy sin ojos está la razón que no llora con aquel humo" (119; Her maidservant puts on her a cloak of smoke; she appears to wear no cloak; she is as much in the flesh as she was before, and in that manner she goes into the street. . . . Smoke, by its nature, makes everyone weep; you would have to be without eyes not to weep at that smoke).

Other poems by Ramírez express sadness at her father's absence, commiserate with him, struck by "principios de gota" (the beginnings of gout), and express sympathy for her mother over her failing eyesight, brought on, it seems, by excessive needlework:

A la madre de la autora que tenía los ojos malos,
y hacía labor con que se le ponían peores

Tus ojos forman querella
ponderando que es rigor,
amar tanto la labor
que ciegues Silvia por ella.
5   Pero como solo ella
te entretiene, (cosa es llana)

tomaré de buena gana
(en esta fineza advierte)
solo por entretenerte
que me zurzas la badana.⁹

(BN ms. 3884 227r)

*To the author's mother, whose eyes were bad
and whose work made them worse*

Your eyes form an argument
thinking that it is harsh
to love labor so much that
you would blind yourself for it Silvia.
But as it's the only thing that
amuses you (it's clear to see),
you should take it with a good will
(take note of this kind gesture)
that just to entertain yourself
you may make me suffer.

This poem provides a glimpse into the world extolled by Luis de León in *La perfecta casada,* a world in which the wife is hard working, self-sacrificing, and uncomplaining, busy with needlework and household chores. In these poems there is no sense that Ramírez holds her father in fear and awe and she clearly loves her mother, expressing concern for her health and well-being. Ramírez's attitude to her father is even more relevant, given available biographical details about the family. Her father, Francisco Ramírez Guerrero, has been described both as an "arrogante y altivo capitán" (arrogant and haughty captain) who had many enemies, and as a good example of the new type of emerging bureaucrat. On his move from his birthplace of Zafra to Llerena he succeeded in winning the hand of Isabel Sebastiana de Guzmán, whose father had intended to

---

9. "[Z]urzas la badana" is not clear but may be read as "zurrar la badana," a term derived from the curing and beating into softness of leather, meaning colloquially "to maltreat somebody with words or actions." It may be that Ramírez deliberately plays with words here—*zurcir* means to sew up a tear in a garment. Such a pun would incorporate both the unhappiness caused to the daughter to see her mother's difficulties and the motif of sewing. That is, her mother is beating her with her needle.

marry her to the heir of the Count of Puebla. Francisco also waged a machiavellian campaign to secure a permanent place as *regidor* (councilor) of Llerena. He traveled to Madrid, where he petitioned to have the number of permanent local *regidores* increased from eight to twenty. He then filled the new seats with his supporters, giving himself a position of unrivalled power in the area (Carrasco García 103–5). Ramírez's poetic plea for a *manto* becomes more interesting in the light of her father's business in Madrid.

The unusually personal nature of Ramírez's poetry is attributed by Entrambasaguas to her provincial upbringing and therefore her distance from the centers of poetic decorum: "Solamente Ramírez—tal vez debido a su alejamiento de los centros literarios—apartóse totalmente de la norma general y escribió poesías no culteranas" (41; Only Ramírez—probably due to her distance from literary centers—departed completed from the general rule and wrote poetry in a nonelevated style). An outsider she may have been in the seventeenth-century social fabric of her class, but her poetry brings forth a privileged, personal view of family life and everyday amusements that is of sociological significance. In addition, the commotion over precedence on the *estrado*,[10] detailed in Chapter 4, shows that provincial life for the upper classes did not differ greatly from city life.

An external observer's opinion of parents's continuing interest in their children tends to confirm that most parents probably did not follow the austerity of Vives but instead reveled in their children's activities, as Lady Ann Fanshawe's memoirs indicate: "[They] take much pleasure to see their little children act before them in their own houses, which they will doe in perfection" (173). Her memoirs reveal much of everyday life in Spain, if only at the highest levels. Even so, there was a distinct change in the way that children were treated once they reached the age of six and were considered ready for instruction. Where before there was little difference in the treatment of girls and boys, now their newfound maturity was measured by the exchange of childhood robes for those modeled on adult lines and by their first communion (Kagan 7–9).

It would be natural to assume that this change in attitude would taint

10. The *estrado* was a raised platform in the salón where women entertained each other while squatting on cushions.

the relationships obtaining between siblings, as boys went away to school and girls stayed at home, and that the closeness of early childhood would dissolve with distance. However, the poetry of Ramírez that so clearly describes her family and their pastimes gives the lie to this assumption. Her attitude is endorsed by the sonnets of Leonor de la Cueva, discussed in the chapter on patronage, that both praise her family's name and show affection for the brother who exhibits the requisite *hombría* expected of a gentleman of his class.

LOVE AMONG SIBLINGS

Early modern Spanish moralists have little to say about the relations between siblings. While boys were sent out to become *criados* (to seek service in another household, usually in expectation of some preferment) or to be educated, or stayed at home to receive advanced education from tutors, girls were expected to follow the activities of their mothers. Lady Anne Fanshawe observes that "[u]ntil their daughters marry, they never stir so much as down stairs, nor [marry] for no consideration under their own quality, which to prevent, if their fortunes will not procure, they make them nuns" (173).[11] In spite of the perceived distances between the sexes, Ramírez writes a number of poems to two of her brothers when they are far from home that express a range of emotions from tenderness to sardonic amusement. The brothers' activities reflect the tightly limited opportunities available to sons of the nobility, where the older son followed the role of the father, and younger sons often went, willingly or not, into the Church.[12]

11. This was the general picture, but the previously mentioned marriage between the parents of Ramírez shows that some parents, at least, bowed to the preferences of their daughters.

12. For a discussion of the sibling rivalry occasioned by the practice of primogeniture among the upper classes, see Kagan, who outlines the patriarchalism of seventeenth-century Spain and the tightly prescribed career of the oldest child who, under the system of *mayorazgo* (primogeniture), would inherit the bulk of the family's wealth. See also Lawrence Stone, *The Family, Sex and Marriage in England 1500–1800* (London: Weidenfeld & Nicolson, 1977), 115. Louis Montrose also discusses the problems that primogeniture in England caused to younger sons through Shakespeare's treatment of the practice in *As You Like It;* see his "'The Place of a Brother' in *As You Like It*: Social Process and Comic Form," *Shakespeare Quarterly* 32, no. 1 (1981): 28–54.

Ramírez's older brother, Pedro (Píramo in her more playful poetry), a year her junior, followed his father into military service as the *alférez* (lieutenant) of his father's company. He later became administrator of the Real Servicio de Millones (administrative office for collecting the *millones* tax [a tax on commodities]) in the city of Lugo. In 1680 he became lieutenant governor of Llerena, where he lived with Ramírez and their sister Antonia Manuela. He never married (Carrasco García 111).[13] Lorenzo, who was born in 1622, was "uno de aquellos clérigos a medio ordenar que tanto abundaban en el siglo de Lope, más amigos de amores que de disciplina" (Entrambasaguas y Peña 21–22; one of those clerics of the minor orders who so abounded in Lope [de Vega]'s century, more devoted to love affairs than to discipline). This opinion accords with two poems Catalina writes to Lorenzo. One, a *décima*, is entitled *A un galán que negaba el galanteo que hacía a una pastelera* (To a young man who denied paying court to a pastrycook):

> Lauro, tu recato es justo,
> pero ¿a el cuál más te llama,
> el crédito de tu dama
> o el crédito de tu gusto?
> 5   Mal con tu elección me ajusto,
> pero, pues determinado
> estás, anda con cuidado,
> porque tu dueño crüel
> no te eche en algún pastel,
> pues te tiene tan picado.

> Lauro, your reticence is right,
> but what else could you call it,
> the reputation of your lady,
> or the reputation of your taste?
> It's hard for me to agree with your choice,
> but, since you are determined,
> proceed with caution,

13. In providing these biographical data, Carrasco García corrects the assumption of Entrambasaguas y Peña that Pedro Antonio was killed at the battle of Rocroy and that a sonnet by Ramírez mourning the death of a soldier was about her brother.

because your cruel mistress
might put you into a pie
she has you so in shreds.

This *décima* trades humorously on the prevailing urban myth that *pasteles,* pies made with chopped meat, were often made with carrion or the flesh of the recently executed. She suggests that he is happy to flirt with a low-class baker's girl, but not to acknowledge her otherwise, provoking the suggestion that the *pastelera* may have the last word.[14] Similarly, Ramírez writes a lengthy *romance,* a small part of which is reproduced below, to this same brother lamenting his imprisonment, apparently effected by his religious superiors to punish his vanity in refusing to cut his abundant hair. It may have been the discipline that caused him to give up the habit and emigrate to Guatemala, in about 1650, where he married (Carrasco García 109). Lorenzo was four years younger than Ramírez, and the poem reveals the fond exasperation of an older sister, as these excerpts show:

Esta noche, hermano mío,
meditando tus sucesos,
me desvelé, que el cuidado
se lleva mal con el sueño.
Y a instancias de la razón
y de mi amor a los ruegos,
propuse hablarte, aunque digas
que es dar voces en desierto
                    (1–8)

. . .

Por órdenes dicen unos
que el tal juez te tiene preso,
y por desórdenes otros,
que es un enigma tu pleito.
                    (49–52)

. . .

14. According to Carrasco García, the *pastelera* did have the last word, as he is recorded as having a bastard son by a *pastelera.* Carrasco García further suggests that this son,

Y perdona que de gorra
se han entrado mis consejos,
cuando, obstinado y temeroso,
te haces sordo a los preceptos.

(81–84) (BN ms. 3917:360)

Last night, brother mine,
thinking of your activities
I lay awake, since cares go
badly with restful sleep.
And impelled by reason, and
by the pleadings of my love for you,
I proposed to speak with you, though
you may say I'm crying in the wilderness.
. . .

Some say that it's by orders
that that judge has you prisoner,
others say its your disorders,
so that your plight is an enigma.
. . .

And forgive me that my counsel
has intruded itself unasked for,
when obstinate and fearful
you deafen yourself to the rule.

She is careful to couch her counsel in terms that would make it difficult
for him to refuse her, begging his forgiveness at her forwardness, yet she
does not scruple to counsel him whether he finds it acceptable or not.
The respectful language is simply a means to an end. Though here she
counsels her own family, she is not alone in giving counsel to men. Writing on a history of women's education, Vollendorf notes the willingness
of at least one woman, María de Guevara, to proffer advice to men: "she
declares that men who do not take women's advice are crazy" (*Lives of
Women* 182). As we have already seen in Chapter 1, the empress was not

---

Manuel, was pointedly left out of the will of the last surviving sibling, Antonia Manuela,
because she disapproved of the affection that Ramírez showed toward him (113–14).

loath to counsel the royal family when she felt it her duty, neither was Luisa de Carvajal y Mendoza slow to proffer unwanted advice to her brother in her correspondence.

The familial closeness and interest in her brothers' activities is also expressed in Ramírez's sonnet to Pedro Antonio, away on military business. In the same manner, Cueva's sonnets to her brother, discussed in Chapter 1, show affectionate concern above and beyond pride in family, rank, and preferment. The loving and emotional ties between the brothers and sisters bear out Lawrence Stone's articulation of the close relationships between siblings of the opposite sex that characterized the early modern English family. This relationship, he claims, did not suffer the envy and bitterness often felt by a younger brother for the family heir (115). In her sonnet to Pedro Antonio, Ramírez utilizes many of the tropes of the conventional love sonnet. Similarly, the poetic *sobrescrito* (address) on a letter to her brother, Pedro, addressed to "el más valiente soldado" (the most valiant soldier), describes him as "el que es mi hermano y mi amante" (ms. 3884 228v; 9; he who is my brother and my beloved). However, where this poem is lively and optimistic, the sonnet of absence is quiet and sad:

Soneto a su hermano Don Pedro

Acertar a decir mi sentimiento
fuera desaire de mi pena grave,
que en el silencio solamente cabe
la significación de mi tormento.

5   De esperanzas de veros me alimento
que es manjar en la ausencia el más suave,
y mudamente mi silencio sabe,
decir callando lo que amando siento.

Y aunque paso esta pena por amaros,
10   no puedo arrepentirme de quereros,
que no dejarme el gusto de adoraros

por ahorrar la pena de no veros.
Que el alma que no tiene ya que daros
gusta de tener ansias que ofreceros.

(ms. 3884. 223r)

Sonnet to her brother Don Pedro

To speak and clear my thoughts
would be to offend my heavy grief,
for only in silence can be found
the full meaning of my torment.

I feed myself with hopes of seeing you
which, in absence, is the sweetest food,
and mutely my silence knows to speak
wordlessly what I feel in loving you.

And though it is in loving you that I suffer,
I cannot regret that I care for you; I would
not deprive myself of the pleasure of adoring you

to save me the pain of not seeing you.
For the soul that can no longer give you
pleasure offers you its yearning.

Because Pedro fulfills the role appropriate to a man and oldest son, away earning honor for the family, to express grief at his absence would be inappropriate. Instead, the octet employs every possible manifestation of silence: "silencio," "mudamente," "silencio," and "callando": "decir callando lo que amando siento" (8). Ramírez's sadness is expressed in silence forced on her by her distance, in the domestic realm, from her brother, away on the masculine business of war. That Ramírez so emphasizes the silence occasioned by her brother's absence suggests that this role was unusual for her. As in Sor Violante's sonnet on the Annunciation, it is the power of silence, women's eloquent burden, that most clearly evokes the relationship.[15] Through silence she expresses strong feelings of love and loss that speak of a genuinely affective relationship, especially in the context of her other family-related verse.

The tercets move from silence to multiple protestations of love that make the "pena" of absence bearable, and this is emphasized by the loca-

---

15. For an enlightened view of the power of women's silence in a different context, see Stacey Schlau, *Spanish American Women's Use of the Word: Colonial through Contemporary Narratives* (Tucson: University of Arizona Press, 2001). Schlau regards women's silence as a rhetorical strategy designed to challenge patriarchal norms (xvii).

tion at the end of each line of the first tercet, of a reiterated crescendo of love: "amaros," "quereros," "adoraros." However, Ramírez ends the sonnet on a declining note of anxiety, occasioned by her concern both to see Pedro and for his safety as a soldier: "Que el alma que no tiene ya que daros / gusta de tener ansias que ofreceros" (13–14). The dangerous reality of his soldier's role in defense of a crumbling European empire is also revealed in another sonnet to a dead soldier that Entrambasaguas supposes to be about Don Pedro's death at the battle of Rocroy in May 1643 (21). However, not only does she write about her brother elsewhere after that date, but Carrasco García provides evidence of his survival, as previously stated.

In providing a sociological picture of seventeenth-century family life, even if only for the upper levels of Spanish society, Ramírez helps to support the contention that within the household there was often real affection between siblings that superseded the differences in education for brothers and sisters and the demands of empire. The companionship of brothers, whose freedom of movement was not impeded by societal mores, must have brought new ideas and interests into the household that influenced the way that Ramírez, Cueva, or other writing women thought and wrote. Ramírez's whole life was passed in Llerena and her poetry derives from her own and her family's activities and interactions.

Lerner has argued persuasively that women, deprived of "cultural prodding," or dialogue and encounter with persons of equal education and standing, were also denied knowledge of the existence of women's history, and were therefore unaware that others like them had made intellectual contributions to knowledge and to creative thought (*Consciousness* 12). Vollendorf and other scholars make the same point, speculating on the degree to which women were aware of other women's writing or whether they operated in a vacuum, although convent writings show evidence of continuity among generations of educated women (*Lives of Women* 169). Ramírez's domesticated poetry indicates that apart from her immediate circle and a level of education that included knowledge of Quevedo's works, she was unaware of the efforts of other women to write against a culture that presumed their inferiority.

CONCLUSION

Given the political upheavals and the economic, subsistence, and public health crises suffered by Spain in the seventeenth century, it might be expected that individuals would not risk investing excessive emotional capital in family members since the potential for losing them was too great. The family provides a unique refuge from the problems of greater society, and as this and the previous chapter have shown, the presence of genuine tenderness and affection among family members is clearly evident in these women's poetry. The degree of filial tenderness registered by Sor Violante in some of her sonnets on the Passion goes far beyond Church requirements for patriarchal conformity in the family. It is evident that she appropriates the Church's propaganda to her own use, advancing and defending the value of the mother-child bond.

Where the principal concern of the moralists is sexual and social propriety, regulated through discipline and the expectations of social and religious hierarchies, these poets show that affection for the family, a pillar of social survival in unhappy times, was a shared affective relationship. Ramírez's frankly affectionate poetry to her father demonstrates a relaxed and familiar bond. It provides an informal view of family life that suggests that fathers were more actively involved in the emotional networks of family than moralizing treatises would suggest. This view is borne out by the constant complaints of moralists that parents were spoiling their children. Similarly, Cueva's poem on the death of a beloved father, shown in Chapter 1 as a foil to the aggrandizing nature of the sonnet to her famous uncle, also projects genuine distress, tenderness, and loss.

The family served as protector, source of religious fervor, social regulator, and means to social advancement in an age before sentimentalism and romantic idealization, and before psychotherapeutic techniques and studies. Affection and solidarity in the family ensured physical and political survival. There were, however, other networks that sprang naturally from familial contact with the outside world. Bonds of friendship between families aided social advancement but also extended further than this, providing women with emotional and spiritual support.

CHAPTER 4

FEMININE FRIENDSHIP

꒦꒷

T HE BENEFITS WOMEN DERIVED from the companionship
and support of other women cannot be underestimated. If the
patriarchal norm prevailed, then the only like-minded people who shared
and understood women's plight were other women. The intellectual and
emotional benefits of friendship can be glimpsed through the poetry and
other writings of those women whose works survive, providing a small
but significant archive of seventeenth-century female thought both religious and secular. Unlike male-authored drama, women's plays in the
period incorporate female friendship as an integral part of the plot, as
can be seen, for example, in the roles of the women protagonists in Ana
Caro's *Valor, Agravio, Mujer,* the mutual support shown between the aristocratic Armesinda and her *criada* (servant and companion) Leonor, in
Leonor de la Cueva y Silva's *La firmeza en la ausencia,* or María de Zayas's
exploration of a female betrayal of friendship in *La traición en la amistad*
(Friendship betrayed). Also, both studied and still to be discovered is the
plethora of works that lie in convent records and which also show evidence of women's control and management of convent affairs and their
assets, as well as the shared intellectual and leisure activities of study and
literary composition.[1] Furthermore, María de Zayas not only argued for

---

1. For more of women's activities in the convent, see Elizabeth Lehfeldt, *Religious
Women in Golden Age Spain: The Permeable Cloister.*

women's education in her writings, but critiqued the victimization to which women could be subjected by their menfolk, calling them to join in friendship for mutual support, as Theresa Ann Smith points out, noting that through her works Zayas directs women toward each other for mutual support, or to the convent, as in the ending of the *Desengaños amorosos* (Disenchantment of love), where they might escape "the brutality of a misogynistic society" (27).

Poems to fellow nuns by Marcia Belisarda indicate a warm familial relationship in which nuns were drawn into the convent community, but the titles suggest that they are written for women of quality who are joining their aristocratic equals. Both hierarchy and patriarchy were the norms across seventeenth-century Europe, and obtained in all aspects of state, society, and the Church, extending even to the convents. Where a sisterhood of joint service, mutual support, and affection might be expected, social and financial stratification meant that the *monjas de velo negro* (nuns of the black veil) sang in the choir and engaged with spiritual matters, while the nuns of the white veil undertook the menial tasks.[2] Sor Ana de San Bartolomé, who was sent by St. Teresa to found convents outside Spain, criticizes the social stratifications of Church and state in her autobiography, where she negatively compares the Spanish methods of enforcing obedience with those of the French.[3] In writing of her work in Paris with another Spanish nun, Isabel de los Ángeles, Sor Ana expresses this difference: "[Y]a ella lo hacía bien, que iba tomando más el estilo de la Francia y dulzura. . . . Y cierto, yo lo hallo mejor y más conforme a la condición de Nuestro Señor Jesucristo, que, si lo miramos, andaba con sus discípulos como hermano y compañero" (qtd. in Arenal

---

2. Concha Torres Sánchez defines this cultural stratification more exactly: the *legas* were sisters of charity, excluded from devotional work; the *freilas* were nuns who served as adjuncts to the military orders; the *monjas de medio hábito* were domestic servants; and the *monjas del coro* were aristocratic women whose duties were limited to the devotional. See Concha Torres Sánchez, *La clausura femenina en la Salamanca del siglo XVII: Dominicas y Carmelitas Descalzas*. Acta Salmanticensia. Estudios históricos y geográficos 73 (Salamana: Universidad de Salamanca, 1991), 68. Vollendorf also defines the class stratification to be seen in convents in *The Lives of Women* (93–94).

3. Ana de San Bartolomé's antipathy to the class question probably had much to do with her own humble beginnings. Arenal and Schlau define her rustic, Castilian vernacular writing as invaluable for students of language of that period, which was undergoing rapid change; see *Untold Sisters* (30).

and Schlau 35; She was now coping very well as she went on taking on more the sweetness of the French style. . . . And truly I consider it better and more in line with the condition of Our Lord Jesus Christ who, if we think about it, went among his disciples as a brother and companion).

The class differences so disliked by Sor Ana were replicated in the Church even to the extent that it was also one of the great customers for the slave traders. Arenal and Schlau have commented on the unself-conscious way in which Madre María de San José writes of the activities of the slave laborers in the daily life of the convent (148). According to Fra-Molinero, an important aristocrat like the Archbishop of Seville could have from seventy to a hundred slaves in his household. The most exploited slaves were black women. Those black slaves who wished to profess as nuns came up against the problems of lack of dowry and questions of *limpieza de sangre,* or blood purity, which excluded them from the religious life. Black women were also particular targets for persecution by the Inquisition (163, 171). Nevertheless, the class structure and questions of blood purity do not detract from the firm and enduring relationships developed between nuns of the same social class, as can be seen from the poetry of Marcia Belisarda and Sor Violante del Cielo.

Outside the convent, conduct books discussed the proper role of women as entirely concerned with the domestic sphere, insisting on silent, obedient, modest, and demure women, whose meddling hands were always to be occupied with sewing, weaving, and other domestic tasks. Constant reminders to husbands of the need to prevent their wives from exchanging visits with their neighbors show that visiting must have been a common practice. Neither were they to allow excessive church visiting or devotional *romerías* (pilgrimages), other potential avenues for social intercourse among women, or, worse, between women and men.[4] Luis de León, for example, notes that among married women it was as if their houses "fuesen de sus vecinas, así se descuidan dellas, y toda su vida es el oratorio, y el devocionario, y el calentar el suelo de la iglesia tarde y

---

4. Jacques Derrida has also commented on the "double exclusion" to which women were subject in "all the great ethico-politico-philosophical discourses on friendship, . . . the exclusion of friendship between women and . . . the exclusion of friendship between a man and a woman"; see Jacques Derrida, *Politics of Friendship,* trans. George Collins (London and New York: Verso, 1997), 642.

mañana" (*Perfecta* 143–44; belonged to their neighbors they took so little care of them, and their whole life was the oratory and devotions and warming the floor of the church night and day). Similarly, Antonio de Guevara, in his *Reloj de príncipes* (Clock of princes), insists that "se debe recatar mucho el hombre cuerdo de que sus hijas y mujer anden vagando de visita en visita, y de estación en estación; ni se debe mover mucho por las devociones" (qtd. in Vigil 157; The wise man should be very hesitant about letting his daughters and wife go wandering from visit to visit and from place to place, nor should they go out much to their devotions).

It is tempting to deduce that as women were even criticized for excessive churchgoing as a means to quasi-legitimized social contact, women's opportunities for social engagement were few. Yet the poetry of women both inside and outside the convent walls reflects genuine affective relationships, as can be seen in the relaxed wittiness and personal nature of Ramírez's and Cueva's poetry, and in Sor Violante's sonnets from within the convent to her aristocratic friends outside. The contemporary views recorded by Barbara Shaw Fairman also suggest otherwise. For example, the wife of an English diplomat, Robert Bargrave, writing in the early part of the century of the *madrileñas* (Madrid women), observed that they were far from being sequestered in their homes, and were much more lascivious and libertine than in other places (171). Lord Roos, who found women of the lower classes immoral and libertine, observed that upperclass women, in spite of their grave manner, "unen ingeniosamente en su trato social cierto pudoroso atrevimiento con aquella gravedad" (172; ingeniously join a certain modest daring to that gravity in their social dealings). Similarly, an anonymous letter, written later in the century, found Spanish women "más animadas, más ingeniosas y de mejor 'carácter,' en el amplio sentido de la palabra" (172–73; more animated, more ingenious, and of greater "character" in the broadest sense of the word). A uniquely personal view of Spanish women in society can also be found in the memoirs of Lady Ann Fanshawe. She too notes the liveliness of Spanish women: "They are generally pleasant and facetious company, but in this their women exceed, who seldom laugh, but never aloud, but the most witty in repartees and stories and notions in the world" (173). Perhaps what gave cause for concern among the conduct book writers was that which the anecdotes by these foreign visitors reveal, for they give Spanish women a lively, intelligent, and rather daring comportment, at variance with their objectification in the discourses of the moralists.

Away from the convent, then, women established socially beneficial relationships through regular visits to church, through visits to each other's homes, and through correspondence, as Sor Violante's poetic plea to Inés/"Nise" for more letters has revealed. Ramírez and Cueva not only enjoyed loving family relationships that were far from silent, they also direct affectionate and mocking poems to friends of both sexes, a pastime presumably enjoyed and responded to in kind by their wider networks of friends and acquaintances.

If women's prescribed roles pertained to the private sphere and tireless domestic activity, those upper-class and educated women who had more access to leisure time utilized the enclosed domestic environment as a site for shared entertainment and companionship. Thus Lady Ann Fanshawe notes that "[w]hen they visite it is with great state and attendance. When they travell they are the most jolly people in the world, dealing their provisions of all sorts to every person they meet, when they are eating" (173). The houses of the wealthier Spaniards offered luxuriously furnished reception rooms in which to entertain guests. The testaments of Ramírez's parents, for example, detail the appointments of the family home: "Hubo para todos camas suntuosas, escritorios, bufetes, objetos de plata, colchas, mantelerías, almohadones de terciopelo o damasco de estrados, y para las hembras, hasta baterías de cocina. También numerosos cuadros" (Gazul, "Familia Ramírez," 527–28; Everyone had sumptuous beds, desks, buffets, silver objects, mattresses, bed coverings, plump velvet or damask cushions for the *estrados,* and even including, for the women, kitchen equipment. Also numerous paintings). As Defourneaux explains, the *salón* was often divided by a wooden screen, on one side of which women entertained their friends, squatting on cushions in the Arab manner, on a raised platform, the *estrado,* while the males on the other side of the screen sat on chairs. Educated women gathered in cultural groups in their homes, "where they used all the refinements of language which the poetry of the time had made fashionable" (149–54). It is this pretension to intellectual pursuits that Quevedo mocks so cruelly in *La culta latiniparla* (The craze for speaking Latin). In spite of Quevedo's satirical attitudes, women's social encounters provided an opportunity to exercise and demonstrate fem-

inine intelligence and wit, as can be seen in the burlesque poetry written
by Catalina Clara Ramírez de Guzmán and Marcia Belisarda.

THE BURLESQUE

Ramírez addresses a number of burlesque poems to family members,
and writes playful and sometimes acid poetry to or about both male and
female acquaintances, showing considerable confidence both in their execution and in her willingness to engage in the masculine pastime of
mocking friends in verse. For example, she directs a burlesque *décima* to
a friend, lampooning her habit of eating aromatic clay, or *búcaro*, a common practice among women as they socialized on the *estrado* with their
drinks of chocolate:

> *A una mujer tan amiga de barro que*
> *se desayunaba con el*
>
> Si en la moneda se paga
> que se pasa Leonor yerra,
> pues se tragara la tierra
> a quien la tierra se traga.
> 5   Salud y color le estraga,
> de su vicio la porfía
> y ella dice cada día,
> queriéndose disculpar,
> que se la quiso almorzar
> porque comerla quería.
>
> (ms. 3884 221r)

> *To a woman who liked clay so much*
> *she had it for breakfast*
>
> If we get paid in the same
> coin we deal in, Leonor errs,
> since the earth might swallow
> whoever swallows the earth.
> It mines their health and color,

a challenge to their vice,
and each day she says,
in wanting to excuse herself,
that she would like it for lunch
because she enjoyed eating it.

Ramírez warns her friend that she is damaging her health by an overin-dulgence in the habit through an amusing poem which suggests that the tables may be turned: she who swallows too much earth will in turn be swallowed by it.

Beyond joking with female friends, Ramírez's poetry shows that wom-en were able to enjoy friendly pastimes with members of both sexes, albeit under a rigid and codified ceremonial procedure. Deleito y Piñuela notes the habitual separation of sexes while also acknowledging that *tertulias* (lit-erary gatherings) for mixed company took place among the upper classes "todo habitualmente dentro de un ritual prefijado" (all habitually within a prearranged ritual). He also observes that ritualistic practices were the norm during visits between women (*La mujer* 32). A serious enmity devel-oped between Ramírez's family and the Almezquita, the son of whom was one of her suitors, over an assumed breach of established protocol:

[N]ació una rivalidad que desembocó en odio y malquerencia por una cuestión de protocolo y jerarquía; . . . Yendo Dª. Isabel de Guzmán y Dª. Francisa de Mendoza a visitar a la mujer del governador de Llerena, D. Juan de Córdoba, disputaron ambas visitantes sobre cuál de las dos había de ocupar el puesto prin-cipal del estrado, originándose una violenta riña que dio en tierra con el afecto y la amistad que unía a las familias respectivas. (32)

A rivalry developed that grew into hatred and ill-feeling over a question of pro-tocol and hierarchy; . . . Doña Isabel de Guzmán and Doña Francisa de Men-doza were going to visit the wife of the governor of Llerena, Don Juan de Cór-doba, when the two visitors had an argument over which of the two should occupy the principal place on the *estrado,* creating a violent dispute that buried the affection and friendship that had united the respective families.

The relationship never recovered from this encounter, although Ramírez did not use any of the Almezquita family as the butt of her burlesque verse, at least not by name.

There is no hint in Ramírez's poetry of the "subtle appropriations and reshufflings of prevailing notions of feminine virtue" mentioned by Ann Rosalind Jones in her discussion of the strategies used by Renaissance women poets to justify their writing ("Fame" 80). Where Jones refers to women poets' use of deference and self-effacement as a method of promoting their own reputation against the masculine right to fame, Ramírez writes secure in her social position and her poetic ability. In one sonnet, for example, the lengthy title provides the reason for its composition, and even before the sonnet begins its target is described as "ridículo" (ridiculous):

> *Respondiendo a un soneto de un hombre ridículo*
> *cuyo apellido era Castaño que habiendole dado*
> *una Dama un vejamen en que él no acertó a*
> *responder más de que se holgaba de ser el instrumento*
> *de la conversación y la antífona, y esto refirió tantas*
> *veces que hizo reparo particular, salió muy obligado*
> *de una que le picaba con más disimulo. Le envió*
> *un soneto gracioso con un hermano de ella tal*
> *mostrándose en el muy agradecido.*

> Si no acierto a decir lo que os estimo
> baste haber acertado en estimaros,
> y cuando sólo trato de obligaros,
> viendoos desconfiar me desanimo.

> 5   ¿Será tal árbol mi seguro arrimo?
> De la verdad podéis aseguraros
> y aunque el fruto me espine de buscaros
> y siempre he de hacer tema de serviros,

> De mi alegría sois el instrumento
> 10 y mi antífona sois de todo el año.
> Veros, Castaño, claro, es lo que siento;

> sólo el ser zaino fuera mayor daño,
> pero si procedéis tan desatento
> más seréis boquirrubio que castaño.

> (ms. 3884, 233v)

Responding to a sonnet by a ridiculous man whose surname was Castaño (Chestnut) who, a lady having given him a poem, was uncertain how to respond other than to say that he enjoyed being the instrument of the conversation and her antiphon. He referred to this so many times that it was particularly noticeable, and he ended up very much compelled by one who goaded him with greater subtlety. He sent her a comical sonnet with a brother of hers, showing in it that he was very grateful.

If I cannot be sure to say what I esteem in you,
it's enough to have succeeded in taking your measure,
and when I simply try to oblige you,
seeing you lose confidence I lose heart.

Can such a tree be my secure support?
You may be assured of the truth
and though the fruits spur me to seek you,
and always with the theme of serving you,

you are the instrument of my amusement
and you are my antiphon all the year.
To see you clearly, Castaño, is what I want;

Being a dark horse would only be worse,
but if you continue to be so inattentive
you will be more a colt than a stallion.

Given the plethora of verse written by Ramírez to her family, it seems likely that the "hombre ridículo" is a friend of the speaker's brother, that she has already produced a burlesque poem to which the subject had been unable to respond readily, and that she feels quite at home engaging in flyting, the poetic exchange of insults as a battle of wits generally reserved for the universities and literary academies.

Ramírez does not hesitate to award all the laurels of this poetic competition to the supposedly weaker and less educated sex. Her equine metaphors embrace both the name of her victim and also the image of a dull slow horse being spurred into action. They suggest that she is riding him, thus both celebrating a particularly masculine type of power and feminizing the object of her cruel wit. With the inclusion of nature and plant imagery, she relegates him, in various ways, to a subhuman category, in which the *castaño* is a horse or a tree, but never a man. Through musical imagery he becomes the *obbligato* of her own composition, and thus always subordinate. She challenges his masculinity at every opportunity, highlighting her disappointment, occasioned by his lack of confidence, in the first quartet: "y cuando sólo trato de obligaros / viendoos desconfiar me desanimo" (3–4). By the second quartet she is questioning whether he is able to protect her as a caballero should: "¿Será tal árbol mi seguro arrimo?" or whether he favors her at all (for example, Covarrubias's definition of the term *tener arrimo* is "tener favor de un señor" [to be favored by a gentleman]). This man, she suggests, is too indecisive to enable her to distinguish either his intentions or his masculinity.

The uncertainty creates a deliberate ambiguity in the tercets, where the speaker describes Castaño as the source of her "alegría," suggesting that rather than making her happy, he makes her laugh: "De mi alegría sois el instrumento / y mi Antífona sois de todo el año" (9–10). Thus the musical harmony and reciprocity implied by "instrumento" and "antífona" is undercut, becoming instead a state of perpetual opposition. It also harks back to the implied riding of the first tercet; now he is an instrument on which she plays her own tune. The puns continue right through to the final tercet: "Veros Castaño, claro es lo que siento / sólo el ser zaino fuera mayor daño" (12–13). The juxtaposition of "zaino," which bears the double meaning of a dark brown horse and a treacherous person, with "castaño claro," again undercuts the masculinity of the "hombre ridículo" to demand that he show his true colors. Finally, Castaño is reduced to a raw youth, a "boquirrubio."

Such a sustained attack on the pride and mental abilities of a young gentleman could only be made less insulting by being part of the banter between friends. There is no sign here of a silent domesticated woman confined to her sewing, the kitchen, and the *estrado,* nor is this the only example of Ramírez's forthrightness and confidence in lampooning the supposedly superior sex. Entrambasaguas has also observed the cruel wit in her poetry, "cuya sátira, retórica de gracia e ingeniosa intención—a menudo cruel—realizada por un estilo conceptista siempre alejado del mal gusto, y legítimo hijo del de Quevedo recuerda vivamente las inimitables obras del gran poeta satírico madrileño" (51; whose satire, a rhetoric of wit and ingenious intention—often cruel—is realized through a conceited style always far from bad taste, a legitimate child of Quevedo, vividly recalling the inimitable works of the great satiric poet of Madrid). However, Ramírez does not restrict herself to lampooning the mental and physical failings of the opposite sex, as scrutiny of her manuscript reveals. The scope of this study does not permit a detailed study of all her verse, but in one *décima,* for example, entitled "A una bizca" (To a cross-eyed woman), she mocks a woman with a squint (ms. 3884 230v), and in another, lampoons male vanity: "A un hombre que por mostrar los dientes blancos se estaba siempre riendo" (ms. 3884 221v; To a man who was always laughing to show off his white teeth). It is significant that Ramírez chooses to ridicule in men that on which they most pride themselves: their assumed natural superiority in intelligence and in action, their attractiveness to women, and their stature and figure. Her sonnet to a small man is perhaps her most devastating and the most reminiscent of Quevedo:[5]

Soneto a un hombre pequeño, D. Francisco de Arévalo

Mirando con antojos tu estatura,
con antojos de verla me he quedado;
y por verte, Felicio, levantado,
saber quisiera levantar figura.

5   Lástima tengo al alma que en clausura
la trae penando cuerpo tan menguado,
Átomo racional, polvo animado,
instante humano, breve abreviatura:

---

5. Gazul presumes that Ramírez would have known part, if not all, of Quevedo's works, and also observes the enmity that existed between her uncle, D. Lorenzo Ramírez de Prado, a famous jurist, and Quevedo, following D. Lorenzo's "respuesta al Memorial famoso en que el gran escritor expuso al rey Felipe IV la situación calamitosa del país y la corrupción de su burocracia" (response to the famous report in which the great writer exposed the calamitous situation in the country and the corruption of its bureaucracy to King Philip IV). This was presumably the *Consejo y consejería de principes,* written in 1617. Gazul describes it as "una réplica aduladora que mancha la buena fama de aquel jurisconsulto" (510; a fawning response that stained the good reputation of that jurist).

¡Di si eres voz!, pues nadie determina,
10   dónde a la vista estás tan escondido
que la más perspicaz no te termina;

o cómo te concedes al oído.
En tanto que la duda te examina,
un sentido desmiente a otro sentido.

(BN ms. 3917 362r)

Sonnet to a small man, Don Francisco de Arévalo

Looking at your stature with spectacles,
I'm still left with cravings to see you;
and through seeing you, Felicio, upright,
to know if you can cut a dash.

I grieve for your cloistered soul,
carried suffering in a body so diminished,
rational atom, animated dust,
human instant, brief abbreviation:

Speak, voice, if you're there! since nobody
can determine where you're hidden from sight;
the most perspicacious can't discern you

nor how you can make yourself heard.
So, while doubtfully seeking you out,
one sense gives the lie to the other.

The quartets provide an absurd description of a microscopic man, while the sestet pretends to search for him. The first quartet includes the line "saber quisiera levantar figura" (3). The term "levantar figura" is principally astrological: "disponer en las doze casas que señalan los lugares donde en aquel punto se hallan los signos del zodiaco, y en ellos los planetas y los lugares de las estrellas fijas" (Cov.; to dispose in the twelve houses that indicate the exact places where the signs of the zodiac are found and in them the planets and sites of the fixed stars). Ramírez subtly suggests that her small subject must remain in a fixed point so that she can focus on him. Two other definitions of the term add to the insulting nature of her sonnet: "hombre ridículo, feo y de mala traza" (a ridiculous man, ugly and of poor appearance); and "el hombre entonado, que afecta gravedad en sus acciones y palabras" (the arrogant man, who affects gravity in his actions and words). As in the sonnet to Castaño, there is only one voice, that of the female speaker.

Wordplay on *antojos* sees her both desire to see him and requiring spectacles in order to see him: "Mirando con antojos tu estatura, / con antojos de verla me he quedado" (1–2).[6] The absurdity of this imagery gives the lie to its frankness and suggests that she is mocking someone she knows well. However, the second quartet is particularly cruel, as in two lines she identifies all that makes a person human, the union of soul, body, and reason: "Lástima tengo al alma que en clausura / la trae penando cuerpo tan menguado" (5–6). She mocks Neoplatonic notions of soul/body duality; if the body is the prison of the soul, this soul suffers unduly by the closer confines of the flesh. As a result, extra pity is engendered for the soul, which naturally aspires to a higher purpose but is here compressed in a kind of torture. She adds to the torture by terminating the quartet with a rapid list of insulting images in which she yet manages to capture his humanity: the "átomo" is rational, the "polvo" is a spiritual substance, the "instante" is human. However, all of this is undercut in the opening lines of the sestet: "¡di si eres voz!, pues nadie determina, / dónde a la vista estás tan escondido / que la más perspicaz no te termina" (9–11). Francisco is silent and concealed from the public gaze, feminized by his tormentor, and hence less than human in the terms of contemporary gender theories. Yet, for all its apparent cruelty, the very hyperbole of this sonnet robs it of much of its vitriol, and the diminutive name applied to the subject, Felicio, suggests both happiness and also that subject and speaker are well acquainted with each other.

Although Ramírez is the only poet of this group to write such powerful verse, there are other examples that adopt a more gently mocking tone. Leonor de la Cueva y Silva, for instance, writes a *décima* to a man she regards as lacking in courtesy:

6. There are a number of similarities between this sonnet and Quevedo's verse; for example, he dedicates a *canción* to "Una mujer pequeña" (a small woman), in which he describes his subject as "tan nonada, que os prometo / que aun no sé si llegáis a ser sujeto" (5–6; so trifling that I promise you / that I am not sure she could be considered a subject). He also feels for the soul, so tightly constrained: "Calabozo de la alma, y tan estrecho . . .

A un descortés, décima

Que le digo a gentilhombre
si es de gorra tan el caso
vuelva atrás en este caso
porque no afrente su nombre;
5   y porque a todos al hombre
con su proceder grosero
sólo en breve decir quiero,
que llega su gallardía
a no hacernos cortesía
por no romper el sombrero.

(Ms. 4127 190)

To a discourteous man, décima

I remind the gentleman that
it is so normal to doff his hat
that he should turn back in this case
rather than affront his good name;
and so that all shall know the
boorish behavior of this man,
I shall just briefly say to what
extent his gallantry goes, that
he would not make us a reverence
so as not to damage his hat.

The "offense" lies in the man's refusal to doff his hat, again suggesting a visitor to the home or a social setting in which Cueva expects to be greeted by him and greeted appropriately. This slight nonsense is reminiscent of Ramírez's poem about the man who smiles constantly to show off his teeth. Marcia Belisarda also indulges in poetic play, although in her case, as a nun, she does not engage in the more acid exchanges of insults of the academies or Ramírez's and Cueva's salons.

The titles of a number of Marcia Belisarda's sonnets, beginning with "Dándome por asunto . . ." (Giving me the topic . . .), suggest that these

---

miro que aun vos tenéis la alma de rodillas" (19–24; Prison of the soul and so narrow . . . I see that even your soul has to kneel). See Quevedo, *Poesía original completa*, 604.

were written for the poetry competitions on specific subjects with which nuns amused themselves. There are many examples of poetry writing by female religious, carried on not only within but also between convents that point to the friendship and community espoused by Zayas while also providing a complete repertoire of poetic styles. Unfortunately, the majority are anonymous and lack personal reference (Custodio Vega 195). For example, Orozco Díaz, in writing of the influence of St. Teresa's writings on her nuns, makes the following observation:

> Es en esta última poesía de sencillo y modesto fin devocional, didáctico y festivo, sin preocupación de originalidad, donde la Santa se identifica y confunde con la obra poética de sus monjas. . . . Mucha de esta producción—de la Santa y de las religiosas—era, pues, improvisación, de la que la mayor parte se perdería pronto . . . y vivía esencialmente dentro del convento como cantos en la tradición oral. (*Expresión, comunicación y estilo en la obra de Santa Teresa [notas sueltas de lector]* 119)

> This last poetry has a simple and modest devotional end, both didactic and festive, without preoccupations about originality, where the saint identifies herself and confuses herself with the poetic works of her nuns. . . . Much of this production—by the saint and the nuns—was, then, improvisation of which the majority was promptly lost. . . . and it survived within the convent as songs in the oral tradition.

Marcia Belisarda's poetry, however, offers a fragment of the potential for clever creativity turned both to religious and secular ends that existed within the convents in the period. As is clear from the structure of her collection, Marcia Belisarda intended her works for wider circulation than the confines of the convent. In her other sonnets she not only claims authorship, but also often provides personal references. In one first-person sonnet she mocks the sonnet form itself, while also lampooning the other poet's gongorism, but the message is concealed in well-composed admiration and self-denigration:

> *Alabaronme un soneto tanto que le pedí con instancia, aunque después de leido no entendí nada y respondí el siguiente confesando mi poco saber*
>
> Vuelvo a enviar el que pedí, soneto, confesando señora y Reina mía

que de tenerle poco más de un día,
mi juicio siento con algún defecto.

5   Cuánto más le adjetivo e interpreto
(curiosa mi ambición en su porfía)
más de mi entendimiento se desvía
su delicado, altísimo concepto.

Alguna soberana inteligencia
10   escribió para sí tan ardua suma,
que no alcanzo aunque más y más discurro;

y, hablando como debo, en mi conciencia,
(otra intención de mí no se presuma)
digo que no es la miel para este burro.

(ms. 7469 42v)

*They so praised a sonnet to me that I demanded to
read it, although having read it I could not understand
it at all and responded as follows, confessing my lack
of understanding*

I'm sending back what I asked for, a sonnet,
confessing, my queen and lady, that
having had it a little more than one day,
I find some errors in my intelligence.

The more I puzzle and interpret this
(my ambition is obstinately curious)
the more its delicate, high conceits
defy my understanding.

Some sovereign intelligence composed
for itself something so wholly difficult
that I cannot decipher it, no matter how I debate,

And speaking as I should, in my conscience,
(presume no other intention of me)
I say that you're casting pearls before swine.

Although Marcia Belisarda confesses to "poco saber," and the anonymous other is her "Reina," or poetic superior, Marcia Belisarda also creates in her writing a well-formed and witty sonnet that gives the lie to her modesty. She confesses to having had the sonnet only a short time, but has already conceded defeat and has not only given it up but is returning it whence it came. However, she undercuts her modest stance suggested in the final line of the first quartet, "mi juicio siento con algún defecto," in being able to return her reply after only "poco más de un día" (3).

At first reading, Marcia Belisarda's sonnet appears to be all it claims, a graceful nod to a superior poet acknowledging the other's greater wit and learning. Moreover, as we do not have the other's sonnet for comparison, this makes an acceptable reading. However, the poet herself describes it in her manuscript as a *burlesco soneto* (burlesque sonnet), and a second reading suggests that the very production of her own sonnet contradicts her claim to "poco saber." This awareness calls into question whether the other sonnet is really clever or an overwrought piece of gongorine excess. There is a degree of sarcasm in the parenthetical comments in the octet, "(curiosa mi ambición en su porfía)" (6), and in the sestet, "(otra intención de mí no se presuma)" (13). In the octet she finds herself surprisingly and daringly ambitious in undertaking such an enterprise, while in the sestet she writes as a nun, noting that she complies with the rule and engages in self-examination of her faults.

As Marcia Belisarda toils over the incomprehensibly difficult writings, rather than reason and logic being employed in a weighty matter that may save her soul, this speaker is engaged in a densely composed poem from which she can extricate neither herself nor the meaning. There is no turn at line eight, as the struggle continues to the final tercet, at which point she concedes defeat: "y, hablando como debo, en mi conciencia, / (otra intención no se presuma) / digo que no es la miel para este burro" (12–14). The terminal proverb at first appears to be an exercise in self-mockery and self-abasement, but it also encapsulates the suggestion that the "burro" (donkey) is the other's sonnet and the "miel" (honey) her own sweet reasoning: the "juicio" called into question in the first quartet.

In writing this sonnet and poetry on the many other *asuntos* (matters) presented to her, Marcia Belisarda expresses not only her skill with language, but also her ability to compose poetry at will and by artistic inspiration. She is both poet and artisan. Like male courtiers, who fulfilled paid functions and wrote poetry for display, Marcia Belisarda shows that educated women in the convent system also went about their assigned tasks and demonstrated their *sprezzatura* (flair) in dashing off a witty poem on demand. Marcia Belisarda's poetry, intended for publication, shows literate women sought to express, by all means available, that given the tools they were the mental equals of their male counterparts. A perusal of Serrano y Sanz's *Apuntes* reveals the numerous poems and sonnets that were written for local and national *certámenes* in the sixteenth and seventeenth centuries, which provided a legitimate outlet for women's verse and hence opportunities for officially sanctioned fame.

Opportunities for women to express the enjoyment of friendships through burlesque verse, as in the above sonnets, must have been rare indeed, but this only serves to make these examples all the more important in a consideration of women's enclosure in the period. They suggest that upper-class women were not only not silent before the opposite sex, but were not expected to be by their male friends, a view bolstered by the comments of contemporaries like Lady Fanshawe and those in Shaw Fairman's collection of anecdotes. These poems suggest that the restrictiveness of the ideal system did not interfere with social interaction at a microcosmic level; indeed its restrictiveness may well have made the bonds of friendship stronger. The poems women write to each other reveal this bond clearly.

SONNETS OF "OTHER SELVES"

Montaigne determined, in his essay on friendship, that women were, by nature, incapable of achieving the spiritual bond of friendship that existed between men because of their "weakness of spirit" (Montaigne 137). He seems not to consider the possibility of friendship between women at all. However, a number of the friendship sonnets by these women do demonstrate that close relationship discussed by Montaigne, where two souls become one and share reliable advice and moral support. Sor Violante del Cielo, for example, gives the lie to Montaigne's views in a highly personal sonnet written to extend support to and praise the beauty of her friend and benefactor, Inés de Noronha, during her husband's absence:[7]

> Ostenta la mayor soberanía
> en la misma humildad, Nise la hermosa,
> quedando por bizarra, victoriosa,
> sin deber a las galas bizarría.
>
> 5   Por no causar, su sol, tanta alegría,
> cuando de una tristeza está quejosa,
> pardas nubes admite rigurosa,
> y en pardas nubes luce más su día.
>
> ¡O tú! que por quedar en todo rara,
> 10   Opuestos admitiste en lo divino,
> bien tu ingenio, tu intención declara.
>
> Pues muestra de tu sol lo peregrino
> En nube tan oscura luz tan clara
> en traje tan grosero amor tan fino.
>
> (*Rimas varias* (1646) 4)

> Nise the beautiful, garbed in humility,
> shows the greater sovereignty,
> being victorious through her own splendor,
> owing none of her glory to gala raiment.
>
> So that her sun shall not cause such joy
> when she is assailed by some sadness,
> she rigorously admits dark clouds,
> yet in dark clouds her day shines the brighter.
>
> Oh you! who being rare in everything
> admitted contraries to your divinity,
> how well your intentions declare your wisdom.

---

7. Vieira Mendes provides biographical details about the lady, noting that she was the daughter of the powerful third conde de Calheta, Simão Gonzalves da Camara, and granddaughter of the first conde, do Castelo Melhor. She married in 1632 and Vieira Mendes suggests that the sonnet could have been written in 1642, when the count left to become ambassador to Paris. See do Céu, *Rimas varias,* 53.

> Since your sun shows your rare beauty,
> a light so clear in a cloud so dark,
> in a habit so coarse, a love so fine.

The title of this sonnet is given in the *Rimas varias* as *A la Señora Condesa de Vidigueira vestida de pardo, por la ausencia del Conde* (To the Lady Countess of Vidigueira, dressing in brown for the absence of the count). However, it also appears, among other verse by Sor Violante, in an eighteenth-century manuscript from the Jesuit College in Coimbra held at the British Library, where the title is given as *A Condesa Vidigueira estando vestida de pardo por su marido* (To Countess Vidigueira being dressed in brown for [or by] her husband). This is not an autograph manuscript and is later than the *Rimas,* but there is sufficient discrepancy in the two titles to suggest that the sonnet may have circulated under different titles, rather than that this is simply scribal error. Given that the count was the publisher of the collection, this raises the possibility that the title was changed when the sonnet went to print in order to avoid embarrassment. As given in the manuscript, the title transforms the import of the sonnet so that it offers moral support and consolation to a friend suffering under a husband's coercive control that extended even to her clothing. However, Sor Violante's acknowledgement of the brown dress also suggests that her friend may have adopted the Franciscan habit, also a favorite burial garment, to mark her husband's absence; such a practice was customary, as a history of Spanish women reveals:

La Marchioness de Villars, esposa del embajador francés en Madrid, refiere en 1679 de esas reuniones que "todas esas mujeres hablan como urracas fuera del nido, muy adornadas con hermosos trajes y pedrerías, salvo aquellas cuyos maridos están de viaje o en alguna embajada. Una de las más bonitas, por ese motivo, iba vestida de gris. Durante la ausencia de sus maridos se consagran a algún santo y llevan con su hábito gris o blanco algunos pequeños cinturones de cuerda o de cuero." (Voltes and Voltes Bou 74)

The Marchioness of Villars, wife of the French ambassador in Madrid, refers in 1679 to those gatherings where "all the women chatter like magpies out of the nest, highly adorned with beautiful clothes and jewels, except those whose husbands are traveling or on some embassy. One of the most beautiful, for this reason, was dressed in grey. During the absence of their husbands they consecrate themselves to a saint and wear with their grey or white habits some small girdles of cord or leather."

The intention in this sonnet is to reassure a friend that her beauty, physical and spiritual, cannot be concealed in an ugly gown, whatever may have occasioned its wearing: "Ostenta la mayor soberanía / en la misma humildad, Nise la hermosa" (1–2). Sor Violante begins by describing what she observes, using the third person, before going on to a direct, second-person apostrophe in the tercets. She skillfully employs metaphors of light and shade, sunshine and clouds, so that the friend is seen to be a source of light and life that outshines her drab garments and even the gala garments of the fiestas. Although she proclaims that the countess wishes to demonstrate her sadness, this only serves to enhance her brilliance: "y en pardas nubes luce más su día" (8). The husband, whose absence or whose command is the reason for the sonnet, is almost completely effaced by this gesture of friendship and admiration, and appears only in the title. The sonnet itself focuses on providing positive images of the woman friend, who is never presented as an objectified individual. Rather, the imagery exudes beauty, light, richness, and quality, while the references to sovereignty and to victory indicate a battle for supremacy, easily won by the countess, as Sor Violante intrudes her "soberanía" into the opening line of the sonnet. As so often in her laudatory poetry, and as already seen in the sonnet to the countess of Penaguião, in Chapter 1, Sor Violante celebrates this countess's ingenuity: "bien tu ingenio, tu intención declara" (11). Finally, however, Sor Violante alludes to the unusual garment as an expression of love, perhaps, after all, by the friend for her absent husband: "En nube tan oscura luz tan clara / en traje tan grosero amor tan fino" (13–14). Whatever the real purpose of this sonnet, it serves Sor Violante well, for it is her friendship with the countess that ensures the publication of her poetry and it is the countess whose excellence shapes the sonnet.

As Sor Violante's sonnet emphasizes the value of female friendship as a social support and comforter, Ramírez writes a love sonnet to an absent friend that blurs the line between the homosocial and the homoerotic, just as Sor Violante does in some of her works already discussed. While the codified nature of this sonnet places it within the milieu of a work intended to display the poet's skills, nevertheless the expression of closeness in the title, *A la ausencia de una amiga, hablando con ella* (On the absence of a friend, talking to her), also indicates the powerful bond that friendship represented to women and the even more important place of unsanctioned conversation.[8] Ramírez's title incorporates the recipient of the sonnet into the thoughts of the speaker, banishing the distance of separation and emphasizing the equality that exists between friends. Yet the pain of absence steals her voice and, able only to talk in whispers, she finds that an unvoiced sentiment has no force:

> Cuando quiero deciros lo que siento,
> siento que he de callaros lo que quiero;
> que no explican amor tan verdadero
> las voces que se forman de un aliento.
>
> 5 Si de dulces memorias me alimento,
> que enfermo del remedio considero,
> y con un accidente vivo y muero,
> siendo el dolor alivio del tormento.
>
> ¿Qué importa que me mate vuestra ausencia
> 10 si en el morir por vos halle la vida
> y vivo de la muerte a la violencia?
>
> Pues el remedio sólo está en la herida;
> mas, si no he de gozar vuestra asistencia,
> la piedad de que vivo es mi homicida.
>
> (ms. 3884 241r)

> When I wish to tell you how I feel,
> I fall silent before you whom I love;
> since such true love cannot be explained
> in voices formed by a sigh.
>
> If I feed my soul on sweet memories,
> I find myself weakened by the remedy,

8. See also Amanda Powell's treatment of this sonnet, in *"'Oh qué diversas estamos'"* (n. pag).

and I live and die by these passions of my soul,
since the pain of them relieves my torment.

Does it matter that your absence kills me,
if in dying for you I find life itself
and live through the violence of death?

Well, the only remedy lies in the wound;
for if I am not to enjoy your presence,
then piteous life is my homicide.

Silence was the only officially appropriate position for a woman to adopt, since speech, and worse, voicing opinions, was always related to a presumed sexual openness and availability. As Ann Rosalind Jones has stated in discussing the formation of Renaissance gender theory, all women, married or not, were constrained to silence. In her cited examples Jones demonstrates the long history of this constraint; for example, Thucydides' belief that "the most praiseworthy woman is she whose praises are kept within the walls of the private house." She also cites Aristotle's analogy of gendered virtue: silence in women balanced by eloquence in men, and its concomitant expression in the Renaissance theory of Barbaro: "Women should believe that they have achieved the glory of eloquence if they will honor themselves with the outstanding ornament of silence." The ideal woman was "unseen, unheard, untouched, unknown—at the same time that she was obsessively observed" ("Surprising Fame" 79). Against this expectation of demure silence, though the import of many of the poems discussed here give the lie to its imposition, Schlau has noted how women writers use silence to great advantage, that what appears to be a "shattering of self" becomes a challenge to patriarchal norms (*Spanish American* xvii). In this instance, Ramírez is writing to another woman, the silence is caused by feelings of loss, but in any event her poetry collection indicates that silence was not part of her lived experience. It freely praises, mocks, and criticizes the behavior and posturing of those around her. The absence of a friend, then, has real poignancy: Ramírez has lost a confidante able to share her opinions, and the committing of words to paper is not sufficient to quell the loss of the other's immediate presence; she has been silenced not by decree but by absence.

While nominally keeping to the structural formalities, the sonnet divides into a primary quartet that sets out the problem, a central group of seven lines that lays down and answers the proposition, and a final tercet that provides the result of the internal debate: that there is no solution while the absence continues. The entire sonnet is infused with terminologies of disease, wounding, life, and death. Her thoughts swing back and forth from her position in Llerena to that of her friend, while the repeated sense of loss is reflected in the chiasmus of "vivo y muero/morir . . . la vida/vivo . . . muerte." The remedy sought in line six is still unresolved at line twelve: "Pues el remedio sólo está en la herida." Using the Petrarchan terms of the bereft lover, Ramírez attempts to salve the wound of absence with sweet memories of the beloved, which lead only to further pain and misery at the realization of the friend's continued absence. There is only one remedy for the pain: the presence of the friend, without whom death and life become one. This possibility, however, remains unfulfilled, and the pain unresolved.

The hyperbolic death-in-absence theme, a common trope in early modern love sonnets, affirms not only the importance of female friendship to women, but also the extravagant nature of language in the period, especially poetic language, when addressing matters of sentiment. The erotic quality of such verse has to be seen in the light of the context in which it was written, when even the term "erotic" had a much less sexually charged meaning than it does today.[9] Hence, Ramírez demonstrates herself to be part of the literary culture of her era, while also paying a compliment to a friend to whom she is evidently very close, or for whom she may feel a sensual attraction. At the same time, her

9. The introduction to a collection of erotic verse of the period illustrates the difference between the meaning of the word "erotic" in the seventeenth and the twentieth centuries: "The dictionary of the Real Academia defines *erótico* as . . . that pertaining or relative to sensual love, whereas at the beginnning of the seventeenth century, the Diccionario de Autoridades . . . explains the word *erotic* in accordance with its etymology in the broadest sense of *amatory.*" And a century earlier, in 1617, the poet Esteban Manuel de Villegas published an *Eróticas* that had nothing to do with the erotic in the sense we understand it today. See Pierre Alzieu, Robert Jammes, and Yvan Lissorgues, eds., *Poesía erótica del Siglo de Oro* (Barcelona: Crítica, 1983), viii. In addition, the Greek *eros,* in Platonic thought, is closely aligned to the creative impulse, to join with the Idea. Nevertheless, in *The Lives of Women,* Lisa Vollendorf provides an interesting discussion of female friendship and female homoeroticism in novels and plays by women of the period (57–89), as does Amanda Powell, in "'*Oh qué diversas estamos*'" (n. pag.).

friend understands well the codified nature of such poetic pleasantries but can also accept it as a genuine expression of friendship and love. The sentiments expressed here closely mirror those of the love sonnet by Violante del Cielo to the absent lover, "Quien dice que la ausencia es homicida" (Who says that absence is homicide), where she explores the paradox of not dying of the fatal illness of separation, a condition she finds far worse than death itself. The sonnet appears in both the *Rimas varias* (1646 [2] and in the British Library Additional Manuscript 25353 [n. pag.]).

Similarly, her view of the true nature of friendship is demonstrated by Sor Violante in her sonnet to "Belisa," probably to her friend Isabel de Castro, that clearly sets out her understanding of the meaning of friendship.[10] Its importance as a revisionist part of literary history is emphasized by Adrienne Martín: "[I]t portrays and extols female friendship while that topic is generally disavowed in Golden Age literature" (60). The sonnet is delivered as a philosophical treatise, a definition of true friendship as beyond price:

> Belisa, el amistad es un tesoro,
> tan digno de estimarse eternamente,
> que a su valor no es paga suficiente
> de Arabia y Potosí la plata y oro.
>
> 5 Es la amistad un lícito decoro
> que se guarda en lo ausente y lo presente,
> y con que de un amigo el otro siente
> la tristeza, el pesar, la risa, el lloro.
>
> No se llama amistad la que es violenta,
> 10 sino la que es conforme simpatía,
> de quien lealtad hasta la muerte ostenta.

10. Olivares and Boyce suggest that this sonnet was probably addressed to her friend Bernarda Ferreira de la Cerda. However, Vieira Mendes determines that the addressee is Isabel de Castro, a friend to whom Sor Violante also dedicated an epistle on a royal death. Vieira Mendes' source is the conde de Sabugosa's *Neves de Antanho*, published in 1919. See Vieira Mendes's note in do Céu, *Rimas varias* (1993), 58. The pastoral name "Belisa" tends to support Vieira Mendes's contention.

Ésta la amistad es que hallar querría,
ésta la que entre amigas se sustenta,
y ésta, Belisa, en fin, la amistad mía.

(*Rimas varias* (1646) 9)

Belisa, friendship is a treasure
so worthy of eternal esteem that
the silver and gold of Arabia and Potosí
are not sufficient payment for its value.

Friendship is a just honor
that one defends in presence and absence,
and in which one friend feels the other's
sadness and sorrow, laughter and tears.

That which is violent is not friendship,
but rather that which is founded on sympathy
from one who prizes loyalty until death.

This is the friendship I had hoped to find,
this is what is sustained by women friends
and this, in the end, Belisa, is my friendship.

Sor Violante regards absence as no barrier to the sharing of experience since communication between true friends is a spiritual matter: "Es la amistad un lícito decoro / que se guarda en lo ausente y lo presente" (5–6). The word *amistad* (friendship) dominates the first lines of each quartet and tercet, and begins and ends the sonnet. First, the poet elaborates her vision of ideal friendship as a treasure beyond price: the quartets are full of positive qualifiers and she includes both Arabia and Potosí to refer synechdochally to the wealth of the world. The reference takes in both the East and the West Indies, a commonly used marker for vast, uncountable riches.[11] However, they are still insufficient to value the true

---

11. Shakespeare, for example, employs this motif in *The Merry Wives of Windsor* when Falstaff muses: "She is a region in Guiana, all gold and bounty. . . . They shall be my East and West Indies and I will trade to them both" See William Shakespeare, *The Merry Wives of Windsor,* ed. and introd. G. R. Hibberd (London: Penguin Books, 1973), ll. 64–66. Similarly, John Donne, in his poem "The Sunne Rising," writes of his beloved: "Look, and tomorrow late, tell mee, / Whether both the Indias of spice and myne / Be where

worth of friendship: "a su valor no es paga suficiente / de Arabia y Potosí la plata y oro" (3–4). Whether together or apart, in Sor Violante's evocation of friendship friends feel each other's emotions: ". . . un amigo el otro siente / la tristeza, el pesar, la risa, el lloro" (7–8). In her discussion of this poem, Vollendorf evaluates the way Sor Violante rejects this masculine material world, choosing an emotional market over the commercial market and forcing a reconception of the connections between ideas of gender inside and outside the convent (*Lives of Women* 99).

Like a practiced rhetorician, Sor Violante shows herself able to argue both sides of her case. Whereas the quartets frame all that is positive and valuable in friendship, the tercets move into the negative mode in the way that religious meditation often employs the *via negativa* to reflect on all that Christ was not: "No se llama amistad la que es violenta, / sino la que es conforme simpatía, / de quien lealtad hasta la muerte ostenta" (9–11). This enables a contrast to be set up in which violence and death occupy balancing and opposite roles to love and sympathy. For Sor Violante friendship demands loyalty until death. It is a faithful and constant spiritual presence that provides mutual support "entre amigas," a friendship discovered, sustained, and offered unconditionally to Belisa. The sting lies in the final tercet line: "Ésta la amistad es que hallar querría" (12). Although in *Tras el espejo* Olivares and Boyce have the last word of this line as "quería," the conditional "querría" is found in the 1646 edition of the *Rimas,* as well as in the British Library's eighteenth-century manuscript, and is also adhered to by Vieira Mendes in her recent anthology. This conditional alters the tone of the poem and implies that Sor Violante is expressing genuine friendship in a relationship she now finds lacking. It also precludes the idea put forward at the sonnet's opening that Sor Violante was simply setting out an objective discussion of the nature of friendship. Sor Violante now regards friendship as an attainable ideal that she has both achieved and offered, as the final lines reveal: "ésta la que entre amigas se sustenta, / y ésta, Belisa, en fin, la amistad mía" (13–14).

Victor Rojas offers several conjectures as to Sor Violante's intentions

---

thou leftst them, or lie here with mee" (16–18); see John Donne, *The Complete English Poems of John Donne,* ed. C. A. Patrides (London: Dent, 1985), 54.

in the sonnet. He suggests that she was writing in the abstract in answer to general questions on the nature of friendship, and that it demonstrates idealism, rather than *desengaño*, as a motivating factor (114). However, in my view, "querría" embodies a distinctly disillusioned tone. Whether disappointed in her friendship with Belisa or not, Sor Violante proves that she fully understands what true friendship of "other selves" means when she continues, paradoxically in terms of the conditional verb, to offer unconditional friendship to Belisa, moving the ideal into the potentially real. Like Martín, I conclude that the expressions of female friendship espoused by Sor Violante merit a more literal reading than they have hitherto been accorded (65). The few known facts of Sor Violante's life, coupled with the content of a number of her other works, have led biographers to conclude that she found human relationships wanting, and that this was one reason for her determination to take the veil. Certainly, in several other sonnets she cures herself of the *desengaño* engendered by failed personal relationships, concluding that such disappointing friendships serve only to turn her ever more faithfully toward God.

Where Sor Violante proffers support to Inés de Noronha and unfettered friendship to "Belisa" beyond the convent walls, this comforting warmth is also seen in the welcoming sonnets written by nuns to celebrate the professions of their sisters. St. Teresa had already encouraged her nuns to write, and she employed poetry as an effective way to express sisterly warmth to new entrants in the convent. In reading Teresa de Avila's poetry, the most striking immediate effect is its joyous and accessible simplicity. Although she employs a range of rhetorical devices, most notably alliteration and anaphora, her verse is comparatively free of the frequent, even excessive, recourse to self-criticism and denigration seen in her prose works. Her poems are principally simple *villancicos,* mostly composed for specific and important activities within the convent, such as holy days and the professing of new nuns. This type of poetry strengthens the image of the convent as a site of mutual support with a modicum of independence, secluded from the problems, stresses, and dangers of quotidian life and, significantly, the pressures imposed by fathers, husbands, and brothers, even though the convent produced pressures of its own. However, St. Teresa was also at pains to stress that friendly relations within the convent should be of a general and communal nature, as a means to avoid jealousy and the factionalism that can arise from particular friendships. In her *Constituciones* (Constitutions) she commands: "Ninguna hermana abrace a otra, ni la toque el rostro ni en las manos, ni tengan amistades en particular, sino todas se amen en general, como lo mandó Cristo a sus Apóstoles" (642; No sister may embrace another nor touch her face or hands, nor have particular friendships. Instead, all should love each other equally, as Christ commanded his Apostles). Such strictures suggest that expressions of mutual affection were common and observable.

In spite of the strictures imposed or recommended by St. Teresa, Marcia Belisarda's poetry, particularly the funeral sonnet to "Anarda," to be discussed in the following section, shows strong commitment to individual friends. She employs rather more complex imagery than that of St. Teresa, as can be seen in the sonnet written to celebrate a profession in her own Convento de la Encarnación (Convent of the Incarnation) in Toledo. Marcia Belisarda sets out her artistic intentions in the title: *A la profesión de Doña Petronila de la Palma en la Concepción Real de Toledo, siguiendo la metáfora de la palma* (On the profession of Doña Petronila de la Palma in [Convent of] the Royal Conception of Toledo, following the metaphor of the palm). Marcia Belisarda clearly had close ties to Doña Petronila, as she does not stop at a sonnet but also writes a *décima* that begins: "Tu nombre mismo acredita / el premio justo que alcanza" (To your very name is credited the just prize) and concludes "La que en méritos de el alma / tres veces la dan la Palma / virtud, profesión, y nombre" (ms. 7469 8r; She who in merits of the soul / three times receives the palm: / virtue, profession, and name):

> En este Real jardín, O palma hermosa,
> os plantó vuestro dueño soberano,
> dispuso y cultivó su sacra mano,
> para que deis la fruta milagrosa.
>
> 5   No ingrata vegetal, sí generosa;
> racional, producid de amor temprano,
> dulces efectos con intento sano,
> mudando el ser de planta en el de esposa.

Advertid pues, que el dueño es infinito,
10   abreviada y finita vuestra vida;
pagadle, esposa fiel, frutos del Alma;

elogios no, verdades os remito;
sed siempre, Palma, a Dios agradecida,
gozaréis en su gloria eterna Palma.

(ms. 4169 8v)

Your sovereign lord planted you,
oh lovely palm, in this royal garden,
arranged and cultivated by his holy hand,
so that you would bear miraculous fruit.

Not a humble vegetable soul, but generous
and rational, you'll produce, out of youthful love,
sweet effects with healthful intent,
changing your being from plant to bride.

Know then, that your lord is infinite,
your own life finite and short.
Pay him, loyal bride, the fruits of your soul;

I send you truths, not flattery;
always be pleasing, Palm, in the sight of God,
and you'll rejoice in the palm of his eternal glory.

The palm is a useful metaphor to link the newly professed nun to both classical and biblical antecedents, for it has many classical allusions, beginning with the birth of Apollo, whose mother, Leto, leaned against the palm tree on Delos as she gave birth to him. This palm became sacred and the symbol of victory in both athletic and military contests (Howatson and Chilvers 310). Horace's first ode mentions chariot races and their victors' palms (1.1), and Shakespeare includes the palm of military victory in two of his Roman plays, *Julius Caesar* (1.2.131), and *Coriolanus* (5.3.117).

Leaving aside these martial and triumphalist images, the date palm flourishes in biblical lands, where the fruits are indeed miraculous in their nourishing and sustaining qualities. Marcia Belisarda's choice of the palm metaphor is a graceful gesture to the name the new nun will leave behind as she enters the convent. It also links the new bride of Christ to both Old and New Testaments and to the Holy Land. In the Song of Solomon the groom addresses the bride: "This thy stature is like to a palm tree. . ." (7.7), while in the New Testament, Christ's entry into Jerusalem was heralded with palms, now celebrated in Palm Sunday. As a pilgrim in search of divine mercy through prayer, the new nun also joins the Christian pilgrims to the Holy Land, the *palmeros* (palmers), who brought back palm leaves from their travels.[12] The garden and nature imagery emphasize both the *hortus conclusus* with its references to virginity and female enclosure, and the wholesome and natural elements of the convent family in an edenic environment of untarnished purity, accentuated by the etymological linking of the "Real jardín" to paradise: "En este Real jardín, O palma hermosa, / os plantó vuestro dueño soberano. / Dispuso y cultivó, su sacra mano" (1–3). The convent becomes a place where the soul will receive the appropriate nourishment for growth. As Vollendorf has explained, the image of the tended garden, the spiritual watering of new plants, was used not only by St. Teresa but also appears frequently in religious writing, citing as further example the work of Sor Angela María de la Concepción (*Lives of Women* 177). Certainly here it suits both Marcia Belisarda's interest in the spiritual nourishment of the novice and her metaphorical deployment of the terminology in a clever poem. As a welcoming sonnet to a new entrant, its positive imagery and gentle tone highlight aspects of health, sweetness, softness, and goodness.

The new nun's "planting" in the convent is attributed to God, here a divine gardener, with references to the Garden of Eden and perfection, but also to Eve's responsibility for the fall of humankind. However, the suggestion of Eve that is inextricably linked with the Garden of Eden and the Fall also looks forward to the redemption of female culpability in the form of the Virgin Mary. As the new plant in the garden metamorphoses into the bride of Christ, she produces the sweet and life-giving "fruta milagrosa." She is not only pledged to Christ but is also a representative of the Virgin, mother of this miraculous fruit, and this in turn is a

---

12. Writing of Teresian iconology, Alison Weber has also noted St. Teresa's identification as "Virgen y Doctora," symbolized by a palm branch and a golden pen; see Alison Weber, *Teresa of Avila and the Rhetoric of Femininity* (Princeton: Princeton University Press, 1990), 164.

reminder that the convent that Doña Petronila will join is the Convento de la Concepción. Marcia Belisarda goes further in emphasizing that this new bride of Christ is not just a passive recipient of God's fertile power, but an intelligent rational woman who chooses this life of her own volition: "No ingrata vegetal, sí generosa; / racional, producid de amor temprano / dulces efectos con intento sano" (5–7). Once again a woman poet takes the opportunity to celebrate female rationality.

The sonnet is carefully divided: the first quartet deals with God's planting and tending of his "palma," while the second offers advice that will lead to the spiritual and rational development of the new nun, with the final line summing up her metamorphosis: "Mudando el ser de planta en el de esposa" (8); that is, from Doña Petronila de la Palma, to the bride of Christ. After the turn, the tercets offer alternating views of heaven and earth. The first tercet offers a reminder of the poverty and insignificance of earthly life, during which the faithful must try to redeem the soul through exemplary living: "Advertid, pues, que el dueño es infinito, / abreviada y finita vuestra vida; / pagadle, esposa fiel, frutos del Alma" (9–11). Finally, the poet reminds the novice that she is not offering empty praise but eternal truths, and she counsels that by living in a way that will please God the new nun will achieve the victory palm of eternal life: "Gozaréis en su gloria eterna Palma." Hence, adroitly, Marcia Belisarda returns the sonnet to where it began, with the "palma hermosa," now transformed. In this way Marcia Belisarda effectively bridges the gap between human frailty and divine majesty, with the metamorphosis into a nun the first step toward the greater metamorphosis of eternal life through divine redemption. Although this is Marcia Belisarda's only sonnet celebrating a profession, her collection contains two other welcoming poems: *A la profesión de una monja bernarda que la hizo en día de la degollación del baptista estando el Santísmo Sacramento descubierto y su nombre Paula* (ms. 7469 8; On the profession of a Bernardine nun who made her vows on the day of the beheading of the Baptist, the Holy Sacrament being displayed, and her name Paula), and *Villancico a Doña María de la Puebla, profesando en la Concepción Francisca de Toledo estando el Santísimo Sacramento descubierto* (ms.7469 56; Song to Doña María de la Puebla, professing in the Conception as Francisca de Toledo, the Holy Sacrament being displayed). Both are expressed with the same tenderness and care as the sonnet and employ similarly complex terminology in combining the human with the divine.

The welcome to a life of religious devotion was a common reason for poetry writing among nuns, as the above sonnet and St. Teresa's poetry can testify. However, the advice offered by Luisa de Carvajal y Mendoza, in one of only three extant poems by her that do not deal directly with divine matters, is a forceful warning call, probably addressed to her cousin, María, to turn to the difficult path of righteousness.[13] For Carvajal y Mendoza this was a difficult path indeed, made always more difficult by her self-confessed determination to suffer and die for Christ. That Carvajal y Mendoza was virtually incapable of comprehending that a sane person may not be prepared to follow a similar path is evident in her sonnet, which is nevertheless addressed to someone whom she dearly loves, and for whose spiritual safety she evinces concern. The title incorporates the suggestion that "Amari" is attempting to follow the Catholic practice of good works: "ocupaciones y correspondencias humanas, aunque con buen fin" (occupations and human activities, although with good intentions); the problem for Carvajal y Mendoza is that they are just not spiritual enough, being grounded far too much in human concerns. In writing this sonnet of sisterly advice, Carvajal y Mendoza asserts that the proper role of a true friend is to share confidences and proffer counsel:

Soneto espiritual de Silva para una señora grave, a
quien ella amaba mucho y deseaba verla muy ocupada
en cosas espirituales, porque era muy para ello, y no
derramada en ocupaciones y correspondencias humanas,
aunque con buen fin

¿Cómo, di, bella Amari, tu cuidado
estimas en tan poco que, olvidada
de quien con tanto amor eres amada,
te empleas en el rústico ganado?

13. Abad observes that the sonnet to Amari is probably intended for her cousin, María de Hurtado y Mendoza. The other is to "Nise," her doncella Inés. See Camilo María Abad, "Nota preliminar a las poesías," in *Luisa de Carvajal y Mendoza: Epistolario y poesías*, ed. Camilo María Abad and Jesús González Marañón, Biblioteca de autores españoles 179 (Madrid: Atlas, 1965), 423. There is also a third sonnet to an unknown "hombre que cayó en la culpa" (man who fell into sin).

5   ¿Hate la vana ocupación comprado?
       ¿Qué nigromántica arte embelesada
       te trae, y de tu bien tan trascordada?
       ¡Ay alevosa fe! ¡Ay pecho helado!

       Vuelve, Amari; repara que perdiendo
10   vas de amor el camino, digo, atajo.
       Y ése que llevas, ancho y deleitoso,

       suele mañosamente ir encubriendo
       entre las florecillas y debajo
       de verde hierba el paso peligroso.

                    (*Epistolario y poesías* 449)

Silva's spiritual sonnet for a lady of quality whom
she dearly loved and desired to see fully occupied in
spiritual matters, because she was very much in
favor of that, and not wasted on human activities
and occupations, even with good intentions

Tell me, Amari, how can you so little
esteem your cares that, forgetting
by whom you are so lovingly adored,
you employ yourself with the rustic herd?

Have vain occupations purchased your soul?
What enchanting arts of black magic
hold you and your well-being so enthralled?
Ah, malevolent fate! Ah, frozen heart!

Turn back, Amari, take care, for I say you
are straying from the narrow way of love.
And that which you follow, broad and delightful

treacherously conceals the perilous path
between the little flowers and
beneath the green grass.

Carvajal y Mendoza addresses her sonnet to a "señora grave." Amari
is a person of quality, yet casts the pearls of her social superiority before
the swine of the "rústico ganado"—in this case not the lower classes but

common humanity—instead of offering them to God. The quartets are filled with questions and exclamations as Carvajal y Mendoza tries to determine what motivates Amari. The third line, "de quien con tanto amor eres amada," is deliberately ambiguous: Amari is beloved by the writer herself (hence her desire to warn Amari before it is too late), and by the source of all Carvajal y Mendoza's inspiration, Christ. Carvajal y Mendoza appears to blame the growing commercialization of society and the concomitant market for consumer goods, where even a soul may be sold, when she asks: "¿Hate la vana ocupación comprado?" (5). As in Sor Violante's sonnet to "Belisa," Carvajal y Mendoza seeks to reject the masculine world of commerce for the world of spiritual devotion. This leads to the conclusion that some evil force has taken possession of Amari: "¿Qué nigromántica arte embelesada / te trae, y de tu bien tan trascordada?" (7–8). The evil power causes her to forget her "true" vocation, that of religion, and her own spiritual well-being. For Carvajal y Mendoza, the way of Amari's present life leads only to darkness and eternal death. The octet ends with two short exclamations that evoke the horror the writer feels at the willing betrayal of faith: "¡Ay alevosa fe! ¡Ay pecho helado!" (8).

Where the octet is a single call to Amari to become aware of her actions, the sestet is a sustained appeal for her to turn back from the easy path to hell, its true nature concealed by the flowers and grasses of human vanity and self-interest: "vas de amor el camino, digo, atajo. / Y ése que llevas, ancho y deleitoso / suele mañosamente ir encubriendo" (10–12). This enhances the urgent tone of the sonnet, and evinces the fervid religious atmosphere that obtained in Counter-Reformation Spain. The plea to Amari, couched in poetic terms that do not veil its vehemence, reveals the poet's belief that Amari's soul is in danger. As friend and kin, she has no recourse but to give due warning.

Luisa's correspondence with her brother shows that for all her professed humility she does not hesitate to proffer advice and counsel where she feels it is needed, further proof of her strong will and independence.[14] The sonnet is unique, not only in its near-desperate emotional appeal, but also because no other sonnet by any of these women seeks to inspire an

14. On Carvajal y Mendoza's paradoxical independence, see Anne Cruz, "Willing Desire: Luisa de Carvajal y Mendoza and Subjectivity," in Helen Nader, ed., *Power and Gender in Renaissance Spain*, 177–194.

individual to abandon her present path and cling to a more devout religious life that precludes all normal human pleasures, within the confines of what was, in any event, a religiously inclined society. In all her sonnets, Sor Violante del Cielo never seeks to make a religious conversion among her well-placed friends though she perhaps offers her own entry into the convent and her disillusion with the world outside as an example. It is typical of her superior intellect and education, however, that she pauses to meditate on friendship, both in her sonnet to "Belisa" and in her religious verse, where she writes a number of sonnets that touch on the theme of friendship but that do not involve contemporary female friendship.

Among Sor Violante's sonnet sequence on the Mysteries in the *Parnaso lusitano,* one meditates on the relationship between Christ and his betrayer in the Garden of Gethsemane, at the moment when Judas comes to give him the betrayer's kiss. Sor Violante argues that, through Christ, this betrayal becomes an act of friendship to all humankind. Nevertheless, it first requires a poetic and intellectual struggle to arrive at this felicitous conclusion. The title, "Sobre el *Amice ad quid venisti?,*" refers to the scriptural story of the betrayal in the garden: "And he came up to Jesus at once and said 'Hail, Master!' and he kissed him. Jesus said to him, 'Friend, why are you here?' Then they came and laid hands on Jesus and seized him" (Matthew 26: 50–51):

> Si sabéis, que este amigo es enemigo,
> ingrato, desleal, fingido, astuto,
> por qué le dais, Señor, ese atributo,
> por qué premio le dais, y no castigo?
>
> 5   Si de su error sois el mayor testigo,
> si a vuestra adoración niega el tributo,
> si sembrando piedad, no esperáis fruto,
> por qué llamáis al enemigo amigo?
>
> Vos sabéis la razón; mas yo sospecho,
> 10   que como en las finezas amorosas
> libráis de vuestro nombre las grandezas;
>
> Amigo halláis, que ha sido un falso pecho,

porque con las ofensas rigorosas
os ha dado ocasión de hacer finezas.

(Parnaso lusitano 12)

If you know that this friend is your enemy,
a disloyal, feigning, sly ingrate,
why, Lord, do you give him this sign,
and the prize instead of punishment?

If you are the chief witness of his error,
if he denies you the tribute of adoration,
if you sow mercy without expecting its fruits,
why do your call your enemy "friend"?

You know the reason, and I suspect
that as in your loving actions you will
unbind the magnificence of your name;

You find him whose heart was false a friend,
because through his harsh offences
he has given you occasion for your miracles.

The speaker of the sonnet is indignant and puzzled that Jesus, with his foreknowledge of his fate, still welcomes the embrace of his treacherous friend and disciple. The querulous quartets reveal that all precepts of friendship have been violated by Judas's actions, yet Jesus' behavior toward Judas is unchanged. Where Jesus continues to treat Judas as his "other self," Judas shows all the worst human attributes; so does the speaker, who, unable to show such Christian tenderness toward a sinner, expresses a human desire for revenge and punishment for injustice. The octet is framed by the double "amigo/enemigo" and "enemigo/amigo," in posing the impossible question: if you know this friend is your enemy, why do you call your enemy a friend? Thus far, Sor Violante's sonnet has the appearance of a correctly practiced meditation on a specific biblical theme, in which she creates the composition of place, and then speaks to Christ as to a friend, but this merely sets up the tercets to reveal Sor Violante's astonishing conclusion.

Continuing to address Christ directly, the poetic voice now determines that Christ, out of his perfect love, deliberately humbles himself before common humanity. Through his more perfect knowledge he is able to see Judas as a friend to all humankind, for it is through his betrayal that Christ complies with his destiny and liberates humankind from the toils of eternal death.[15] Sor Violante's sonnet condemns human frailty, in the person of Judas, but celebrates Christ's sacrifice, joining both in an act of friendship, the kiss that seals the fate of the divine victim and brings hope to the world. Her determination that Judas's act of betrayal was, in reality, an act of friendship demonstrates women's willingness to assert friendship as a good and to retain that friendship in the face of all provocation: a trusting faith that is not always well paid, as her sonnets comparing human and divine love reveal. However, it is not women's love that these poems reject, but rather the activities of the world.

Sor Violante's sonnets often suggest that her personal interactions in the world outside the convent were not satisfactory, and this may be borne out in the foundering of her relationship with Andrade through the machinations of her family. Three of her sonnets compare the difficulties of human love with the perfection of the divine: "Daños del amor humano, bienes del amor divino" (On the ill effects of human love, the goodness of divine love), "Firmezas del divino amor, inconstancias del amor humano" (The constancy of divine love, the inconstancy of human love), and "Mal paga del mundo es colirio para ver y buscar a Dios" (The world's ill treatment is the eye's remedy for seeing and seeking God). These reveal, through the misery occasioned by lost or failed friendships, the great importance of companionship, shared confidences, and mutual support to seventeenth-century women. The following examination of the third of these sonnets will serve as an example:

> Esta pena, mi Dios, este tormento
> que me causan agravios repetidos,
> castigos son bien al error debidos
> de querer fabricar sin fundamento.
>
> 5 ¡Oh qué peligro corre el sufrimiento
> entre agravios, Señor, no merecidos!

15. Early Gnostic sects appear to have considered this point, and Tertullian, in about the year 200, gave some credence to it in his "Liber de praescriptione haereticorum." See Catholic Encyclopedia Online: "Judas."

Mas paguen, paguen siempre mis sentidos
las torres que fundaron en el viento.

Paguen la confianza que tuvieron
10   en humana amistad, pues no llegaron
a prevenir lo que tan presto vieron.

Dichosos los que en Vos se confiaron
solamente, mi Dios, pues no cayeron
por más que el edificio levantaron.

(Parnaso lusitano 51)

This pain, my God, this torment,
caused me by repeated affronts,
are well earned punishments for my errors
of wanting to build without foundation.

Oh what dangers suffering brings,
Lord, among unmerited insults!
But my feelings shall pay and pay again
for the castles I built on the wind.

They'll pay for the trust they placed
in human friendship, for they never
foretold what they soon came to see.

Blessed are they who trusted in you
alone, my God, since they did not fall
no matter how high they built their tower.

Although this sonnet retains a conventional quartet/tercet rhyme scheme, it more naturally divides into a six/eight-line structure. The shifting insubstantiality of human relations is compared unfavorably with the utter dependability of divine love in the first six lines, through the use of a familiar proverbial phrase and a well-known biblical reference, reflecting the common nature of human affections and *desengaño*. The turn comes at the sixth line. From there follows the repetition of "Paguen . . . paguen . . . paguen," which emphasizes both her own foolishness in expecting more than it is within human capacity to give, and also how dearly the emotions suffer when reliance on human friendship founders on the vacillations of human intercourse compromised by self-interest.

The speaker compares her fate with that of those who leave aside relations with their fellows, devoting themselves entirely to God: "Dichosos los que en Vos se confiaron / solamente, mi Dios, pues no cayeron" (12–13). However, by couching the whole of the sestet in the simple past she implies that in the seventeenth century such faith is no longer possible. Gone are her friendships and, by implication, gone also are those lucky few who loved God exclusively, as if she refers to long-dead saints and philosophers. In doing so the poet reflects the common perception of a disillusioned seventeenth century that the world was decaying, that times were out of joint, and that true joy and perfectibility lay in a golden past.

These sonnets of "other selves" contrast strongly with commonly held masculine ideas that women were, by nature, incapable of forming and maintaining deep abiding friendships. The sonnets and other verse written by nuns to mark the entrance of new nuns to their sisterhood demonstrate the importance, not just of their marriage vows to Christ, but also of the bonds that bind women together in shared poverty and obedience. In writing sonnets to their "other selves," these poets affirm that they fully understand the purpose of the love sonnet as a codified form of display and graceful compliment. However, that they write such sonnets also points to the considerable importance that women placed on the solidarity they received from friendships and shared confidences, as can be seen in Sor Violante's sonnet on the brown dress and Ramírez's sonnet to her absent friend. These are more than mere expressions of wit. Sor Violante defines the nature of friendship from a woman's perspective very precisely in her sonnet to Belisa, and compounds her message by identifying the bleak nature of false friendship in her sonnet on the betrayal in the garden. The above poems show that women did not have to be familiar with Aristotle's affirmation of friends as "other selves" in order to discover a valid and important source of solace, companionship, and shared experience. It is because they enjoy such fruitful relationships with their friends that sonnets marking their deaths are so poignant.

FRIENDSHIP AND DEATH

The same codification of poetic display seen in the Petrarchan love poetry and some of the sonnets discussed above is also evident in a host of encomiastic funeral sonnets directed both to personal friends and to high-born or powerful people in the seventeenth century.[16] Many women seized the opportunity during the national outpourings of funeral verse at the deaths of royalty to express themselves in print in a seemly way, as has also been noted by editors of women's poetry collections:

La oleada de poesías necrológicas, que eran publicadas en obeliscos o en coronas fúnebres, ofrece considerable interés para nuestro estudio por el elevado índice de participación de mujeres y las posibilidades que brindaba a éstas para hacer públicas sus composiciones, aunque solo fuera dentro del género que aquellas ocasiones requerían. Era, generalmente, una literatura de circunstancias, de limitada inspiración personal y vacía de emociones sinceras. (Navaro 47)

The wave of obituary poems that were published in obelisks or in funeral *coronas* offer considerable interest for our study for the high level of participation by women and the possibilities that were offered to them to make their compositions public, even if only within the genre required by those occasions. It was generally an occasional literature of limited personal inspiration and empty of sincere emotion.

However unwise it may be to search for sincerity in a baroque sonnet, I contend that women did not only write funeral sonnets simply to insert themselves into historic public moments. Beyond the ritualized public displays of poetic emotion at the deaths of public figures, they also exhibit in their poetry personal intimate grief, only partly assuaged by Christian belief in the eternal life of the soul. Some of the dedicatees were both personal friends and women of substance and renown, such as

16. Serrano y Sanz notes surviving works from at least eleven women who wrote such sonnets in the seventeenth century alone: among them, Violante del Cielo's sonnet on the death of Lope de Vega. A number of sonnets also appear by women writing in the New World: most notably, Sor Juana Inés de la Cruz's sonnet on the death of Felipe IV. Other popular subjects for such verse were Prince Baltasar Carlos, the cardinal-prince Don Fernando, and Queen Isabel de Borbón. For the latter, María Nieta de Aragón wrote, and apparently published, six sonnets on her death, under the title *Lágrimas a la muerte de la Augusta Reyna* . . . (Tears on the death of the august queen . . .) Por Dª. Maria Nieto de Aragón. Madrid Diego Díaz de la Carrera. 1645. No. 245 in Serrano y Sanz, *Apuntes para una biblioteca de escritoras españolas.*

Sor Violante's friend and fellow poet Bernarda Ferreira de la Cerda. Others were purely friends and companions, such as the "Anarda" of Marcia Belisarda's sonnet, to be discussed below. Straddling the two forms of funeral poetry are the sonnets composed by Sor Juana Inés de la Cruz on the death of her beloved patron, friend, and supporter the vicereine of Mexico, the Marchioness de Mancera, in which she celebrates the outstanding physical beauty of the subject and likens her to the sun, with all its regal and divine connotations. Though Sor Juana lived and wrote in the New World, I include these sonnets because the marchioness represented Spanish royalty and as such created a bridge between the Spanish Crown and the new colonies. Furthermore, it was through the marchioness that Sor Juana's poems were first published, in Spain:

En la muerte de la Excelentísima Señora Marquesa de Mancera

De la beldad de Laura enamorados
los Cielos, la robaron a su altura,
porque no era decente a su luz pura
ilustrar estos valles desdichados;

5   o porque los mortales, engañados
de su cuerpo en la hermosa arquitectura,
admirados de ver tanta hermosura
no se juzgasen bienaventurados.

Nació donde el Oriente el rojo velo
10   corre al nacer al Astro rubicundo,
y murió donde, con ardiente anhelo,

da sepulcro a su luz el mar profundo:
que fue preciso a su divino vuelo
que diese como el Sol la vuelta al mundo.

(*Lírica personal* vol. 1, *Obras completas* 299)

On the death of the most excellent Lady the Marchioness of Mancera

The Heavens, enamored of Laura's
beauty, captured her to their heights,

for it was not decent that her pure light
should illuminate those unblessed valleys.

or so that the mortals, enraptured
by the beautiful architecture of her body,
captivated to see such beauty,
should not judge themselves so blessed.

She was born where the Orient's red veil
rushes to give birth to the rubicund Star,
and died where, with ardent desire,

the deep sea gives a sepulcher to its light:
for it was essential to her divine flight
that like the Sun she should circle the world.

Through the sun imagery of the sestet, Sor Juana is able to include the marchioness's role as representative of Spanish majesty and to show that majesty is not limited by gender. This imagery, normally associated with the king's person, acts in two ways: it emphasizes the idea that the vicereine's places of birth and death span the world, as do the sun in its diurnal round and Spain's dominion over its colonies. References to the sun also foreground its importance in Mexico's pagan past; while the sun's inexorable east-west movement also brings to the fore the assumed permanence of Spanish world domination, the *monarquía* on which the sun never set, and to whose governing classes the marchioness belonged. Underlying all of this is the simple, historical fact that the Marchioness de Mancera died at sea and hence, as the sun appears to do, passed into the sea that became her grave.

Sor Juana wrote three sonnets immortalizing the dead noblewoman. In this first she rehearses the severing of the marchioness's beautiful soul from her equally beautiful body; in another, beginning "Bello compuesto en Laura dividido" (Combined beauty in Laura divided), she finds solace in the observation that it is necessary to suffer this "divorcio riguroso" (rigorous divorce) in order to achieve eternal union of body and soul at the end of time. Sor Juana insists on the unparalleled beauty of the subject in all three sonnets, an important factor for the poet in the context of salvation, since physical beauty was in this period seen as the outward manifestation of inner purity and goodness. The line "Pero ya ha penetrado mi sentido" (but now it has pierced my senses), which opens the second quartet of the second sonnet serves a dual purpose; it begins to resolve the questions of the first quartet and represents the genuine piercing of the poet's "sentido": the grief occasioned by the loss of her beloved friend. The three sonnets function on a rising continuum of personal involvement. In the first, Sor Juana stands back to observe that the heavens, jealous of her beauty, have stolen the subject; the second questions the division of such a perfect body and soul, and seeks the answer in divine providence; the third opens directly with the poet's personal suffering: "Mueran contigo, Laura, pues moriste, / los afectos que en vano te desean" (1–2), and acknowledges still-current humoral theory, in the shedding of black tears:

> Mueran contigo, Laura, pues moriste,
> los afectos que en vano te desean,
> los ojos a quien privas de que vean
> hermosa luz que un tiempo concediste.
>
> 5 Muera mi lira infausta en que influíste
> ecos, que lamentables te vocean,
> y hasta estos rasgos mal formados sean
> lágrimas negras de mi pluma triste.
>
> Muévase a compasión la misma Muerte
> 10 que, precisa, no pudo perdonarte;
> y lamente el Amor su amarga suerte,
>
> pues si antes, ambicioso de gozarte,
> deseó tener ojos para verte,
> ya le sirvieran sólo de llorarte.
>
>   (*Lírica personal* vol. 1, *Obras completas* 300)

> There died with you, Laura, since you died,
> the feelings that desire you in vain,
> the eyes deprived of what they would see,
> your beautiful light, conceded us a short time.
>
> My unhappy lyric in which you form
> echoes, cries a lament for you until

these ill-made flourishes become
black tears from my sad pen.

Death itself is moved to compassion,
that, perforce, it could not spare you;
and Love laments his bitter fate,

for if, before, ambitious to joy in you,
he desired to have the eyes to see you,
now they serve him only to weep for you.

The poet claims in the second quartet to have lost her muse: "Muera mi lira infausta en que influíste / ecos," hence the death of her *lira*. As she attempts to inscribe her love and grief on the page, the ink is portrayed instead as tears from her weeping pen that impede her creative impulse. The black tears also incorporate the idea of the melancholic philosopher and recall that, according to humoral theory, the coldness of the melancholy humor created the necessary mental state for intellection. The theory of melancholy as a natural precursor to scholastic achievement, mental brilliance, and artistic achievement in the Renaissance is limited to the masculine sphere. Melancholic male scholars are characterized as having a cold, dry temperament, whereas women bear the melancholic characteristics of coldness and wetness, identified in the period with excessive emotion, hysteria, and mental weakness. Soufas argues that the melancholic tendencies considered typical of the female mind are frequently invoked in the writings of female scholars as a means to enter the debate about melancholy and its limitations on the female. Their appropriation of the ambiguities and tensions inherent in the theory articulate challenges to notions about the female mind and body (171–84). Here Sor Juana claims the status of melancholy poet-genius attributable to masculine writers, but also disclaims these qualities due to the effects of black melancholy on her emotions, occasioned by the marchioness's death. Although she undercuts her own articulation of female melancholy as a creative urge, by completing three elegant sonnets in celebration of the marchioness she also reenters the debate with written proof that gives the lie to her words.

As Sor Juana performs a quasi-official function in eulogizing the dead marchioness, she also, in the process, reveals that in spite of her Christian faith the loss of her friend grieves her deeply. In the same way, Marcia

Belisarda writes a sonnet to the dead "Anarda" that seeks both to immortalize the dead woman in print and also to assuage personal grief, insisting that her friend's spiritual perfection will ensure her a place in heaven. Hence death is essential to enable her true life to begin:

> Fatal Rigor, ejecutando aleve
> la Parca (corta el hilo de una vida)
> astuta, recelándose, vencida
> de su bizarro ardor en tiempo breve.
>
> Postrada yace, al fin de un soplo leve,
> Lozana planta, que en edad florida
> a poca tierra infausta reducida,
> desengaños causando, a llanto mueve.
>
> Fue Anarda toda gala, entendimiento,
> deidad de ingenio, alma y hermosura
> que luego en sí lograrla el cielo quiso.
>
> No atienda, no, a su falta el sentimiento
> a un punto en que ganó sí, por ventura,
> Gloriosa vida en un morir preciso.
>
> (BN ms. 7469 57v)

> Harsh Fate, treacherous, cunning
> Atropos (cuts the thread of a life)
> sly and mistrustful; despoiled of her
> valiant ardor in a short space.
>
> Prostrate she lies, snuffed by a gentle sigh,
> a luxuriant plant, who in her time of ripeness
> is reduced to a handful of unhappy earth,
> causing regrets, moving tears.
>
> Anarda was all brilliance, perception,
> goddess of wisdom, soul, and beauty,
> all that heaven wished to find in her.
>
> No, do not direct your sentiments to her loss,
> but to the point at which, through fortune,
> she found glorious life in necessary death.

Marcia Belisarda does not begin the sonnet in resigned Christian faith. Rather, she focuses on the swift ease of death's stroke, apostrophizing an implacable treacherous Death that takes Christian and heathen alike: "Fatal Rigor" refers to the classical Fates rather than a Christian reaping of pure souls, as Atropos cuts the thread of Anarda's life. The descriptive qualities and immediacy of the octet indicate Marcia Belisarda's presence at this leavetaking. Personal grief is expressed in the strained structure of the sonnet. The rhyme scheme remains intact, perhaps to show that underlying personal tragedy the normal rhythms of life and death continue inexorably forward. Death's moment occupies only the first two lines, followed by an immediate disappointment, in the poet's view, of death's momentary triumph which is over by the end of the first quartet. She then moves into description of the changes wrought in her friend at that instant as, rapidly despoiled of her earthly beauty and vigor, she sighs her last breath. It is a compelling picture, in which a woman's entire life, color, personality, intelligence, beauty, and vivacity are reduced to a handful of earth. As Marcia Belisarda grieves over Anarda's early death, "en edad florida," she calls in the lines of the funeral service and of St. Paul, and turns from the pagan Atropos to the Christian Bible.[17]

There is a major change at the turn, emphasized by the transition from present to past tense. In the brief space of that last breath, and the passage from octet to sestet, the poet absorbs the shock of loss and moves on to celebrate her friend in a tercet funeral oration: "Fue Anarda toda gala, entendimiento, / Deidad de ingenio, alma, y hermosura" (9–11). The references to "gala, entendimiento" and "ingenio" imply that the dead woman may have been a contestant in the convent's poetic jousts (the titles of her own sonnets suggest that Marcia Belisarda was an enthusiastic participant). This would make the loss of a companion who shared and perhaps equaled her intellectual interests and capacities particularly poignant. Like Sor Violante, she seizes the opportunity to celebrate the dead woman's unusually superior intellect and the sonnet ends optimistically. Fortified by her own faith, the speaker turns away from the dead Anarda to the wider world with words of advice and faith that also serve to bolster her

17. The reference to humankind as composed of earth is found in St. Paul's Epistle to the Corinthians (1 Corinthians 15: 42–50).

own spirits: "No atienda, no, a su falta el sentimiento, / A un punto en que ganó sí, por ventura, / gloriosa vida en un morir preciso" (11–13). Janice Raymond has studied the notion of "spiritual friendship" in convents, observing that "[n]uns expressed commitment to each other in a mode of communication that is peculiar to spiritual friendship, along with a highly pietistic tone that is typical of this 'companionship of souls'" (86).

Further evidence of genuine fellow feeling between the nuns and for departed colleagues is to be seen in a poem, also by Marcia Belisarda, entitled *"Otra [romance] a una Religiosa que lloraba sin medida la muerte de otra que la había criado"* (Another [romance] to a religious who cried uncontrollably for the death of another who had raised her), in which she strives to console her friend as she grieves for the woman who had taken the place of a mother. The *romance* begins: "No llores del mal que sientes" (Do not cry from the sadness you feel); the concluding verse still tries to stem the tears:

> No llores, cántete endechas
> tu dulce voz que a mi ver
> si en ella atenta te miras
> Narciso serás después.
> Canta, baste que llore
> quien te quiere bien
> pues de entrambos la pena
> viene a ser.
> Canta, canta.
> Darás gloria a la pena
> como a la causa.
>   (ms. 7469 45r)

> Don't cry, let your sweet voice
> sing a lament, for it seems to me
> that if you fix your eyes on her
> you will then become a Narcissus.
> Sing, enough of your weeping
> for she whom you love well,
> for the sorrow comes between you.
> Sing, sing,

glorify your misery
and its cause.

As a celebrated poet in her own time, Sor Violante del Cielo composed a number of funeral sonnets to honor famous or powerful individuals. These differ markedly from the expression of personal experience
evident in the sonnet by Marcia Belisarda above.[18] However, like Sor
Juana Inés de la Cruz, Sor Violante del Cielo was also on friendly terms
with the nobles and notables whose lives she immortalized. She enjoyed
a close friendship with the famous Portuguese poet Bernarda Ferreira de
la Cerda, who, according to Serrano y Sanz, was born in Oporto in 1595
and died in 1644, and was celebrated in verse by both Manuel de Gal-
legos and Lope de Vega, suggesting that she was highly regarded as a poet
by her male peers.[19] Sor Violante wrote a *canción* to Bernarda and her
daughter, published in the *Rimas varias,* and directed two sonnets to her
friend on her death; these appear in the *Parnaso lusitano.* In them she celebrates the woman's poetic gifts and links Bernarda's heavenly and earthly immortality. Both sonnets are extremely hyperbolic, as the poet strives
to do justice to the memory of her friend and, perhaps, to demonstrate
her equality in poetic power. There is little sense of the loss that Marcia
Belisarda strives to control; rather, they are a triumphant celebration of
Bernarda's life and achievements. That Sor Violante thought Bernarda's
verse admirable and exceptional is clear in the first sonnet by the frequent
references throughout the quartets to the dead woman as the governing
muse on Parnassus who has sipped the waters of the Pierian Spring. Thus
Bernarda is portrayed simultaneously as a mortal and a goddess:

18. Examples of such occasional sonnets are those written to mark the deaths of the
Duchess of Aveiro (*Rimas varias [1646]* 56), the *dama de corte* Maria de Ataide (Vieira
n. pag.), General Andrè de Albuquerque, who died in the battle won by the Portuguese
against *"os Castelhanos em Elvas"* (the Spaniards in Elvas) in 1659 (*Parnaso lusitano* 67), and
two to Maria Luiza de Noronha, *"Senhora de doze annos"* (a young lady of twelve years)
(*Parnaso lusitano* 66–67). Some of these have been discussed in Chapter 1.

19. Vieira Mendes describes Bernarda as the daughter of the chancellor of Portugal, Inácio Ferreira Leitão. She published the first part of *España libertada,* dedicated to
Felipe III, in 1618, and *Soledades de Buçaco* in Lisbon in 1624. The second part of *España
libertada* was published in 1673 by her daughter, Maria Clara de Meneses. do Céu, *Rimas
varias* (1993), 82. Bernarda Ferreira de la Cerda is also recorded as entering poems in two
poetic jousts: Montalbán 1636, folios 42, 46 and 137, and Grande de Tena, 1639, folio 134v.
See José Simón Díaz, ed., *Siglos de Oro: Índice de Justas Poéticas* (Madrid: CSIC, 1962).

Depuso lo mortal, buscó dichosa
esfera superior con veloz paso,
la Musa que imperando en el Parnaso,
música investigó más sonorosa.

5   Por ser, si bien humana, excelsa diosa,
tanto extrañó su sol terrestre ocaso,
que, dejando las aguas del Pegaso,
al cielo renació luz portentosa.

Las Musas, que con dulce melodía
10   lloran de tanto bien la eterna ausencia,
transformen la tristeza en alegría;

que Bernarda, deidad de la elocuencia,
si Musa suspendió con su armonía,
estrella obligará con su influencia.

(Parnaso lusitano 64–65)

She left the mortal and, fortunate,
sought the highest sphere with rapid flight,
that Muse who, though ruling on Parnassus,
looked for a more sonorous music.

In being, though human, a superior goddess,
her sun so enthralled the terrestrial dusk
that, leaving the waters of Pegasus,
she gave the heavens a renewed, portentous light.

The Muses, who with sweet melody
lament the eternal absence of so much good,
convert their sadness into joy

that Bernarda, goddess of eloquence,
who stopped the Muse with her harmony,
will submit the stars to her influence.

This first sonnet is filled with light, movement, and sound as Bernarda, already master of the music of the spheres, seeks music even more heavenly, that of the angelic choir. Her soul speeds through the heavens at the moment of death. Sor Violante attributes astral powers to Bernarda after death, as she who can give the Muses pause will be able to influence the stars that affect the lives of mere mortals below: "si Musa suspendió con su armonía, / estrella obligará con su influencia" (13–14).

The theme of a superlative individual who occupies both the earthly and the heavenly realms is repeated in the second sonnet:

Otro al mismo sujeto sobre la vida
de su fama, y gloria

Murió para vivir eternamente
entre excelsos luceros colocada,
la que tuvo en el mundo de admirada,
lo que tiene en el Cielo de viviente.

5   Murió para saber la absorta gente,
que era humana deidad tan aclamada,
si bien muestra en quedar eternizada,
que fue solo mortal por accidente.

Murió Bernarda en fin, mas de tal modo,
10   que asegura al amor virtud tan cierta
(por medio de la Parca ejecutiva)

Que logra, cuando muestra dejar todo,
en el Cielo una vida nunca muerta,
en el mundo una fama siempre viva.

(*Parnaso lusitano* 65)

Another, to the same subject, about her
living fame and glory

She died to live eternally,
placed between brilliant stars,
she who was admired in the world
will have in heaven a living soul.

She died so that the rapt people should know
that she who was acclaimed a goddess was human,
though she shows well, in being eternalized,
that she was only mortal by accident.

Bernarda died, finally, but in such a way
that love assures her certain virtue
(by means of Death's instrument)

May she achieve, in this show of leaving,
a life that never dies in heaven,
and in the world an ever-living fame.

Bernarda's singular qualities ensure her acceptance into heaven, while the
poetry that survives her ensures her continuing fame on earth. Extrava-
gantly, Sor Violante claims that it was necessary for Bernarda to die in
order to be seen by the world as human and not a pagan goddess, and
the sestet remains in the classical world in attributing Bernarda's end to
the classical Parca: "Murió Bernarda en fin, mas de tal modo, / Que asegura al amor virtud tan cierta (Por medio de la Parca ejecutiva)" (9–11).
This sonnet repeatedly counterbalances life and death and heaven and
earth, with Bernarda occupying both realms. The final tercet is typical
of Sor Violante's style and her liking for chiasmus as earth and heaven,
death and life weave and change position, all coming to the concluding
observation of her dual eternity; her good, Christian soul, her godlike
mastery of poetry, will ensure her eternal fame on earth and her eternal
life in heaven: "Que logra, cuando muestra dejar todo, / En el Cielo una
vida nunca muerta, / en el mundo una fama siempre viva" (12–14).

Women took their opportunities to inscribe themselves into the national literature in composing sonnets marking the deaths of notable
figures, but their commemorations of the dead were not always written simply to show their prowess as poets nor to participate in national
events. They also expressed genuine grief, loss, and love for those companions who had shared their experiences and who provided companionship, support, and understanding of the difficulties women faced in
seventeenth-century Spain.

CONCLUSION

In studying these sonnets of friendship, it becomes clear that wom-
en were not universally silent and meek, but nor were they struggling to
change the Counter-Reformation system that sought to reduce them to

the level of nonentity. Rather, they appear to shrug off societal expectations as these sonnets celebrate their normal everyday existence, in which they pay and receive visits to friends, mock each other's peculiarities, celebrate each other's small successes and pleasures, and derive from their friendships the succor of mutually affective and enjoyable relationship. As María del Pilar Oñate has pointed out, in this century "cosa nueva es que la mujer salga a la defensa de su sexo" (141; it is a new thing that woman goes to the defense of her sex), and this can be seen in the robust flyting engaged in by Ramírez and Cueva. Nevertheless, as Ann Rosalind Jones also reveals, "every woman poet recognized the necessity of winning men over to her side as mentors and as critics" ("Fame" 80). Women were in no position to demand an equality that tradition, the Church, and officialdom opposed; hence friendships with the opposite sex provided possibilities within which to practice their art, promote social harmony, and show women's intellectual capabilities.

The religious faith of these poets, evinced in the sonnets of consolation, is also displayed in their sonnets of divine love, where the model of humankindness and friendship is Christ. Christ, as will be seen in Chapter 6, on Carvajal y Mendoza's mystical poetry, also forms the subject of highly erotic verse in which the poets seek to fuse themselves with his body and soul. Furthermore, in erotic poetry written by both secular and religious women, the poets explore themes of desire and loss, show a determination to take control of the amatory situation, demonstrate their familiarity with the Petrarchan mode, and do not hesitate to deflate male pretension in the matter of love.

CHAPTER 5

WOMEN'S LOVE SONNETS

ᔥ❦

WOMEN WHO COMPOSED LOVE POETRY stepped into a masculine field, bound by tradition, where the female was the silent and idealized object of unrealized love, merely a rhetorical exercise carried forward from the courtly love mode. When Malón de Chaide discusses the ideal of a love that must be given freely, he is not talking of love in the modern, post-Romantic sense.[1] He describes that Neoplatonic ideal, a chimera of female excellence, where a woman's perceived lack of intellect, coupled with her physical beauty, provides her with spiritual gifts above those of man, enabling her to rise above the masculine norm and communicate with the angels (I. Maclean 24). According to Malón de Chaide, the lovers' souls are united both in human terms and in the divine: "[E]l amor llamase potencia unitiva, que une al amante con el amado, sacándole de sí y llevándole a lo que ama y allí lo transforma y hace uno con él . . . síguese que el amado es señor de todo el amante, y el amante se transforma en el amado" (69; Love may be called a unitive power that joins the lover with the beloved, taking him out of himself and carrying him to that which he loves and there transforming it and making it one with him . . . it follows that the beloved is entirely the

---

1. Malón de Chaide (1530–1589) was an Augustinian mystic, a brilliant author, preacher and writer. A student of Luis de León, his most famous work is *La conversión de la Magdalena,* published in Barcelona in 1588.

master of the lover and that the lover is transformed into the beloved). In this he differs from other Renaissance theorists of divine love, such as St. Francis de Sales, for whom the comparison of divine and human love is simply a simile.

Writing of Castiglione's influential *Book of the Courtier,* Joan Kelly notes Castiglione's likening of the beloved lady to the prince, in his theory of Neoplatonic love. However, she also notes that in a structured hierarchy of superior and inferior, though the lady appears to be served by the courtier, the theory causes her to become symbolic of the reversal of domination, wherein the prince comes to serve the interests of the courtier. The Renaissance lady "is not desired, nor loved for herself. Rendered passive and chaste, she merely mediates the courtier's safe transcendence of an otherwise demeaning necessity" (195). As with the Renaissance lady, so too with the *dama* of the Baroque, where women served as the bartering tool for socially desirable marriages and to smooth the path of patronage.

In addition, and bound up with the Counter-Reformation, is the change from the freer troubadour tradition to more repressive attitudes toward women, their education, and their relationship to men. Michel Foucault locates a change in European attitudes to sexuality in the seventeenth century, when sexuality became more repressed, bound to language, and subjugated in a discourse that defined and delimited sexual practices (17). Cruz, however, discovers this repression in Spain a full century earlier, due to "the supposed threat of miscegenation posed by the country's ethnic and religious minorities" ("Juana" 89). These social and ideological changes in the sixteenth and seventeenth centuries robbed Hispanic women of a poetic voice that had sung of love in the *kharjas* of Al Andalus, if only to an internal public of other women (Bergmann and Middlebrook 146). Furthermore, Ana Navaro observes that the reduced margin of freedom afforded by the limits of women's education deprived them of the free expression of emotion, while inflexible literary models robbed their literary expression of spontaneity. This latter assertion is perhaps too sweeping in light of recent scholarship and of the poetry discussed in this book. However, as Navaro also observes, "es difícil encontrar entre las poetisas de la Edad de Oro manifestaciones de la intimidad emocional como la expresaron las musulmanas de la Edad Media" (51; It is difficult to find among the women poets of the Golden Age manifestations of the emotional intimacy expressed by the Muslim women of the Middle Ages).

Nevertheless, surviving love sonnets by seventeenth-century women prove them to be capable sonneteers, practiced in the rhetoric of love, which they appropriate to their own ends. Navaro deplores the custom of concealing their identities under pseudonyms and surmises that an evaluation of anonymous feminine literature of the period would show a freer expression of amorous intent, extending from the purely sentimental to the sensually erotic (51). Yet the sonnets of the women under consideration in this study show their determination to break the seal on female silence. They express their views on the love debate, and their thoughts are not veiled in anonymity. Furthermore, their poems provide opportunities to explore their emotional lives.[2] This is not to suggest that the poetry is autobiographical but rather that it expresses an attitude to the emotions prevalent among their contemporaries, and therefore part of their own experience. Their viewpoint is, however, feminine rather than protofeminist in that they do not rail against the patriarchal system that nourishes and sustains them as members of the upper strata of Spanish society. Their discourse is reserved to the direct and personal, to emotions and feelings that render lived experience in fictive terms. In this they express, to a degree, the Renaissance feminism described by Constance Jordan:

By representing woman as a type in whom are incarnate virtues specifically associated with femininity—mercy, patience, temperance, and so forth—feminists began to argue not only for the worth of woman but also for the feminization of society as whole. Correspondingly, they spoke of a degenerate kind of masculinity. (Jordan 137)

However, the poems resist categorizing, for they do not always represent this feminine type; some poetry shows women to be refreshingly aware of their failings. While they do not argue for a feminization of society, their poetry is also more than just a rhetorical exercise, and some of the

---

2. Amanda Powell's recent chapter on women's love poetry to women also includes discussion of some of the poems mentioned in this chapter (*"Oh qué diversas estamos"* n. pag.).

sonnets to be discussed here, particularly those by Cueva, do speak of a "degenerate kind of masculinity." Their works are not only conscious expressions of artistic endeavor, designed to win praise from companions of both sexes, but also expressions of their attitudes to the activities surrounding them. Thus they comment on moral and social failings, both male and female, and express their view of women as rational, intelligent, and morally upright, and certainly equal in these qualities to the masculine view of male conduct.

This feminine viewpoint can be viewed from two angles: first, assuming the continuing influence of Petrarchism in the Spanish love lyric of the seventeenth century, through the manner in which these women poets negotiate the Petrarchan mode, both utilizing and subverting it, creating sonnets in which a feminine voice articulates the pains of unrequited love. The second angle is through female appropriation of typically masculine themes of display and desire, wherein they create a male-voiced discourse in order to criticize male attitudes or to call for sexual equality. Such ideas are most clearly expressed in the love poetry of Marcia Belisarda, Leonor de la Cueva, Catalina Clara Ramírez, and Sor Violante del Cielo. Furthermore, in four sonnets that form part of her play *La firmeza en la ausencia,* Cueva celebrates women's moral and intellectual strength and challenges gender expectations of feminine *mudanza* (inconstancy).

As they insert themselves into modish, literary-academy and drawing-room activity, these women write confident witty sonnets. They do not embark upon a lengthy journey through the interior trials of unrequited love in a sequence of thematically related verse.[3] While they discourse on the pain of absence and the agonies of unspoken love, where the object of love is portrayed as male he is not the masculine equivalent of the *dama esquiva* (disdainful lady) of male love poetry. Instead, he is often exposed to ridicule or censure, and it is often he who is mutable and loquacious. This is most clearly the case in sonnets by Cueva, such as "Muestra Galicio que a Leonarda adora" (Galicio shows that he adores Leonarda). These function to admonish the faithless male lover, who is

3. Only Sor Violante composes a sequence, in her sonnets on the Mysteries of the Rosary published in *Parnaso lusitano;* but in the *Parnaso* the subjects of her verse are exclusively divine and religious.

frequently shown to exhibit the fickle and deceitful behavior traditionally attributed to women.

Ann Rosalind Jones has observed of early modern women poets who entered the debate over female intelligence and who wished to publish their work that they resisted their exclusion from cultural production: "By drawing on ideological support outside their texts and by compromising with limits on women's speech within them, poets who were not courtesans found ways of mediating social dictates and the conventions of love poetry" (*Currency* 34). This technique is evident in Sor Violante's *Rimas varias;* she also seeds her collection with liberal applications of poetry designed to appeal to patrons, as discussed in Chapter 1. Similarly, Marcia Belisarda's appeals to reason and the deployment of a male speaking subject work to deflect criticism.

WOMEN AND PETRARCHISM

The titles of many of the sonnets indicate at least circulation among a limited coterie. These sonnets too mediated social dictates and poetic convention and in doing so conformed to masculine style, while at the same time expressing particularly feminine concerns with regard to social restrictions and conventions. For example, women were seldom, if ever, permitted to choose their own husbands, and no poet extends the imagery of her love poetry to include marriage, not even as an epithalamion.[4] However, neither is theirs the conventional view of ideal beauty for Petrarchan contemplation and dissection, though they sometimes utilize Petrarchan themes, no doubt inspired by the examples available to them. Rather, they explore the subject of love as an abstract feminine ideal of recognition, acceptance, and reciprocity, beyond the capacity of some of their male subjects.

Writing of Petrarch's *Rime Sparse,* Nancy Vickers describes it as a pri-

---

4. As has been noted in Chapter 2, on the family and marriage, Catalina Clara Ramírez de Guzmán writes a solitary poem to celebrate the marriage of one sibling, Ana Rosalea. In addition, Feliciana Enríquez de Guzmán, whose works do not form part of this study, concludes the second part of her published play, *Tragicomedia de los jardines y campos sabeos,* with an epithalamic *soneto a las bodas de Maya y Clarisel* (Sonnet on the marriage of Maya and Clarisel). Louis C. Pérez, *The Dramatic Works of Feliciana Enríquez de Guzmán* (Valencia: Albatros, 1988).

mary canonical text produced out of his appropriation of a complex network of descriptive strategies into a single transformed model. She considers that his role in the historical interpretation and internalization of woman's "image" by both men and women cannot be overemphasized (265). Some of these women's poems gesture to the Petrarchan mode, although they do not enter it entirely. The most striking aspect of this poetry is the adoption of a feminine voice, for the female speaker occupies the space exclusively reserved for the Petrarchan lover who adores his lady. Eschewing silence as a mark of modesty, the female poets instead silence the male objects of love in order to express their discontents. Strikingly, given the fragmentation of women's bodies often found in the masculine mode, in these love sonnets there is no blazon, and no fetishizing of fragments of the beloved's body, dress, or possessions. Although death features frequently as a typically Petrarchan symptom of the disease of love, it does not allude, as it often does in male poetry, to orgasm. Nor is the binary distinction of life and death/*engaño* and *desengaño* (delusion and disenchantment) evident. Rather, *desengaño* furthers self-realization in the speaker and deepens understanding of the love dilemma. Love poetry becomes educative.

The beloved is portrayed as a living whole being to whom the speaker expresses feelings, hopes, and criticisms. Thoughts and emotions attributed to the *amante* (lover) or the *amado* (beloved) are privileged over the passive and atomized body of the traditional model. Whereas, in the masculine Neoplatonic love convention the ideal is perceived through contemplation of the silent beloved object or her parts, here it is necessary to contemplate the whole person, who is not silent and probably not perfect. Nor is the speaker masochistic in a continued pursuit of the often cruel beloved. Instead, the complaint is frequently delivered as the end result of *desengaño*, achieved through appraisal and realization of a situation in which the persona is not going to achieve his or her ends. This can be seen in sonnets by Cueva and Marcia Belisarda: for example, Cueva's "Alcindo, ya murió en tu desengaño" (Alcindo, there now dies in your disenchantment) and "Puse los ojos ¡ay que no debiera!" (I laid my eyes, oh, but I should not have!), or Marcia Belisarda's "Para una novela" (For a novel).

It is also clear from the titles of many of the poems ("Encomendóseme . . ." [I was entrusted with . . .], "Dándome el asunto . . ." [Giving me the topic . . .]) that love poetry was not always produced as the result of personal meditation leading to a distillation of emotion in sonnets and *liras*. As in male courtier poetry, it was also a means of amusement among friends, or an opportunity for display complementary to the masculine poetry of the academies, performed to praise the wit of male members and the beauty of the veiled women in the audience.[5]

Writing in a male voice and under a nom de plume was one way for women to publish works without attracting censure for their immodesty. Yet the impression given by these women's sonnets is that the male voice is employed instead to critique male pretensions, or to engage in intellectual play, activities certainly not sanctioned by seventeenth-century moralists. The poems of Ramírez, already discussed in Chapter 4, and those of Cueva, demonstrate that these *damas* enjoyed social relationships with members of the opposite sex, in which poetic interchanges were part of social intercourse. Sor Violante too, during the course of her friendship with Paulo Gonçalves de Andrade, wrote and received love poems that were more than a mere sharing of rhetorical skills.[6] Educated women were therefore familiar with the poetic fashions of their time and with the complex conceits of a Góngora or a Quevedo, and had opportunities to read the love poetry of their male counterparts as well as traditional Petrarchan love sonnets.

When Marcia Belisarda writes a sonnet that begins "Filis de amor hechizo soberano" (1; Filis, under love's sovereign spell), it is not the interior musing of an anguished and disappointed lover, although she gestures toward a number of Petrarchan conventions, particularly in floral imagery and color. The speaker of the poem is in the objective position of an observer, outside the action, and the manuscript title indicates that the topic was given to her in poetic challenge: "Dándome por asunto cor-

---

5. For a detailed study of academy poetry in seventeenth-century Spain, see Jeremy Robbins, *Love Poetry of the Literary Academies in the Reigns of Philip IV and Charles II* (London: Tamesis, 1997).

6. Sor Violante exchanged love poetry with Paulo under the pastoral nomenclature of "Silvano" or "Lauso" and "Silvia." See, for example, Pociño López, ed., *Sóror Violante do Céu (1607–1693)*, 33. Vieira Mendes also notes that their names appear linked as "Lauso" and "Silvia" in numerous laudatory compositions by some of Portugal's most notable poets of the period. Vieira Mendes, "Apresentação," 11.

tarse un dedo llegando a cortar jazmín" (Giving me for a topic cutting
one's finger reaching to cut jasmine). Although Marcia Belisarda incorporates life and death, represented in the classical allusion to Filis as "Atropos bella" (beautiful Atropos), she never moves into the carpe diem tropes
favored by Golden Age male poets. In fact, the slight nature of the topic
undercuts the Petrarchan mode altogether. Even where the traditional colors of red and white, portrayed in the blood and the jasmine, are utilized
in the second quartet, they do not form part of a blazon. Instead, Marcia
Belisarda's sonnet becomes a critique of Filis, a silly and vain young woman proud of her minute accomplishment in cutting a flower:

> Filis, de amor hechizo soberano,
> cortar quiso un jazmín desvanecido,
> y de cinco mirándose excedido
> quedó del vencimiento más ufano.
>
> No bien corta el jazmín cuando tirano
> acero en rojo humor otro ha teñido,
> mintiendo ramillete entretejido
> de jazmín y clavel la hermosa mano.
>
> Atropos bella a la tijera cede
> piadosa ejecución, si inadvertida,
> a su mano dolor ocasionando;
>
> que si alma con su sangre dar no puede,
> en vez de muerte dio al jazmín la vida,
> de amor el dulce imperio dilatando.
>
> (Ms. 7469:88r)

10

> Filis, under love's sovereign spell,
> wished to cut a wayward jasmine,
> and excelling herself in taking five
> felt ever more proud of her conquest.
>
> Scarcely is the jasmine cut when the
> tyrant steel has stained another crimson,
> feigning on her lovely hand an entwined
> sprig of jasmine and carnation.

Beautiful Atropos piously cedes the
execution to the scissors as, unheeding,
they occasion pain in her hand;

for though she cannot give a soul with her blood,
instead of dealing death she gave the jasmine life,
increasing the sweet empire of love.

Marcia Belisarda converts the sonnet into an anti-Petrarchan admonition concerning human vanity appropriate to the nun's calling. Though love brackets the sonnet in the first and fourteenth lines, its content has little to do with love or its problems. Rather than seizing the moment in the always uncertain course of life, the poem returns life to the plant through the nourishment of Filis's blood, claiming thereby to infuse and colonize the floral world with love: "en vez de muerte dio al jazmín la vida, de amor el dulce imperio dilatando" (13–14). Where, in Petrarchan poetry, there is interplay between the girl and the flower that leads to reflections on the tyranny of time and its effects on fleeting beauty, here Marcia Belisarda emphatically returns to the present. The wounding of Filis's hand works against the traditional model of poetic atomization and the flower remains nothing more than a fragrant backdrop to the young woman. What Marcia Belisarda's sonnet does, however, is to highlight the empty triviality of many young women's lives, denied education, and bound to the home, the *estrado,* their embroidery, and empty conversation until they are married off to husbands chosen by their fathers.

In this sonnet the objective speaker is an observer in the marginal space occupied by women in society, but often the *yo* (I) of women's love sonnets is problematic. Writing of Sor Juana's love sonnets, Georgina Sabat de Rivers notes that one of their most unusual aspects is that Sor Juana varies the norm in her expression of the poetic self, which is sometimes a woman addressing a male beloved, sometimes the complaining male, and sometimes an ambiguous figure whose gender is unidentifiable (105). This is also true of some of the poetry by Sor Violante already discussed in Chapter 1. However, although like Sor Juana these poets also employ masculine and ambiguous voices, the speaking subject is often feminine, suggesting that women made more use of the female poetic voice than may previously have been thought.

The *amor cortés* (courtly love) tradition determines that the female object of poetic desire be portrayed in masculine terms as the *dueño* (master) of the male *amante,* who is able, thereby, to project his own image before his reader. Cueva, in particular, presents poems in which the poetic voice is masculine, speaks about women, and purports to reveal masculine thinking, which can only have enriched the enjoyment of her female audience. This male-voiced poetry will be discussed in greater detail below. The problem for women poets is that, in joining a certain "school" of poetry writing, they must perforce use the method already laid down, a masculine style intended for male readers. Yet such impersonation enables the female poet to participate in a male discourse considered to be beyond her mental capacity. If we read the *dueño* as male and the *amante* as female, an altogether different vision of female agency is revealed.

A good example of this may be seen in Cueva's undermining of the Petrarchan mode in a manner similar to that of Marcia Belisarda. The sonnet is a gloss on the phrase "¿De qué sirve querer un imposible?" (What purpose is served by an impossible love?). The speaking voice is nominally ambiguous, but poetic concern about the free-roving eyes that have caused the problem of love suggest a female speaker, for there are no restrictions on the male gaze. She begins by apostrophizing a personified love, blaming him for her predicament, and employing common Petrarchan themes of death, fire, and shipwreck:

> ¡Basta, amor, el rigor con que me has muerto!
> ¡Cese un poco, rapaz, tu ardiente fuego!
> Pues ya del alma el señorío entrego,
> por los ojos no más, a dueño cierto.
>
> 5   Y aunque es el bien que adoro tan incierto
> que no pasa de vista, a sentir llego
> tu fuerza de manera que me anego
> en mil mares de amar sin hallar puerto.
>
> Riño unas veces a mis libres ojos,
> 10   mas por respeto de lo que han mirado,
> detengo el castigarlos lo posible.

Y viendo que padezco estos enojos,
digo entre mí a mi pecho enamorado:
¿De qué sirve querer un imposible?

(BN ms. 4127: 259–60)

Enough, Love, of your death-dealing torture!
Stop your ardent fire, rapacious one!
For now I surrender the mastery of my soul
to a certain master, though only with my eyes.

And though the beloved I adore is so indistinct
that he cannot be seen, I feel your
force so strongly that I'm drowning in a
thousand seas of love, without safe harbor.

Sometimes I struggle with my wandering eyes,
but out of respect for what they have seen,
I do not punish them as I should.

And seeing that I suffer these problems
I say to myself in my enamored heart:
What purpose is served by an impossible love?

Rather than seeking to eternalize the beloved figure, Cueva's persona attempts to rid herself of love altogether, for the sonnet raises a social question: What purpose could be served in surrendering so much as one's eyes to a "dueño cierto" who may not meet the approval of the family? Where a male reader would read the sonnet as an attempt to enter the tradition, a female reader may instead see patriarchal restriction as the basis for its conception.

The poet's insistence that the persona has surrendered only through the eyes suggests a female speaker restricting her immodest behavior to her gaze, while her knowledge of Renaissance theories of love is revealed through the linking of the eyes and the soul. Thus far, with the exception of the ambiguous subject, the sonnet follows a traditional line. Already by the second quartet, however, the beloved, rather than being fleshed out into a vision of unattainable beauty, either male or female, is effaced from the poem into invisibility. Nevertheless, the poet continues the traditional themes of the *amante,* helpless in the toils of love, in the same imagery of shipwreck and drowning that she uses in her sonnet of patronage on the "pretendiente," discussed in Chapter 1: ". . . a sentir llego / tu fuerza, de manera que me anego / en mil mares de amar sin hallar puerto" (6–8).

Cueva appears at first to propose for her persona the traditional role of the male lover, helplessly captivated by the *cierto dueño,* tossed about and controlled by the machinations of a capricious Cupid. But, as a female, this *amante* does not conform to the social requirements; she does not control her eyes, permitting them to feast immodestly on the figure: "Riño unas veces a mis libres ojos, / mas por respeto de lo que han mirado, / detengo el castigarlos lo posible" (9–11). This calls for a rereading of the quartets because there the irresistible figure is revealed as barely visible, and this rereading converts the sonnet into an anti-Petrarchan complaint. This is not a Neoplatonic reaching for the ideal, as the speaker herself reveals in the final tercet, bringing herself abruptly out of her reverie in the final line gloss: "Y viendo que padezco estos enojos, / digo entre mí a mi pecho enamorado: / ¿De qué sirve querer un imposible?" (12–14). Rather than pursuit of the higher good through the obsessional recitation of the beloved's charms, Cueva instead claims that the *amante* is in love with the idea of love, an insubstantial and false ideal, ultimately not fulfilling and far from the reality of arranged marriages and female enclosure. This theme of insubstantiality of the beloved object appears to be a preoccupation of women's love lyric. It is also explored in a sonnet to be discussed below, by Sor Violante del Cielo: "Quien dice que la ausencia es homicida" (Who says that love is a homicide). Similarly, Sor Juana's famous sonnet "Detente sombra de mi amor esquivo" (Stop, shadow of my elusive love) explores this theme. For women, the unattainable ideal is not a vision of the divine but of emotional freedom within their own environs. This tragic attraction to an impossible independence is frequently revisited in sonnet complaints to the absent lover.

The themes of the absent and longed-for lover and the pain and torments of love, central to Petrarchan and Golden Age poetry, enjoy a long pedigree extending back to antiquity, as may be seen in the lovers' complaints of Ovid's *Heroides.* There, however, the bereft heroines offer specifically directed epistolary complaints to a Jason or an Aeneas. The lovers' complaints that form the focus of much of the love poetry of the four poets discussed in this chapter are less directed and therefore more universal. The titles often indicate that the women compose their works according to a preordained subject. However, though these may be produced as displays of wit and for entertainment, from them can be deduced the central preoccupations, not only of these women, but also of their anonymous female companions, as to the nature and problems of love. In the Renaissance and in the pre-Romantic period poetry was composed according to the rules of poetic decorum rather than as an expression of personal emotion. Nevertheless, the highly personal sonnets of Ramírez reveal that for women poetry served as more than merely literary expression, just as the burlesque sonnets of Quevedo, for example, certainly expressed opinions common to the period in a highly entertaining, if often cruel, way.

These women's sonnets reveal that absence presented particular problems and fears to Hispanic women of the seventeenth century, a preoccupation that should be seen against a social background where men were frequently away, either at court, in the colonies, or at war. Given that women were generally not permitted to choose their suitors, the emotions expressed in these sonnets also represent not only vestiges of the courtly love themes of earlier generations, but also a profound grief at the impossibility of choice for women, an impossibility exemplified by the experience of Sor Violante and Gonçalves de Andrade. One of several poems by Sor Violante dealing with the absent beloved evokes the universal nature of these problems for women by effacing the beloved object to almost complete nonexistence, in a manner reminiscent of Cueva's sonnet apostrophe to impossible Love.

In the *amor cortés* model the male is the active subject and the female the passive object, but in Sor Violante's sonnet the persona is unequivocally female, while the beloved is not gendered. This method of composition creates a number of effects. It suggests that Sor Violante seeks a social world not subject in every aspect to gender constructions, hence broadening the message of her poem beyond that of a mere love sonnet. In effacing the differences between male and female, the nongendered object makes the expression of emotional pain a more universally experienced phenomenon than does the masculine model. Sor Violante rejects the conventional death symptoms as inadequate in expressing the depths of despair suffered by the bereft lover. She determines immediately that the Petrarchan notion of absence as death dealing does not fully explicate the totality of suffering caused by the beloved's absence. For Petrarch, the absent beloved is a rhetorical device through which he reveals his poetic skill. For Sor Violante and her female contemporaries, the expressed misery is more than rhetoric and is worse than death, because it does not end:

> Quien dice que la ausencia es homicida,
> no sabe conocer rigor tan fuerte,
> que si la dura ausencia diera muerte,
> no me matara a mí la propia vida.
>
> 5   Mas ¡ay! que de tus ojos dividida
> la vida me atormenta de tal suerte
> que muriendo sentida de no verte,
> sin verte vivo, por morir sentida.
>
> Pero si de la suerte la mudanza
> 10   es fuerza me asegure la evidencia
> que tanto me dilata una tardanza:
>
> No quede el sentimiento en contingencia,
> que el milagro mayor de la esperanza
> es no rendir la vida a tal ausencia.
>
> *(Rimas varias* (1646) 2)

> Whoever says that absence is a homicide
> does not really know such harsh rigor,
> for if anguished absence were to kill,
> life itself would not be killing me.
>
> But oh, in being separated from your eyes
> life torments me in such a way
> that in dying from feelings of not seeing you,
> I yet live, not seeing you, feeling I'm dying.
>
> But if the vacillation of fate is as
> strong as I am assured it is by the
> evidence I see of such prolonged delay,

feelings cannot endure uncertainty;
the greater miracle of waiting and hoping
is not to surrender my life to that absence.

The hyperbolic death imagery is neither surprising nor unusual, for Sor Violante works within the Petrarchan mode, even though she finds it wanting in this instance. As Leonard Forster has noted, "[a] convention working with hyperbole inevitably utilizes imagery concerned with death: if the lover's longing is not fulfilled he dies" (17). Here, absence is proposed as lethal three times in just the first quartet, and though the death theme continues throughout the sonnet it still proves insufficient to express the persona's overflowing suffering. As she weaves between death and life, she creates a Petrarchan paradox, a purgatory where life and death are conflated. As one is indistinguishable from the other, they parallel Sor Violante's nongendering of the sonnet's absent object as a model for a nongendered world. Suspended between life and death, the speaker concludes in marveling that such a state can be sustained by simple hope: "No quede el sentimiento en contingencia, / que el milagro mayor de la esperanza / es no rendir la vida a tal ausencia" (12–14). The pain of absence is portrayed as entirely the speaker's; there is neither an expression of mutual pain at parting, nor of a cruel *esquivo/a* whose indifference brings death of a different kind. Paradoxically, however, the very ephemeral nature of the beloved reproduces in the reader the absence that the persona elaborates in the sonnet. Thus, instead of the Petrarchan interiority of the speaker's feelings, the pain of parting becomes shared, reflecting the inclusiveness and mutuality of female relationships and female emotional expression. Sor Violante revisits this theme in very similar terms in other sonnets, written in Portuguese, which are not reproduced here, such as "Vida que não acaba de acabar-se" (Life, which never ceases to end itself) and, more particularly, "Se apartada do Corpo a doce vida" (Sweet life leaves the body), which completes a complex rhyme scheme wherein the last word of every line is either *vida* (life) or *morte* (death). This latter sonnet deals with the speaker's love for "Silvano," whose name is reiterated four times in successive lines in the quartets. These sonnets are numbered 21 and 22 in the 1646 edition of the *Rimas varias*.

This participation of the female as the speaking subject of erotic desire has been explored in considerable depth by Deborah Lesko Baker in a study of Louise Labé's poetry. Baker notes that the Sapphic influence (in the French tradition, an expression of intense heterosexual desire) in Labé's first elegy does not erase the Petrarchan presence but works to challenge its exclusivity. Furthermore, Baker highlights Labé's plea for solidarity among women, both in respect of the independent pursuit of study and writing and in relation to their unhappy love relationships (91–98). Labé's volume of prose and poetry was published in 1555, a full century before these Spanish women were voicing their poetic anxieties about love and subjectivity, suggesting a considerable audience, both temporally and geographically.

Similar emotional evocations of absence to those expressed by Sor Violante are seen in a sonnet by Inarda de Arteaga. Here, however, she does not so much seek to share the misery of separation with the beloved as to express it openly and specifically to the absent *amado*, in a desolate poem of desertion. Although she is not central to this study, her work nevertheless warrants inclusion since the sonnet expresses the inequalities between the sexes in terms of the freedom of movement allowed to men but denied to women. The fickle male becomes a shifting periphery to the still center of the bereft speaker. Little is known of Arteaga, who appears to have lived on the cusp of the sixteenth and seventeenth centuries. Her only known works are the sonnet discussed here and an encomiastic *décima* in praise of Agustin de Rojas' *El viaje entretenido:*[7]

Alegres horas de memorias tristes
que, por un breve punto que durastes,
a eterna soledad me condenastes
en pago de un contento que me distes.

Decid: ¿por qué de mí, sin mí, os partistes
sabiendo vos, sin vos, cuál me dejastes?
Y si por do venistes os tornastes,
¿por qué no al mismo punto que vinistes?

7. This *décima* is published in Ana Navaro, ed., *Antología poética de escritoras de los siglos XXVI y XVII* (Madrid: Castalia, 1989).

¡Cuánto fue esta venida deseada
y cuán arrebatada esta venida!
Que, en fin, la mejor hora fue menguada.

No me costastes menos que una vida,
la media en desear vuestra llegada
y la media en llorar vuestra partida.

(BN ms. 3890 120)

Happy hours of sad memories
which, for the brief instant you lingered,
condemned me to eternal solitude
in payment for the contentment you gave me.

Tell me: Why did you go from me, without me,
knowing how, without you, you left me?
And if you can return to whence you came,
why not to this same place return again?

How much this arrival was desired
and how wrenched from me this coming!
In the end even the best hours became withered.

You cost me no less than a life;
half in desiring your coming
and half in lamenting your going.

No other love poem discussed here re-creates so fully the desolation of this poem, which evokes the extended complaint of Penelope to Ulysses in the *Heroides* (Ovid 11–19). Nevertheless, social history provides us with a number of reasons why a woman may have been left by her lover other than through his cruel indifference—among them plague, subsistence crises, the requirements of empire, and the economic decline of the seventeenth century that, for example, decimated the city of Medina del Campo. This decline is enshrined in Cueva's sonnet "Al miserable estado y desdichas de Medina," discussed in Chapter 1.

Arteaga's sonnet is created as a complaining apostrophe, epistolary in its personal nature, in which the opening line encapsulates the story of the persona's lost love in an image of past happiness and present sadness. The speaker plays with time and emotions, as momentary pleasure brings her a lifetime of sadness, and *horas* functions both in terms of remembered pleasure and present misery. Without the lover the persona's life has ceased to move forward, condemning her to an eternity of waiting and complaining that must have been the lot of many women whose menfolk went to war or to the New World, never to return.[8] The loneliness of the speaker, together with the cessation of both life and pleasurable emotion, is emphasized in the retrospective nature of the language and in the ebb and flow of arrival and departure. A succession of polysyllabic verbs end each line, adding a sobbing, sighing quality. The frequent linking of the two protagonists in *vos* and *mí* continually returns the reader to the cause of the speaker's distress as it reiterates the joy of meeting and the pain of parting. Here the speaker differs from Petrarch and from patriarchal gender norms, for the sonnet's terminology of meeting and parting suggests personal and sexual intimacy. Therefore, the most painful aspect for the speaker is her ignorance of the cause of this desertion and the male lover's cruelty, revealed in his awareness of, and lack of concern for, the pain that his desertion will cause: "Decid: ¿por qué de mí, sin mí, os partistes / sabiendo vos, sin vos, cual me dejastes?" (5–6). This creates an unbridgeable gulf between female expectation of honorable masculine behavior, supposedly the norm, and the reality of the male beloved's perfidy and slipperiness in discarding the persona seemingly without effort. The speaker attempts to reason with the object of her love; if he can leave one place to come to her, and then leave her, why can he not return again to her side?: "Y si por do venistes os tornastes, / ¿por qué no al mismo punto que vinistes?" (7–8).

The tercets bring *desengaño* and resignation to her fate, as she admits that the enduring absence of her lost lover has caused even her happiest

8. Antonio Domínguez Ortíz provides detailed evidence of the subsistence crises and successive epidemics of plague at the beginning, middle and towards the end of the century. He also reveals Spain's loss of manpower through the expulsion of the Moriscos (Valencia, for example, had its population reduced to 40% of pre-expulsion levels). Apart from this there were losses through war, service to the empire in the Low Countries, Naples and the New World, as well as defense of Spain's own boundaries. His data show a marked decline in the decade 1640–50. The population does not begin to rise again until after 1680 and in 1700 is still far from recouping its 1596 level of 8.5 million, reaching only 7 million for the whole of Spain. Domínguez Ortiz, *La sociedad*, 101–13.

memories to wane and lose their sustaining force. Again, the loss of love is identified with loss of life. In the typical hyperbole of the love sonnet the speaker claims that the absent *galán* has consumed her entire life, divided between desire and grief. However, even within the context of conscious artistic representations of Petrarchan love, when the speaker of a female-authored poem suggests that one undying love has consumed her life, she challenges the conventional gender expectations of her era. Similarly, Ann Rosalind Jones has observed of Mary Wroth's "Pamphilia" that Wroth's abandoned woman turns her humiliating position into proof of her heroic constancy (*Currency* 143). Since women were regarded by Church, science, and moralists alike as helpless in the toils of their own physiology, and therefore weak-headed, mutable, moody, and easily seduced if left to their own devices, any statement by a woman that women could sustain loyal devotion in the face of fickle masculinity represents an important stand against traditional views of feminine *mudanza*.

That women should feel the pain of extreme grief and loss seems to have been lost on male poets and writers. The privileging of male grief to the exclusion of female affective identity, thus refusing women the possibility of Petrarchan subjecthood, has been discussed at length by Juliana Schiesari. Schiesari describes this preeminent male loss as conferring on the male subject a melancholic heroism quite denied the female. However, Schiesari has also noted, in reading Renaissance Italian women poets, that they revise the tradition by rejecting "the metaphysical figure of woman as a mere icon of male desire." Schiesari asks what happens when the female as "a mere pretext for a melancholic voice" becomes herself the "I" of the poem (166–67). This question is in part answered by Ann Rosalind Jones's discussion of the silent Ovidian heroines, Echo and Philomel, who, in the hands of Gaspara Stampa, no longer merely listen, but become speakers of their own desires and accusers of the "cruelly absorbed lover" ("New Songs" 268–69). Schiesari affirms that the mourning of loss in women's verse becomes a broader mourning for the lost possibilities that women suffer under patriarchal dominance, due to "their lack of an accredited lack" (169).

In seventeenth-century Spain it was still fashionable to write love poetry that acknowledged the Petrarchan mode. However, the sonnets discussed here show that while women were aware of the requirements of

Petrarchan verse, they subscribed to them in small measure. Instead, they provided their female speakers with an objective, external view of love, or with the means to speak of the harsh reality of female loneliness in the absence of the beloved that elucidates the objectification of women under both Petrarchan poetics and the patriarchal seventeenth-century reality with which they lived. However, an altogether more positive aspect of these women's writing can be seen when they appropriate the masculine subject in order to show their ingenuity and education.

TRANSVESTITE SUBJECTS

Many of the sonnets written by seventeenth-century female poets were written specifically to participate in a canon that conventional wisdom about female intelligence regarded as impossible, and to display to a male audience women's ability to write successful poetry in the masculine mode. These aims required careful poetic organization, as has also been noted by Olivares and Boyce with regard to poetry by Cueva: "[T]iene en cuenta siempre al lector hombre y los decretos del género; implícitamente solicita su aprobación de lo bien que ella los obedece, de lo bien que escribe como hombre e imita su poesía amorosa" (*Espejo* 24–25; She always has the male reader in mind and the rules of the genre; she implicitly solicits their approbation of her success in obeying them, of how well she writes like a man and imitates their amorous poetry). To be able to pass herself off as a capable and witty male poet gives the lie to the idea of the female as an inferior male. Cueva is in no position to change the social system within which she lives, but neither does she always write within the masculine system. That she demonstrates her awareness of and capacity to engage in this type of writing only makes more meaningful the poems in which she writes against the masculine canon.

Cueva is not alone in writing sonnets in the male voice. Both Marcia Belisarda and Sor Violante del Cielo also write mimetic sonnets that reflect masculine fantasies about women and desire. Cueva, in a sonnet entitled "Introduce un galán desfavorecido de su dama, quejándose de su crueldad" (Introducing a gallant, out of favor with his lady and complaining of her cruelty), engages in all the Petrarchan ploys of her male contemporaries in portraying the male lover as involved in battle, besieging the beloved. Marcia Belisarda, the poet who most celebrates reason, joins Cueva in writing a sonnet that takes the male view, entitled "Para una novela" (For a novel), but she goes further in creating a typically masculine description of the fickle and mutable woman which, from the pen of a woman poet, takes on a distinctly ironic tone. This is in stark contrast to her sonnet "Si no impide mi amor el mismo cielo" (If heaven itself does not impede my love), where, in adopting a male voice, she resorts to reason to control a love disdained. However, Sor Violante, the most poetically accomplished, treats love more conventionally as an incurable disease in a sonnet entitled "Para el amor no hay remedio" (There's no remedy for love), included in the eighteenth-century British Library manuscript but not in the *Rimas varias,* suggesting a later date for its composition than 1646.

Cueva's title, "Introduce un galán desfavorecido de su dama, quejándose de su crueldad," makes clear her intention to write a traditional love sonnet in the *amor cortés* mode, expressed by a male lover ruled by passion, with the *esquiva* (disdainful woman) as the object of desire:

> Basta el desdén y bastan los rigores,
> Clori, no más crueldad, no más enojos.
> Serena un poco tus divinos ojos
> y suspende sus rayos matadores.
>
> 5 Cesen desprecios, cesen disfavores,
> Que por flores no es bien que des abrojos
> a quien te rinde un alma, por despojos,
> no indigna de gozar tus favores.
>
> ¡Ah ingrata Clori! ¡Ah ingrata, que a mis quejas
> 10 tienes el alma y pecho de diamante!
> y parece que vives con mi muerte.
>
> Mas, cruel Clori, aunque penar me dejas,
> y aunque me matas, he de estar constante,
> con tu desdén luchando hasta vencerte.
>
> (ms. 4127: 237)

> Enough disdain and enough of your hardness,
> Clori, no more cruelty, no more anger.

Calm a little your divine eyes, and
stop their homicidal rays.

Stop the criticisms, cease your disfavor,
It is wrong to exchange thistles for flowers
when he who surrenders you his soul as spoils
is not unworthy to enjoy your favor.

Oh ungrateful Clori! Oh ingrate, who turns a
diamond heart and soul to my complaints!
It seems that you live off my death.

But, cruel Clori, although you leave me to suffer,
and though you kill me, I shall be constant in
battling your disdain until I win you.

Here, the persona declares himself of sufficient rank to court Clori:
". . . te rinde un alma, por despojos, / no indìgna de gozar de tus favores"
(6–8); the quartets call for a truce in the war with repeated imperatives:
"Basta/bastan, serena, suspende, cesen," while the tercets reiterate the traditional, courtly love imagery of the cruel beauty: "¡Ah ingrata Clori! ¡Ah
ingrata, que a mis quejas / tienes el alma y pecho de diamante! / y parece
que vives con mi muerte" (9–11). The lover converts Clori into a parasite,
whose power and beauty are enhanced in direct proportion to the life
she extracts from him. The first line of this tercet is cleverly structured;
in employing melodic rhythm and a succession of synelephas a sustained
cry of pain is directed to Clori's diamantine obduracy, yet the highly hyperbolic language of the sonnet, coupled with the poet's use of the ven-
triloquized male voice, undercuts its message of pain, converting it into a
mockery of the sonneteer's traditional complaint.

Similarly, Marcia Belisarda's sonnet "Para una novela" reiterates male
views of emotionally labile and morally untrustworthy women. The use
of the subjunctive in the first quartet suggests that the speaker is rehears-
ing an apparent outburst by the absent lover, also named "Clori":

En suspiros y llanto arroje el pecho
la causa que ocasiona mi dolencia,
aunque tras sí con rígida violencia
se lleve el corazón pedazos hecho.

5 Destiérranme de Clori, a mi despecho,
 celos que ésta me intiman cruel sentencia,
 mas su gusto matando con la ausencia
 ha de quedar mi agravio satisfecho.

 Pues a otro dueño concedieron palma
10 de amor ¡oh ingrata, aleve!, tus favores,
 a tu ruego cual áspid ser intento,

 cerrando en mis oídos puerta al alma,
 porque bien no se sirve a dos señores
 si no es teniendo al uno mal contento.

         (BN ms. 7469: 57v)

Though the cause of my suffering
may rend her breast in sighs and tears,
behind her, with hard violence,
are dragged the shards of a broken heart.

Jealousy has exiled me from Clori,
who pronounces my cruel sentence,
but in killing her pleasure with my absence
I shall have my grievances satisfied.

Since you conceded the palm of your love
and favors to another, oh treacherous ingrate!,
I shall try to be an asp to your pleas,

closing in my ears the door to my soul,
for it is impossible to serve two masters
without making one of them discontented.

  The speaker does not clarify whose heart is broken in the first quartet. Indeed, the whole sonnet is deliberately ambiguous, blurring subject, object, and gender expectations. Hence, Clori, if she is the object, may be dragging her own broken heart, as is suggested by the sighs and tears, or the heart of the rejected lover behind her. The "telling" of the story of Clori justifies the title but also suggests, in its novelty, that this poet seeks to undercut a message which, on the surface, is denigratory of the female and sympathetic to the male. Legal terminology in the second quartet, incorporating sentencing, exile, and the satisfaction of a grievance, gestures again to the Petrarchan mode, but also to the world of men, since women have no part in the justice system.

The irony Marcia Belisarda inserts into her sonnet points to the burlesquing of male love poetry, for here it is Clori who dispenses a "justice" considered utterly unjust by the speaker. Although the speaker indicates that he has no choice but to accept his plight, in the tercets he turns to first-person discourse in order to castigate Clori directly. The structure is also strained, for although the rhyme scheme remains dedicated to the tercet norm, the intention of the poet is clearly to separate the castigation of Clori into paired lines. The first pair accuse, the next express the lover's intentions, and the final two provide a biblical proverb as a warning to fickle lovers. Again there is mockery in the tercets. The aggrieved male will become an asp in rejecting a beloved who has already rejected him in the quartets. It is his ears that will close the way to his soul, rather than the conventional eyes: an allusion, perhaps, to the verbal excesses with which women were charged. This woman, however, is silent and the tercets await instead her pleas for forgiveness. The adoption of the unusual figure of the deaf "áspid" further supports my contention that this sonnet takes issue with masculine dominance and pretensions, as the poet/nun resorts to the Psalms to undermine the injured dignity of the speaker: "The wicked go astray from the womb, they err from their birth speaking lies. They have venom like the venom of a serpent, like the deaf adder that stops its ear, so that it does not hear the voice of charmers or of the cunning enchanter" (Psalm 8: 3–4). The rebuffed lover becomes the butt of feminine criticism, for this psalm begins: "Do you indeed decree what is right, you gods?" Rather than castigate the "ingrata," the poet subtly suggests that the male lover is equally at fault.

Remaining with Scripture, the poet concludes in the New Testament. She quotes from the Sermon on the Mount to affirm that in the fiction of the poetic love debate it is not the woman who is master, but always the male: "No one can serve two masters; for either he will hate the one and love the other, or he will be devoted to the one and despise the other" (Matthew 6: 24). In making Clori the servant of two masters, the speaker overplays his hand: in the *amor cortés* tradition, it is the female beloved who is the nominal master of the suffering lover/servant. The sonnet finishes, therefore, in reality. Whether or not Clori has two "masters," she remains in the position of inferiority. Marcia Belisarda exposes the masculine love complaint as a rhetorical sham and women as simply pawns in political, economic, and familial alliances.

In such works, Cueva and Marcia Belisarda write in carefully crafted homage to the masculine art of sonnet writing, while subtly criticizing the system they appear to emulate. In contrast, Sor Violante defies structural conventions in pursuing the love-as-disease theme in her sonnet "Para el amor no hay remedio" (There is no cure for love), which sustains ten alliterative and repetitive lines:

> ¿Qué importa Lisi que mi amor ofendas?
> ¿Qué importa amor que mi dolor aumentes?
> ¿Qué importa duelo que mi sangre afrentes?
> ¿Qué importa llanto que mi fuego enciendas?
>
> 5 ¿Qué importa muerte que mi fin pretendas?
> ¿Qué importa pena que mi agravio alientes?
> ¿Qué importa honor que mi venganza intentes?
> ¿Qué importa duda que mi ofensa entiendas?
>
> ¿Qué importa celos que abrazéis mi pecho?
> 10 ¿Qué importa pruebas que digáis mi engaño?
> ¿Qué importa estar en lágrimas deshecho?
>
> Si aunque de todo tengo el desengaño
> está ya por mi mal el daño hecho
> y no encuentro remedio por el daño.
>
> (BN ms. 32353 n. pag.)

> Does it matter, Lisi, that you wound my love?
> Does love matter if you augment my pains?
> Does it matter that I suffer if you affront my blood?
> Does weeping matter, with which you light my fire?
>
> Does death matter, that you seek my end?
> Does suffering matter, that you inflame my pain?
> Does honor matter, that you tempt my vengeance?
> Does doubt matter, that you understand my offense?

Does jealousy matter, that burns my heart?
Do proofs matter, that you deceive me?
Does it matter to be dissolved in tears?

Although I am disenchanted by it all,
the damage, to my sorrow, is now done
and I find no remedy for my wound.

These piled questions enumerate all the symptoms of the Petrarchan disease of love: "dolor," "duelo," "llanto," "muerte," "pena," "duda" and "celos," including a typical paradox: "¿Qué importa llanto que mi fuego enciendas?" That they overflow the usual octet/sestet structure only serves to emphasize the disordered mental state of the male lover. Yet, at the same time, the repeated "Qué importa" detracts from the Petrarchan message and reveals a more disillusioned attitude to love in the final tercet: "Si aunque de todo tengo el desengaño / está ya por mi mal el daño hecho" (12–13). Ultimately, Baroque *desengaño* proves insufficient to cure the ills of the lover; the final line returns him to the helplessness of his plight: "y no encuentro remedio por el daño" (14). Arguing through the causes of his pain does not bring the relief he seeks. The sonnet collapses back into the helplessness of Petrarchan engagement, with the speaker unable to achieve his ends or to let them go.

In simultaneously utilizing the courtly love mode while altering the structure so as to reinforce the despair felt by the persona, Sor Violante emasculates him; he does not take control of the beloved nor cast her aside, showing a distinct lack of *hombría*. However, this sonnet cannot be read purely from the point of view of the masculine persona, for there is no way of knowing whether Sor Violante intended her speaker to be male, in spite of the female object and the traditionally Petrarchan theme. It was this gender ambiguity in her works that caused nineteenth-century scholars to question her sexuality, as has already been discussed. However, women writing in this male field were compelled to utilize the tropes that indicated their ability to do so, for the pattern was already set for them. Gerda Lerner makes the same point about women's marginal position in a history written by men (*History* 52–53).

The question of the persona is also left unresolved by Marcia Belisarda and Leonor de la Cueva. By writing in the male mode they broaden the perspective of the reader and make a space for themselves as authors and for their female companions as audience. Preconceived notions of female inferiority cannot be brought into the equation. Furthermore, they efface the differences, perpetuated in male-authored works, that situate women only as the manipulated object of their masculine fantasies. When women participate in these poetic activities as readers, they too participate in the debate about women; hence the choice of speaking subject becomes critically important to the understanding of women's position in the patriarchal scheme. This shifting voice—masculine, feminine, or neither of these—is an enabling strategy in altering women's perceptions of their own worth and capabilities.

When Marcia Belisarda writes mimetic sonnets in the male voice, she goes further than to appropriate an existing mode, either for purposes of display or criticism. She also resorts to the male prerogative of reason, as in her sonnet entitled "A consonantes forzosos sobre que habían escrito sonetos con asuntos diferentes diferentes personas, diéronme por asunto no desmayar a vista de un desdén" (In set rhyme about how different people having written sonnets on different matters, I have been given the topic of not swooning in the face of a rebuff):

> Si no impide mi amor el mismo cielo,
> no bastarán cuantos rigores miro
> a ponerle del alma en el retiro,
> porque en razón fundado toma vuelo.
>
> 5 Y aunque cansarte en porfiar recelo
> y en querer porfiar de mí me admiro,
> la causa del dolor porque suspiro
> no admite de temor prisión de hielo.
>
> Si mi gusto no logra sus antojos,
> 10 por negarles tus ojos luces bellas,
> y en vez de amor me pagas con enojos,
>
> no formaré de algún rigor querellas,
> sino sólo, Jacinta, de tus ojos,
> puesto que están conformes las estrellas.
>
> (BN ms. 7469 18r)

If heaven itself cannot stop my love,
then no matter how many rigors I see they're
not enough to put her from my soul into seclusion,
for love founded on reason takes flight.

Though I may tire you in enduring mistrust
and though I astonish myself in wanting to persist,
the cause of the pain that makes me sigh
will not admit the icy prison of fear.

If my desires do not achieve what they seek,
since they are denied the lovely light of your eyes
and instead of love you pay me with disdain,

I shall not form a quarrel from such rigor,
except only, Jacinta, of your eyes,
given that they are aligned with the stars.

For Marcia Belisarda, the masculine *yo* justifies her appeal to reason, yet her authorship undermines the presumed masculine supremacy and questions its gendered suppositions. Here Marcia Belisarda is again writing within an "academy" of her companions; hence she does not adopt the love-as-war theme favored by Cueva, the legal arguments of her own sonnet to Clori, or the love-as-disease theme used by Sor Violante. Instead, she begins with a conditional that links the poet-nun to the voice of her speaker: "Si no impide mi amor el mismo cielo." However, with or without heaven's sanction, the persona determines to employ reason as a cure for the ills of disdain and the passions of love, as the remainder of the quartet reveals: "no bastarán cuántos rigores miro, / a ponerle del alma en el retiro, / porque en razón fundado toma vuelo" (2–4).

This opening does not sound like the complaint of a distracted and rebuffed lover, but suggests instead the application of reason and intelligence to the will, as favored by religious meditation techniques. It is such an approach that enables the speaker not to "desmayar a vista de un desdén." Nevertheless, Marcia Belisarda pursues the traditional line of the hapless lover, painfully imprisoned in the icy disdain of the beloved: "la causa del dolor porque suspiro / no admite de temor prisión de hielo" (7–8). This prison is not the paradoxically burning ice of the Petrarchan love lyric; it is transparent and friable, engendering the hope that the prison itself may be melted in the warmth of a mutual gaze.

In Marcia Belisarda's sonnet reason conquers the pain of unrequited love. The final line links the religious aspect of the first line to astrological thinking: "no formaré de algún rigor querellas, / sino sólo, Jacinta, de tus ojos, / puesto que están conformes las estrellas" (12–14). If the stars are appropriately aligned, the lover hopes to achieve his desires, but in order to see the stars he seeks in vain Jacinta's eyes. Hence his only complaint is to be denied the eyes through which he seeks to discover his fate. In Renaissance love theory the gaze consisted of beams passing directly from the soul through the eyes. When lovers' eyes met, their souls also joined in mutual harmony. Marcia Belisarda links Jacinta's gaze to the heavens and to the soul, only to find that, while reason brings a measure of control, it is not quite enough to quell the passions. Nevertheless, the artful nature of this construct, in which she solves an emotional "problem" with reason, is entirely undercut by the title's clear indication that the sonnet itself is a work of reason and wit, a clever and rhythmic piece of artifice that completes a philosophical excursion through the powers of the soul, not in religious contemplation but in play. Her artfulness in no way deprives her poem of its message that women are capable of reason. In fact, the message is enhanced by the apparent ease with which reason can be employed.

Marcia Belisarda's appeal to reason is repeated in her paired sonnets to and from the "dama seglar" (secular lady) to be discussed below. While reason places her in a masculine space, the appeals to heaven, stars, and the soul return Marcia Belisarda to her convent and her religious companions. Conversely, Cueva, in "Introduce un galán desfavorecido de su dama, quejándose de su crueldad," already discussed, and perhaps because she may be writing for male readers, finds in her *galán* the moral strength and fiber lacking in the *galanes* of her other sonnets, where men are frequently found wanting. In her conclusion, Cueva celebrates male courage and constancy in the war of love, ranging Clori's murderous attitude with the *amante's* siege methods: "y aunque me matas, he de estar constante" (13). In the process, the poet tells her male readers that, like Chaucer's Wife of Bath, her speaker knows what women want, and that is to have control of their menfolk. However, where Chaucer frames this as a negative characteristic, buttressing his argument with the words of

St. Paul, Cueva affirms that women admire persistence and constancy in their male contemporaries.

While these women show their capacity to write in the field of male love poetry, they go further in composing male-voiced sonnets in which the *yo* frequently expresses frustration and jealousy in the face of firm controlled female modesty. In so doing they extol the dignity and moral worth of their formless and silent female objects, and hold up to scrutiny the generally low opinion of women held by men. The commonplace of female inferiority was reinforced over and over by the concordance of Aristotelian teachings, Renaissance medical theories, and the teachings of the Church.[9] However, these poets mock the Aristotelian and Galenic view of females as inferior or deformed males, doomed to reduced mental and physical capacity by reason of their cold moist humors. Instead, the male, whether subject or object, is imbued with all the undesirable characteristics normally attributed to women, being emotional, garrulous, flirtatious, unfaithful, and irrational. In contrast, women are portrayed as rational and morally strong, and all this within the role cast for them by men of chaste silence. For example, in Cueva's "Soneto a Floris" (Sonnet to Floris) the cause of the male lover's dilemma is not the *mujer esquiva,* but her absence, as "he" indicates in the opening lines:

> Ausente estoy de tus divinos ojos;
> en fin, ausente y lleno de desvelos.
> Si al ausencia cruel siguen los celos,
> confieso, Floris, que me dan enojos.
>
> 5 ¡Ay! ¡Quién gozara de tus rayos rojos
> sin tantos sobresaltos y desvelos!
> Pues mientras duran los nublosos velos
> ¡He de tener la rienda a mis antojos!
>
> ¿Cuándo se ha de acabar, Floris divina,
> 10 La rigurosa pena de no verte
> Y el cobarde temor de tu mudanza?

9. For a detailed exposition of the Renaissance theories of female inferiority, see Ian Maclean, *The Renaissance Notion of Woman: A Study in the Fortunes of Scholasticism and Medical Science in European Intellectual Life* (Cambridge and New York: Cambridge University Press, 1980).

Que aunque eres en firmeza peregrina,
vive mi amor dudoso de perderte,
aunque más le sustenta la esperanza.

                              (BN ms. 4127 188)

Absent am I from your divine eyes;
In truth, absent, sleepless, and full of cares.
If cruel absence is followed by jealousy,
I confess, Floris, that jealousy troubles me.

Ah! Who could enjoy your radiant rays
without suffering upsets and sleepless nights!
But while the cloudy veils endure
I have to keep a rein on my desires!

When will it end, divine Floris,
this rigorous pain of not seeing you
and the cowardly fear of your fickleness?

For while you're rare in your firmness,
my love lives in doubts about losing you,
though it sustains itself with hope.

Without access to the mutual gaze the speaker cannot enumerate Floris's charms, and his struggle for self-control in the quartets suggests his banishment, as does his plaintive cry in the tercets: "¿Cuándo se ha de acabar, Floris divina . . . ?" (9). This concrete absence moves the mood away from contemplation, for the speaker has nothing to contemplate. Nevertheless, his revelation in the quartets of the devastating effect of her eyes shows that they dominate him, whether he can see them or not. This mistress is entirely the master of his passion: "¡Ay! ¡Quién gozara de tus rayos rojos / sin tantos sobresaltos y desvelos!" (5–6).

The inevitable effect of the absence is to arouse the male speaker's suspicions as to the beloved's actions; there can be no trust in a system that insists on women's congenital inability to control themselves. At the same time, Cueva attributes emotions normally applied to the female to the suffering lover: he is jealous, he is irritated by the separation, and he suffers unresolved "antojos" (cravings, especially those of a pregnant woman) and cowardly fears. Even though he demonstrates all the typical symptoms of the Petrarchan lover, being sleepless, sick with worry, and depressed by separation from the beloved, it all comes down to control. If he is not able to see the beloved, he is immediately assailed by the certainty that she is being unfaithful. The necessity to curb physical desire is doubly expressed with a delightful pun on *detener* (to detain) at the end of the quartets that both pulls him up and lets him go: "¡He de tener la rienda [tener la rienda = to give a horse his head] a mis antojos!" (8).

Pregnant with desire, the male lover is filled with doubts and uncertainties represented in the "nublosos velos" of absence that come between him and the sun of his beloved and in his fear of feminine *mudanza*. By contrast, the female subject is "peregrina" in her "firmeza," as Cueva again erases the differences between the sexes. The female object neither entices nor denies, nor does she have shape or color, except for the "rayos rojos" of her commanding eyes. Rather than a cool and virginal moon, Cueva's "rayos" suggest she is the sun, too dazzling to look at, as she moves and determines the diurnal round. A pun on "peregrina" (rare and beautiful but also a pilgrim or a traveler) notes Floris's rare qualities and also creates a paradox: she is both firm and mobile. The fears of the lover are finally soothed, as in Sor Violante's earlier sonnet, by hope: "Aunque más le sustenta la esperanza" (14). Like Everyman, the speaker finds that only hope remains after every other emotion and quality has been expended. This is not the only sonnet in which Cueva feminizes the male lover. In another gloss, entitled "Glosa—Todo lo pierde quien lo quiere todo" (Gloss: Who wants everything loses everything), Cueva's speaker tells a cautionary tale of the fate awaiting the mutable male lover:

> Muestra Galicio que a Leonarda adora,
> y con segura y cierta confianza
> promete que en su fe no habrá mudanza,
> que el ser mudable su firmeza ignora.
>
> 5   Mas de su amor a la segunda aurora
> muda su pensamiento y su esperanza,
> y sin tener del bien desconfianza,
> publica que Elia sola le enamora.

Con gran fineza, aunque si bien fingida,
10   a Leonarda da el alma por despojos,
y luego con un falso y nuevo modo

dice que es Elia el dueño de su vida.
Pues oiga un desengaño a sus antojos:
Todo lo pierde quien lo quiere todo.

(BN ms. 4127 206)

Galicio shows that he adores Leonarda
and with secure and certain confidence
promises that he is unshakable in his constancy,
that his firmness knows no mutability.

But a second aurora arouses his love,
moves his thoughts and his hopes,
and without doubting his success
he proclaims that he loves only Elia.

With great and well-feigned goodwill
he gives Leonarda the spoils of his soul,
then, with a false and new manner,

says that it is Elia who's the mistress of his life.
But hear this disappointment of his desires:
He who wants everything loses everything.

The speaking subject is unable to focus on only one beloved object, too feeble and dishonorable to choose between the two. Cueva delivers a moral proverb in the final gloss: he who wants everything loses everything.

Navigating in the narrow space between intellectual expression and undesirable and damaging fame, women like Cueva, Sor Violante, and Marcia Belisarda, in adopting the male persona, reveal their capacity to see the love debate from the other side of the mirror, to join the male speaker who holds up the image of his beautiful beloved as an image of self-worship. In the process the mirror becomes subtly distorted and opportunities are thus created to circumnavigate the limits on female speech. Writing of the power of discourse, Luce Irigaray has noted how female sexuality is never defined with respect to any sex but the masculine. Such a definition usually provides a negative image that offers male sexuality "an unfailingly phallic self-representation" (69–70). What these poets reveal in their male-voiced sonnets is that they too take issue with these negative assumptions. They reflect on the shortcomings of the love debate, particularly its one-sided nature, as well as on commonplace masculine presumptions about the female intellect. Furthermore, as they employ and lampoon masculine expression, they challenge gendered opinions of writing women as *varonil* (masculine).

LOVE AND SELF-KNOWLEDGE

The constant theme in the love poetry by these female poets, even as it ranges over a variety of topics and styles, is that men and women were not as different as contemporary scientific and religious teaching suggested. The poets argue that both sexes are capable of transgressing norms, of emotional attachment, and, more importantly, of reason, and therefore of learning by experience. Cueva, for example, writes a series of sonnets *a petición* (by request) in which the female speakers acknowledge their own moral defects, discovered through the *desengaño* engendered by dishonorable male conduct. This realization brings them to a state of independence and freedom. Cueva, as a secular poet, expresses *desengaño* as representing lived experience in the less than satisfactory interchange between the sexes. Marcia Belisarda, the religious, espouses an intellectual debate with the distance of considered wisdom.

Marcia Belisarda writes an exchange between a *galán* and a *dama seglar* (secular lady) in a pair of sonnets that utilize similar terms to argue the same point from opposed sides, in the Scholastic manner. Since, as the poet herself points out, the *dama*'s response deploys the same language, it is clear that the sonnets are written as an exercise in intelligence and wit. However, this does not dilute the message of reason and intelligence that Marcia Belisarda wishes to convey.[10] Adding to the impression that she wishes to join a philosophical debate about physical appetite and its con-

---

10. Belisarda also writes *décimas* and a *romance melancólico* to *pensamiento* (respectively 53v and 31r of Ms. 7469). The *décimas,* particularly, deal with memory, intellect and will, while the *romance* determines that wrong thinking brings the ill of which she thinks.

trol, the author/nun emphatically distances herself from the persona in the first sonnet, insisting that it is the *galán* speaker who addresses a *dama seglar.* The second sonnet, which responds to and refutes the argument of the first, locates the *dama seglar* in a superior position to the "male" speaker of the first sonnet. It is she who argues from reason, from the rational soul, while the *galán* argues for satisfaction of the appetite:

> Mal haya un apetito refrenado,
> un disimulo y un encogimiento,
> un recato, un temor, un desaliento,
> para que se interprete un hombre honrado.
>
> 5   Si en el tiempo fatal se halla el cuitado
> hecho Tántalo al husmo del contento,
> agresor general de pensamiento
> sin que a la parte se le dé traslado.
>
> Yo por huir de aqueste inconveniente
> 10   digo que sois el norte de mi vida,
> sois el incendio que mi amor inflama
>
> Y en consecuencia de lo antecedente
> esta alma alborozada se convida
> a ser la mariposa de esa llama.
>
>   (BN ms. 7469 n. pag.)

> A restricted appetite is an ill thing,
> a pretence, a shrinking away,
> a withdrawal, a fear, a loss of spirit,
> thus it's to be explained by an honorable man.
>
> As in the time of the Fates the unfortunate finds
> himself made a Tantalus at the whiff of pleasure,
> it is an aggressor to all thought, since he
> cannot move himself to that part.
>
> And to flee from this inconvenience,
> I say that you are my life's North,
> you are the fire which my love inflames

And as a consequence of the foregoing
this rejoicing soul invites you
to be the moth to that flame.

In this first sonnet the male speaker argues for base satisfaction as
a positively masculine quality: "Mal haya un apetito refrenado" (1). He
inserts the fate of Tantalus in the second quartet as a sort of cautionary
tale; if left unsatisfied, desire will dominate the man's ability to think
rationally and therefore to develop his *pensamiento*. Reason is purport-
ed to be the dominating difference between male and female, for wom-
en are "burdened with passionate humors and wandering wombs, both
of which are unchecked by (male) reason, and . . . they are disabled by
the lack of a phallus, which renders them wounded or deficient males"
(P. Smith 16–17). In this sonnet, Marcia Belisarda's *galán* puts medieval
medical theories to his own use. Rather than reining in the appetite by
resorting to reason, he instead seeks to satisfy appetite as a means of paci-
fying the animal side of his nature and thereby allowing his *pensamiento*
to take control. This sophistical argument sees the male speaker attempt
to appropriate both action and contemplation to his own benefit.

In the classical myth, Tantalus is castigated for offending the gods.
His punishment is purely at the sensual and physical level; he is placed in
a pool to his neck but cannot drink from it, fruits are tossed by the wind
from his reach and he is driven both by physical frustration and the need
for survival. Marcia Belisarda's *galán* seeks to avoid the fate of Tantalus
by persuading the "fruits" that he desires, the sexual favors of the *dama,*
that restraint is unhealthy and that she should place herself within his
reach. Yet, by focusing his argument on bodily cravings, Marcia Belisarda
denies him reason and intelligence, and feminizes his argument: men are
expected to be practiced in the art of conversation, while wheedling per-
suasion and logorrhea are what males complain of in women.

By expressing his desire for the *dama,* by making her the "norte" of
his "vida," and inviting himself to dance in her flame, the *galán* opens
himself to the fate that he seeks to avoid. In the first tercet there is confusion as to the indirect object of the action in its final line: "Yo por huir
de aqueste inconveniente / digo que sois el norte de mi vida, / sois el in-
cendio que mi amor inflama" (9–11). Either his inflamed love breathes

on and intensifies the *dama*'s fire, or the heat of her nearness engenders a burning desire in the *galán*. The two conventional images create a circularity in which, as the Petrarchan moth of the lover's soul breathes on and poeticizes the beloved object, he also seeks to awaken her own flame. However, the "esta alma / esa llama" of the final line creates a distance between the lover and the *dama* that the *galán* cannot bridge. In this sonnet, Marcia Belisarda deliberately gives no space to the silent, invisible *dama;* since the *galán* and the *dama* are engaged in Scholastic debate, she allows him to speak, uninterrupted, while she ponders her response.

In the second sonnet the *dama* demonstrates her rational and intellectual control of the argument and makes clear in the second quartet that the ideas she espouses are her own:

> Bien haya un apetito refrenado,
> que en ocasiones el encogimiento
> no es cobardía, menos desaliento,
> cuerdo reparo sí de un hombre honrado.
>
> 5   Presumo que de juicio está menguado
> aquél que a ejecuciones el contento
> atribuye, si ya de pensamiento
> no es del mismo apetito vil traslado.
>
> Para mi gusto es este inconveniente
> 10   y es conveniente, pues, para la vida
> de mi amor que le templa y no le inflama.
>
> Esto supuesto de lo antecedente
> no vive, a lo primero se convida
> y al fin de noble amor solo se llama.
>
>   (BN ms. 7469 n. pag.)

> A restrained appetite is a good thing,
> for on occasion a shrinking is not
> cowardice, nor is it lack of spirit,
> but the wise caution of an honorable man.
>
> I presume that it is diminished judgment
> which attributes contentment to

actions, if this vile appetite is not
yet removed from one's thinking.

This inconvenience is to my taste, and it is
convenient, then, for the life of my love,
that you should soothe and not inflame it.

That assumption of the foregoing will
not survive; at first one invites and
at the end calls only for a noble love.

The *dama* argues that to control physical desire is the most intelligent recourse for a man of honor, yet the code of *hombría* determines that a man must gain honor through prowess. Furthermore, the *dama* expresses the philosophical view that contemplation is preferable to action, particularly when the pursuit is purely for physical satisfaction. In doing so, Marcia Belisarda's feminine voice adopts an ideally masculine role. The *dama* ignores the body to privilege the mind and the intelligence, and does not shrink from expressing her own preference for the Christian ideal of containment toward which a rational man should naturally strive, as the opening of the sestet reveals: "Para mi gusto es este inconveniente / y es conveniente, pues, para la vida / de mi amor que le templa y no le inflama" (9–11). In advising the *galán* to exercise appropriate control, to warm her passions rather than to kill them with excessive heat, the *dama* neither rejects nor invites him, but maintains a balancing control, demanding of him the most noble and pure love. In a neat wordplay on *llama/llamarse* (meaning both a flame and to call or name), Marcia Belisarda converts the flame of the *galán*'s final word to a call for more noble aspirations in love: "Esto supuesto de lo antecedente / no vive, a lo primero se convida / y al fin de noble amor solo se llama" (12–14).

It is clear that in these sonnets Marcia Belisarda demonstrates her ability to enter the male realm of philosophical debate. In privileging matter over form in the *galán*'s argument, she professes a manifesto of equality, where irrationality and the irksome demands of the body are shared and not women's alone. Conversely, the *dama* employs Church doctrine to argue for containment of the passions for the good of the soul. She therefore takes on the role of priest or confessor who stands as a mediator between the sinner and God and who employs doctrine in his preaching to educate his flock and to ensure orthodoxy. In using the same terms to create two opposing arguments, Marcia Belisarda demonstrates the inherently deceptive nature of the masculine art of rhetoric and the fickleness and slipperiness of language. She proves that a practiced rhetorician can argue either side of an argument with equal facility, and she demonstrates the gendered attributes contained within language, depending on who is using it. Given that facility with language is an admired trait in the male, but frowned on in the female, Marcia Belisarda thereby casts doubt on the veracity of male verbal production and demands a more reasoned approach to individual intelligence and rationality, as human rather than exclusively male traits. Above all, she asserts that women too are capable of reason and self-control.

With regard to women's struggle to prove to themselves and to others their capacity for abstract thought, Gerda Lerner has observed that it has skewed their intellectual development as a group, since their major intellectual endeavor has been to counteract patriarchal assumptions of their inferiority. It is this struggle that Marcia Belisarda enters with her poetry of reason, and her life experience is borne out in Lerner's observation that learned women were mostly single and often cloistered. The intellectual precociousness that was encouraged in youth was discouraged later, forcing women to choose between marriage and enclosure, in other words "the life of a woman or the life of the mind" (*Consciousness* 30).

While Marcia Belisarda finds strength in distanced argument and moralizing, always from the vantage point of reason, Cueva turns to bitter experience in the education of her female lovers. They and their author occupy a secular world, while the titles suggest that Cueva writes to order and that social restrictions on contact with the opposite sex before marriage were not as stringently observed as the moralists would have liked. For example, Cueva writes two sonnets in which the female speakers courageously acknowledge their outrageous behavior according to the prevailing social standards. However, in each case the cause of the problem is the male, portrayed as insincere and untruthful for encouraging one lover while promised to another. The sonnets are placed next to each other in the manuscript. Both claim to be written by request, and their didactic purpose is indicated in their lengthy titles as, for example: "Soneto a petición: Introduce una dama que se aficionó a un galán que estaba prendado de otra y dándole a entender su amor la correspondió, hasta que vino a saber que quería a otra y enojada le hace este soneto dando de mano a su amor" (Sonnet by request: Introducing a *dama* who, attracted to a *galan* who was in love with another, and giving him to understand her love, he reciprocated, until she found out that he loved another when, angry, she wrote him this sonnet, casting his love aside). These titles not only indicate social intercourse between the sexes, but that the nominally superior males were seen to act as Eve figures in tempting the young women. The women do not scruple to show their interest, defying the restrictions on where a *doncella* could safely cast her eyes. This restriction on wanton gazing was clearly still in force in the following century. When Carmen Martín Gaite makes observations about the female gaze in the eighteenth century, she shows that Enlightenment thinking had done nothing to alter the patriarchal preconceptions that governed the lives of seventeenth-century women:

To look up, to look someone straight in the eye was what girls had to avoid if they wished to give guarantee of their chastity. The proper attitude was summed up in a concept inseparable from that of maidenhood, crystallized in the *recato*. . . . The reiterated preachings of maidens' reserve stressed far more the exterior appearance of reticence than the causes leading to an unvirtuous action; what really harmed a woman's reputations was not being reserved enough. What was not seen did not exist. (72)

Cueva's sonnets both refute and endorse male attitudes. Initially, in the opening line of the above-named sonnet, she indicates that the young woman fails in her *recatamiento* (modest prudence): "Puse los ojos ¡ay que no debiera!" (1; I laid my eyes, oh, but I should not have!). However, the remainder of this quartet leaves open the question as to the cause of her regretful exclamation. This may be either her failure to observe the social obligation to keep her eyes downcast, or her inappropriate gazing at a man already claimed by another. The problem then moves from the socially transgressive female to a mutually transgressive infidelity entered into by both parties, though the title shows the speaker to be an innocent victim of male duplicity:

Puse los ojos ¡ay que no debiera!
en quien ya de las flechas de Cupido
mostraba el tierno corazón herido,
para que yo, sin esperanza, muera.

5   Huir fácil me fue de la primera
ocasión que a tal daño me ha traído,
con resistir mirar tan atrevido,
mas fui mujer y al fin mujer ligera.

Grillos amor me puso a los sentidos,
10   y la causa cruel de tantos daños,
con sus regalos aumentó mis glorias;

pero sabiendo ¡ay Dios!, que eran fingidos
he sepultado en caros desengaños
mi firmeza, mi amor y sus memorias.

                        (BN ms. 4127 258–59)

I laid my eyes, oh, but I should not have,
on one whose tender heart showed the
wounds of Cupid's arrows, so that
now I, bereft of hope, might die.

It was easy for me to flee on the first
occasion that brought me to such peril,
by resisting a so daring gaze, but I
was a woman, in the end a loose woman.

Love put my senses in chains,
and the cruel cause of so many sorrows
augmented my glories with his gifts,

but knowing, oh God! that they were feigned,
I have entombed in dearly bought disillusion
my resistance, my love, and his memory.

Throughout the quartets the persona accepts the culpability for her
inappropriate action. Since she acknowledges her error, resulting in *desengaño,* the poet places her in a morally superior position. The persona

accepts that her failure at self-control is due to female weakness: "mas fui mujer y al fin mujer ligera" (8). However, she also discloses her attempts to resist the "mirar tan atrevido" of the *galán* already promised to another. In addition, the second quartet expresses the *dama*'s awareness not only of the emotional hurt that the flirtation engenders, but also of the compromised social position in which she finds herself, as *daño* serves both causes: "Huir fácil me fue de la primera / ocasión que a tal daño me ha traído, / con resistir mirar tan atrevido" (5–7).[11] The speaker blames a personified love for her predicament, for love has robbed her of reason and captivated all her senses: "Grillos amor me puso a los sentidos" (9). She yokes the mischievous boy-god to the dishonorable lover who encourages her love with gifts: "la causa cruel de tantos daños / con sus regalos aumentó mis glorias" (10–11). *Desengaño* comes with the realization, in the final tercet, that she is being deceived by the lover's pretense, and she finds within herself the strength to resist.

Contiguous to this sonnet in the manuscript is a companion work where the female speaker is more forceful in rejecting the fickle lover, Alcindo. From the first quartet his failings are set up against the strength and dignity of the speaker:

> Alcindo, ya murió en tu desengaño
> un verdadero amor, el mas constante;
> ya contrastó su fuerza de diamante
> tu desprecio cruel para mi daño.
>
> 5   Ya he conocido por mi mal tu engaño.
> Eres cual viento leve e inconstante;
> ni sabes ser galán ni firme amante,
> y así pienso tratarte como a extraño.
>
> Aunque alegres, mis ojos, te han mirado,
> 10   por pagarte en lo mismo que tú vendes,
> es su contento, como tú, fingido,

---

11. In her manuscript, Cueva emphasises the gaze in this line by enclosing it in dashes, thus: *con rresistir—mirar—tan atrebido.*

que pues tanto desprecias siendo amado
y un firme amor tan declarado ofendes,
tu memoria de hoy más cubra mi olvido.

(BN ms. 4127 257–58)

Alcindo, now has died in your disenchantment
a true and most constant love.
I have already compared its diamond strength
with your cruel disdain, to my ill.

Now, to my ill, I have uncovered your deception.
You were like the wind, slight and inconstant;
you do not know how to be a *galán* or a firm lover,
and thus I am decided to treat you as a stranger.

Although my eyes have gazed on you rejoicing,
to pay you in the same coin that you sell,
their contentment is, like you, feigned,

and since you so scorn being loved,
and since a firm love, thus declared, offends you,
your memory, from today on, I'll bury in oblivion.

Unlike the first sonnet, where the lonely, interior search of the conscience acts like a confessional, progressing from presentation of the problem to its solution, this one apostrophizes Alcindo. Again, the descriptive terms applied to the fickle *galán* are those ascribed to women by male poets, playwrights, and moralists, who locate female fickleness in their inferior humors. This supposed physiological inevitability gives men no reason to suppose that women learn from their mistakes. Cueva's poetry indicates that, whether or not women subscribed to Renaissance humoral theory in their daily lives, she regards women as intelligent, rational, and capable of learning.

The female lover's firmness and constancy are contrasted positively against the *galán*'s inconstancy, infidelity, and deviousness in the second quartet: "Eres cual viento leve e inconstante; / ni sabes ser galán ni firme amante" (6–7). In suggesting that Alcindo behaves neither like a *galán* nor a lover, the speaker indicates some experience in this field. She attributes the cause of her suffering to her own open declaration of her feelings,

feelings that leave her exposed to the "desprecio" of the *galán*. *Desenga-ño* arises from her realization that the *galán* fails to respond appropriately because he is "prendado de otra." Through her portrayal of his duplicity Cueva again punctures the masculine appropriation of honorable behavior. Moreover, as she shows women to be more experienced at the game of love than they are supposed to be, she also discloses that women are more capable of self-discipline and control than are their male counterparts.

HEROIC CONSTANCY: *La firmeza en la ausencia*

Cueva's interest in promoting the cause of female strength, loyalty, and moral courage is reflected not just in isolated poems in her manuscript but also in her one extant play, *La firmeza en la ausencia* (Constancy in absence).[12] The female protagonist, Armesinda, successfully defends herself against the political power, wiles, and physical strength of the King of Naples. She therefore defies all the norms of the patriarchal system, saving her honor and the life of her beloved, Don Juan, in the process. Cueva's choice to name her hero "Don Juan" is surprising, given the associations of that name with the classic philanderer. However, his doubt that Armesinda will be able to resist the king, together with Cueva's choice of name, may be a further, ironic tilt at male weakness. Cueva may also have enjoyed playing with the potent symbolism of names, as she gives her own name to the lower class *criada*.

In order to achieve the requisite degree of independence and freedom to act in her protagonist, Cueva has to dispossess her of any living male relative who could take control of her life and place her in the masculine-

12. While all other sonnets are taken directly from the poets' manuscripts, the sonnets from the play, quoted in this chapter are taken from Teresa Scott Soufas, *Women's Acts: Plays by Women Dramatists of Spain's Golden Age* (Lexington: University Press of Kentucky, 1997). The scope of this study does not permit a full discussion of the play. I focus on the four sonnets uttered by the four lovers. For treatment of other aspects of the play and Cueva's challenge to patriarchy, see Sharon D. Voros, "Fashioning Feminine Wit in María de Zayas, Ana Caro and Leonor de la Cueva," in *Gender, Identity and Representation in Spain's Golden Age*, ed. Anita K. and Dawn L. Smith Stoll (Lewisburg: Bucknell University Press, 2000), 156–77; or Teresa Scott Soufas, "Absence of Desire in Leonor de la Cueva y Silva's *La firmeza en la ausencia*," in *Gender, Identity and Representation in Spain's Golden Age*, ed. Anita K. Stoll and Dawn L. Smith (Lewisburg: Bucknell University Press, 2000), 142–55. *Women's Acts: Plays by Women Dramatists of Spain's Golden Age* (Lexington: University Press of Kentucky, 1997).

controlled marriage market. As Peter Stallybrass has observed, in the early modern period the category "woman" is a property category, an idea prevalent since the Commandments linked "wife, maid, ox, and ass side by side as a man's assets" (127). Cueva makes Armesinda's isolation explicit: "Desde mis primeros años, de padres desamparada" (2014–15; Unprotected by parents since my earliest years). In the course of the play Cueva produces a suite of sonnets devoted to absence, trust, and firm devotion. In Act 1 the king, who cannot control his lust for Armesinda, sends Don Juan away to war. Don Juan laments to his *lacayo* (servant), Tristán, that absence and jealousy are the death of love. Before his departure, Don Juan and Armesinda pledge loyalty in matched sonnets that are equaled in a sonnet exchange between the *criada*, Leonor, and Tristán.

These two pairs of sonnets are fascinating for a number of reasons. This is no Petrarchan interiorizing of rarefied love, nor are the female protagonists chastely hidden from sight. These sonnets are delivered face to face, between the two pairs of lovers, whose eyes meet in solemnization of their vows. Moreover, in spite of the affectionate companionship that the play makes clear between Don Juan and his *lacayo* and between Armesinda and her *criada,* distinctions of class are acknowledged and revealed through the fates the four lovers wish on themselves should they fail to keep their word, a distinction that allows for considerable comic effect in the sonnets of the two servants. Nevertheless, differences of class do not detract from the close confidences enjoyed by the servants and their aristocratic employers. Tristán's and Leonor's fate lies in the realm of the domestic, the kitchen and ever-present vermin, as Leonor's vow reveals:

> Si yo olvidare, cielo, eternamente
> el amor y las gracias de Tristán,
> con campanas me atruene un sacristán
> y beba en el verano agua caliente;
>
> 5 persígame un galán impertinente,
> no halle flor en el campo por San Juan,
> en piedra dura se me vuelva el pan,
> y tenga lamparones en la frente;

no halle descanso ni contento en cosa;
10   pulgas me piquen en cualquiera parte,
y si durmiere, que me den enojos;

quede, cuando llorare, lagañosa,
si yo dejare, mi Tristán, de amarte,
porque eres el candil de aquestos ojos.

(1.2.654–66)

Should I ever forget, heavens,
the love and the graces of Tristan,
may I be deafened with bells by a sacristan
and may I drink hot water in summer;

may an impertinent *galán* pursue me,
may there be no flowers in the fields by St. John's Day,
may my bread turn to hard stone,
and may I have boils on my forehead;

may I find no contentment nor rest in anything;
may fleas bite me in every part,
should I sleep, may it give me troubles;

and may I stay bleary-eyed when I weep,
should I cease, my Tristan, to love you,
because you are the light of these eyes.

Tristan's sonnet promise is even more fervent:

Pues si yo te olvidare, mi Leonor,
ni borrare del alma tu retrato;
con sus ratones me persiga un gato,
con sus golpes me aturda un herrador;

5   ande hecho estafermo de un señor,
de mis favores haga un necio plato,
con preguntas me mate un mentecato,
y atraviéseme el cuerpo un asador;

parezca cocinero de convento,
10   no tenga en esta guerra buena suerte,
un escudero goce mis despojos;

y póngame a guardar un monumento,
si yo, Leonor, dejare de quererte,
porque eres las niñitas de estos ojos.

(1.2.667–80)

Well, if I should forget you, my Leonor,
or erase your portrait forever from my soul;
may a cat and her mice harass me,
may a blacksmith stun me with his blows;

may I be turned into a knight's quintain,
may an idiot make a dish of my favors,
may a fool kill me with his questions,
and a roasting spit pierce me through and through,

may I seem a convent cook,
have no good fortune in this war,
may a squire enjoy my spoils,

and may I be put to guard a monument,
if I, Leonor, cease to love you,
for you are the very pupils of these eyes.

The vows of the aristocrats, however, revolve around disparagement, loss of honor and status, and worse, loss of chastity, as in Armesinda's vow that she may be enjoyed by a "vil esclavo," and the words of Don Juan show:

Armesinda to Don Juan

Si yo, ingrata, olvidare tus amores,
ni burlare, mudable, tu esperanza,
en un golfo de celos sin bonanza
me anegue de tu ausencia en los rigores;

5   de mi edad juvenil, las frescas flores
marchite en mayo el tiempo y su mudanza

haga de un envidioso confianza,
y un vil esclavo goce mis favores;

no tenga en cosa que procure gusto,
10 penas me sean las mayores glorias,
persígame tu sombra en cualquier parte,

viva muriendo, en cautiverio injusto,
y atorméntenme el alma tus memorias,
si yo, don Juan, dejare de adorarte.

(1.2.605–18)

If I, ungrateful, should forget your love,
or, being mutable, cheat your hopes,
may I drown myself in a gulf of jealousy
without safe harbor from the rigors of your absence.

May the fresh flowers of my young age
wither in May from the caprices of time,
may I make a confidante of an envious one,
and may a vile slave enjoy my favors.

May nothing give me pleasure,
may the greatest glories be sorrows to me,
may your shade pursue me everywhere,

May I live dying, in unjust captivity,
and may your memory torment my soul,
if I, don Juan, should cease to adore you.

D. Juan to Armesinda

Pues si dejare un punto de quererte,
ni olvidare jamás tu rostro hermoso,
no halle en cosa que emprenda fin dichoso,
y en flor me coja desastrada muerte;

5 tenga en todas mis cosas mala suerte,
con el rey me enemiste un mentiroso,
no vuelva de esta guerra victorioso,
y máteme la pena de no verte;

gócete el rey, y rompa mis despojos,
10   ostente los favores de tu mano,
pase mi cuerpo de esta a la otra parte

con mi espada delante de tus ojos
la mano del más rústico villano,
si dejare, Armesinda, de adorarte.

(1.2.619–32)

Well, if I should cease in any way to love you,
or forget forever your beautiful face,
may I find no fortunate end to my endeavors
and may disastrous death reap me in full bloom;

May I have bad luck in everything,
may a liar make enmity for me with the king,
may I not return victorious from this war,
and may the pangs of not seeing you kill me;

May the king enjoy you, destroy my remains,
and show off the favor of your hand;
may I be run through from one side to the other

before your very eyes, with my own sword,
at the hands of a rustic simpleton,
should I cease, Armesinda, to adore you.

The author nevertheless injects a considerable degree of emotional equality into the sonnets. The self-imposed submission to vile horrors are bracketed, in each of the four sonnets, by near-identical opening and closing lines: "Si yo olvidare . . . / Si yo dejare . . ." in those of Tristan and Leonor; "Si yo olvidare . . . Si dejare . . . / Si dejare . . . Si dejare . . ." in those of Armesinda and Don Juan. The effect of the vows, whether couched in rustic or regal terms, is the same. In all four sonnets, absence from the beloved is figured as death, and all four speakers wish ultimately for death if they do not comply with their own stringent standards. Although the early modern vision of desire as at once impossible and a kind of death is everywhere present in literature of the period, this is not the case in Cueva's play. Nowhere does she suggest that the desire between the two pairs is impossible. Absence is artificially constructed through the malign figure of the king, who abuses his power to assuage his lust and who is, paradoxically, the epitome of the patriarchal model. Social order and the requital of desire will be achieved through the application of one woman's constancy and intelligence.

Those whose duty it is to obey have no choice in this enforced absence, as the *caballero* has sworn fealty to his lord and the servant has no option but to follow his master into involuntary exile and war. This action reflects the appropriate behavioral codes for the patriarchal society of early modern Spain, though the *comedia* plays cynically with the hypocrisy and corrupt abuse of power by the king, who should be the model for social propriety, and who besieges Armesinda for a year and a half, before Don Juan and Tristán are finally able to return. Even when threatened with death by the king, Armesinda determines not to break her word or compromise her honor. She becomes a model that counters the traditionally misogynist view of women as unreliable and weak, and hence forms a balancing figure to the debased king.

As Cueva features the king's ignoble behavior, she also upholds the idea that integrity, honor, and moral strength can exist in all levels of society and in both sexes, and that they are not the prerogatives of the men of the dominant class. This is a direct challenge to the gender, class, and ethnicity presumptions of the ruling male elites of seventeenth-century Spain. Gerda Lerner has articulated the need for such a challenge in the writing of history because of patent contradictions in what is written and what actually happens. The traditional model is elitist, leaving out more than half of humankind, not only women, but most men, and all classes and races other than the privileged group. That is, men and women have participated actively in the world, yet we are told of a past in which men act and women are acted upon. In observing that the first known slaves were women of foreign tribes, Lerner draws together the strands of class, ethnicity, and gender into a single Other whose fate is operated on by those in power: that is, those who write history (*History* 131–33). In this vein, Cueva's own dominant social position does not prevent her from observing that women are less active than acted upon within her own social milieu. However, she proves, through the play's title and plot, that

women can also act: it is the strategic deployment of her heroine's ingenuity, intelligence, and moral strength that resolves the social problems
raised in the play.

The correct political order is reestablished when the king's attentions
are deflected on to an even more noble target, a French princess. Hence,
Cueva achieves closure at both the political and the personal levels. Although she does not seek change in the governing system, Cueva does
critique the morally repugnant possibilities inherent in absolute power.
In the play's sonnets Cueva foregrounds equality between men and wom-
en in terms of their integrity, ingenuity, and mutual trust. In the *comedia*
she proclaims an equality between men and women in their capacity to
surmount problems and determine their own political and personal relationships. Furthermore, she insists that relationships of gender equality,
albeit strictly within one's own class, are socially beneficial.

CONCLUSION

This chapter has revealed that these women were capable sonneteers of love. Furthermore, they took the opportunity, in appropriating a
particularly male pastime to their own use, to defend women against
the misogynists' claims of weakness, fickleness, and mutability. They
also express female attitudes to male failings and challenge the prevailing masculine appropriation of honor and probity. Though it would be
dangerous to take the sonnets of a few educated women as representative
of the whole, there are sufficient examples here, by women from a wide
geographical distribution of the educated upper classes, to suggest that
women's access to social intercourse with male equals was more common than has been suggested in masculinist histories, or recommended
in conduct manuals, and that women freely expressed their views about
the social failings and successes of their male contemporaries. While in
this regard they fall far short of the revenge stories of a María de Zayas,
these sonnets show strong and independent women expressing themselves through their ideas and most emphatically not through their bodies. Without the colorful blazon of the adored body, these poems become
a feminine manifesto about the possibilities of human love, shorn of its
idealizing perspective, and hence providing a lens through which to de-

termine the realities of love and physical attraction between the sexes. The possibilities thereby released in the love lyric are taken up with even greater fervor in relation to mystical love of the divine. It is this mystical love that will form the thematic substance of the next chapter, through a discussion of the works of Luisa de Carvajal y Mendoza.

CHAPTER 6

LUISA DE CARVAJAL   *More Martha than Mary*

⚜

IN 1601, LUISA DE CARVAJAL Y MENDOZA wrote a letter to
a friend, a nun at the court of the archduchess of Flanders, from
her small and impoverished, yet independent, home in Madrid. In it, she
confided that "[t]odos estos días estoy deseando que me dejen tomar la
pluma en la mano para aliviarme de las pesadumbres y ocupaciones que
traigo" (*Epistolario* 109; every day I desire to be left to take up the pen in
my hand to relieve myself of the pressures and occupations that I carry).
Although the relief she sought in this instance was to be found in writing to her friend, her comment indicates that, among the chosen difficulties of her ascetic life, Carvajal y Mendoza sought comfort in the written word. The solace she derived from this exercise must certainly have
extended to poetic composition, since all her poetry was written in Madrid during the 1590s. Abad concludes that when Carvajal y Mendoza finally set up house in London she was too preoccupied with her mission
to write poetry, and notes that in Madrid "hubo momentos en que su
vida mística, llegada a cierta tensión, la obligó a desahogar en esa forma
los afectos del alma" (*Epistolario* 422; there were moments in her mystic
life when a certain tension appeared, obliging her to unburden herself of
the feelings of her soul in this manner). Several poems are datable, in relation to known facts of her life, to 1597.[1]

1. Olivares and Boyce suggest that her works were composed between 1593 and 1601;
see *Espejo*, 491.

The circumstances of Carvajal y Mendoza's life are so extraordinary that it becomes impossible to read and discuss her works without taking into account the suffering she was made to endure while still a young girl and the self-inflicted difficulties of her adult life.[2] It is important that an analysis of Carvajal y Mendoza's sonnets takes into account these tensions and conflicts, as well as her own avowed determination to seek martyrdom. Of her fifty poems, nine are sonnets. An analysis of seven of these will demonstrate the nature of Carvajal y Mendoza's mysticism and her poetic capabilities.

The foundations of Carvajal y Mendoza's determination to endure a martyr's death, and her desire to suffer as Christ, reside in her early life, for even in the heightened religious atmosphere of the Counter-Reformation her childhood was excessively devout, arduous, and tormented. Born into a noble family in Jaraicejo, Extremadura, in 1566, Carvajal y Mendoza was orphaned at the age of six and was sent to live with her aunt, a *dama* at the court of Philip II. Here she first made contact with the Jesuits through her aunt's confessor. On the death of her aunt, she was moved to Pamplona, under the guardianship of her uncle, the Marquis de Almazán. Her exceptional piety from an early age is noted in her autobiography and in subsequent writings about her life. This attitude was assisted by her uncle, who prescribed and oversaw her unusually broad general and religious education. However, he also imposed penitential practices that were by any measure excessive, but which amount to appalling abuse when the facts of her life are known. She was only fourteen years old when the systematic torture and humiliation began, administered by two servants especially employed for the task.[3]

Carvajal y Mendoza began her self-imposed religious reclusion when her uncle moved to the court in Madrid in 1588. Until the deaths of the

2. There have been numerous writings about Carvajal y Mendoza's life. Her militant political efforts in London ensured that she appeared in the Calendar of State Papers and in the dispatches of Felipe III's London ambassadors, as well as in the Downshire papers, which give voice to Archbishop Abbot's negative opinions of her vocation. Unless otherwise stated, I draw details of Carvajal y Mendoza's life from Camilo María Abad, *Una misionera española en la Inglaterra del siglo XVII (1566–1614)* (Santander: Universidad Pontificia, 1966).

3. Southey went so far as to describe the marquis as an "incarnate fiend" in his exploration of Muñóz's *Vida* which he included in *Letters Written during a Journey in Spain and a Short Residence in Portugal by Robert Southey,* 3rd ed, 2 vols. (London: Longman, 1808), 277.

marquis and his wife in 1592, she pursued the path of poverty and self-denial in a separate apartment in their house in the Calle Mayor, this being the limit of her uncle's toleration of her aims. With the deaths of those in control of her life, she was free to pursue her determination to follow in Christ's footsteps, as she herself wrote, in the clearest terms:

[A]lcé los ojos a Dios y díle inmensas gracias, porque me vía del todo sola y libre para irme, sin ningún estorbo, tras los desprecios y desamparos de Cristo, que tanto deseaba mi alma . . . [Nuestro Señor] me arrojó desde donde estaba y dio conmigo en una gran soledad (aunque dentro de los límites de la babilonia de Madrid), cortándome del trato de mis deudos, amigos y conocidos . . . Yo entonces conocí su mano, y adoréla, y determiné de entrarme tras él por sus pisadas sin más dilación. (Abad, *Misionera* 69)

I raised my eyes to God and gave him immense thanks, because I realized I was completely alone and free to follow, without impediment, the condemnations and abandonments of Christ which my soul so desired. . . . [Our Lord] tore me from where I was and placed me in great solitude (even in the limits of the Babylon of Madrid), cutting me off from dealings with my relatives, friends, and acquaintances . . . and then I knew his way and adored it and determined to follow behind him in his footsteps without further delay.

The fulfillment of her determination, her successful and dangerous apostolic mission to London, shows how, in spite of a solemnly sworn vow of absolute obedience, she was able to pursue her own ambitions, thus securing herself a remarkable degree of independence.

Also important in the analysis of Carvajal y Mendoza's poetry is her deep devotion and attachment to the Jesuits, which may have stemmed from her early contact with them when under the care of her aunt. She wrote her poetry while living in a tiny house, described by Abad as "aquella ruín casita" (that ruinous little house), adjacent to their church in the Calle Toledo in Madrid (Abad, "Semblanza" 27). Here Carvajal y Mendoza pursued a life of extreme poverty with a few companions, begging for her food at the church door, dressing in the poorest of clothing, and seeking every opportunity for self-abasement and humiliation that she felt brought her closer to the experience of Christ's suffering. Throughout her life Carvajal y Mendoza remained close to the Jesuits, exchanging letters with Father Creswell, vice-superior of the English Mission and administrator of the foundation created when Carvajal y Mendoza endowed the society with her considerable inheritance to create an English novitiate in Louvain (Abad, "Semblanza" 71).

At the time when Carvajal y Mendoza was writing her poetry in Madrid, directed to Christ or to his mystical presence in the communion bread, Spanish Christian mysticism was at its apogee through the writings of such influential figures as Francisco de Osuna, Luis de León, Malón de Chaide, St. Teresa of Avila, and St. John of the Cross. For example, in the *Abecedario espiritual* (Spiritual alphabet) Osuna describes the mystical linking of the soul with Christ: "El ánima que se junta al invisible esposo por amor, ninguna consolación recibe del presente siglo, mas de todas entrañas suspira a aquella que ama, hierve, tiene ansia, fatígase y hácese vil la salud del cuerpo por estar traspasada con la llaga del amor" (Osuna 385; The soul that joins herself to the invisible spouse through love receives no consolation from the present century, but sighs with all her being for that which she loves. She burns, is anxious, exhausts herself, and makes herself ill in body through being pierced with the wound of love). In Spain, apart from a few luminaries such as Ramón Llull, mysticism had had to wait until the Reconquest and the religious fervor of the Catholic kings provided a suitable environment for it to flourish. This sudden efflorescence of fifteenth-century Spanish religiosity relates also to the advent of printing and the reform of the religious orders undertaken by Cisneros (Surtz 2). In this period, the Song of Songs, a source for Carvajal y Mendoza's sonnets, figures strongly in the mysticism of Malón de Chaide and St. John of the Cross. For Malón de Chaide, the Song of Songs is a paean of love between Christ and the Church that mirrors human love: "Y porque los *Cantares* de Salomón son una égloga pastoril, en la cual se introducen un pastor, que es Cristo, y una pastora, que es la Iglesia, es menester tomar la proporción de lo que acá en los amores humanos suele pasar, a lo que pasa en los divinos" (72; And because the Song of Solomon is a pastoral eclogue into which a shepherd is introduced, who is Christ, and a shepherdess, who is the Church, it is necessary to measure what usually happens here in human love against what happens in the divine).

Although mysticism in the Western tradition can be traced back to Plato, the union with the One sought by Plato seeks to leave the senses aside. In *The Republic* Plato discusses the best means to approach the highest principle, the Idea of the Good, on which all other ideas depend. He advocates arousing the understanding *(nous)* by abstracting the mind from the senses, toward pure reality (Louth 8–9). Nevertheless, in the *Phaedrus,* he expresses the passion with which the soul recognizes true beauty in the form of the beloved: "When one who is fresh from the mystery, and saw much of the vision, beholds a godlike face or bodily form that truly expresses beauty, first there comes upon him a shuddering and a measure of that awe which the vision inspired, and then reverence, as at the sight of a god" (251A). This imagery is very similar to the *afecto* (passion) of Carvajal y Mendoza's sonnets, as will be seen below.

It was the fifth-century mystic Pseudo-Dionysius, also known as Denys the Areopagite, who first compounded an understanding of Christ's real presence in the liturgy, the sacraments, and the Scriptures into a mystical theology. Grace Jantzen has argued that the more this mystical theology was united with Church liturgy (she uses the example of the Eucharist), the more it was removed from women and taken into the exclusive control of men (87). The effect of this control can be seen in Carvajal y Mendoza's sonnet "¡Ay! soledad amarga y enojosa" (Oh bitter and wearisome solitude!). Denied what was for her the unique comfort of daily communion by her male confessor, she attempts to convey the anguish this causes in verse. However, although Church-led attempts to codify mystical theology enabled a firmer control of heterodox thought and claims of mystical experiences, Carvajal y Mendoza's remarkably strong character ensured that eventually she always succeeded in getting male acquiescence to her desires. In spite of all the difficulties experienced by the English Catholics, she was almost always able to take communion daily during her time in London. She was also successful in having the host kept on the chapel altars of the Spanish, French, Venetian, and Flemish embassies, an unusual achievement as the host was normally only displayed in a church (Abad, *Misionera* 228–29). Carvajal y Mendoza writes of her delight in having it near her in the Spanish embassy: "Ahora han puesto en la capilla el Santísimo Sacramento, con que me hallo enriquecidísima. Cae muy cerca de mi escalera y es fácil, sin verlo nadie, ir allí muchas veces" (*Epistolario* 159; Now they have put the Holy Sacrament in the chapel, so that I find myself greatly enriched. It is very close to my staircase and it is easy to go there often without anybody seeing).

Carvajal y Mendoza is known to have had the works of St. Teresa of Avila and St. John of the Cross when she was in Madrid (Abad, *Misionera* 348–49).[4] Her verse frequently follows the latter's thought and that of Denys the Areopagite. Their Christian view moves beyond the Platonic "Idea" and the more universal understanding centered on the relationship of God to his hierarchical Church of Malón de Chaide to an ecstasy shared equally by God and the individual soul. For Denys, the type of symbolic mysticism seen in Carvajal y Mendoza's poetry is part of the process necessary to achieve the apophatic state. Denys does not distinguish between *eros* and *agape,* though *eros* is "more divine." Both unite and bind in effecting fusion in the beautiful and the good. Denys describes this fusion as ecstasy that draws the soul out of itself toward the object of its love (Louth 175).

What also becomes clear in reading Carvajal y Mendoza's sonnets is that, for all her professed desire to rob herself of her body and to find shared joy between her soul and her Savior, the body remains insistently present, both as a canvas on which to paint Christ-like suffering and as a participant in the pleasure of physical union. Her attachment to this latter evocation of the body will be examined in my discussion of her sonnets "En el siniestro brazo recostado" (Reclining against the left arm) and "De inmenso amor aqueste abrazo estrecho" (This tight embrace of immense love), which draw on the Song of Songs for their imagery. When Carvajal y Mendoza found a more positive outlet for her physical and spiritual energies in England, she moved away from the quest for apophatic union. Her poetry remains in the emotional and the symbolic, although she never abandons her devotion to the body of Christ.

For the Spanish mystic, love poetry could be turned to divine purposes in the same way that the beloved of male-authored Petrarchan-style sonnets became the ideal to be worshipped by the poet lover as a divine figure. It was then used to express the perfection of love by and for Christ, joining rapt, unitive mysticism to the artistic resources of six-

4. Carvajal y Mendoza is known to have had or read Luis de Granada's *Oración y meditación; Memorial de la vida cristiana* and its *Adiciones.* She also read St. Cyprian, St. John Clímacus, Augustine's *Meditations* (probably in the original Latin), and St. Teresa's *Vida,* to which she alludes in a letter to Father Creswell from London in December 1611. Apart from this, of course, she read the Fathers of the Church; the Scriptures she had committed to memory. See Abad, *Misionera,* 348–52.

teenth-century poetic practice. The mystical poetry of St. John of the Cross and St. Teresa, for example, sought to put into words the inexpressible joy of the soul's union with God in divine marriage and the hollowness of earthly life by comparison. For this purpose, John of the Cross, in particular, turned to the Song of Songs as a means to express the inexpressible in the *Cántico espiritual* (Spiritual canticle). These ideas were far from new, being founded on a pre-Christian platform, later amplified by such influential Christian figures as Origen and St. Bernard of Clairvaux.

The third-century Alexandrian philosopher Origen appears to be the first influential Christian thinker to link God and the Church in the Song of Songs. Origen's argument for virginity as purgation, necessary on the path to achieving illumination and, finally, union with the divine, is detailed in the prologue to his *Commentary on the Song of Songs*, where he defines the difference between carnal and divine love:

[J]ust as there is one love, known as carnal and also known as Cupid by the poets, according to which the lover sows in the flesh; so also is there another, a spiritual love, by which the inner man who loves sows in the spirit. . . . And the soul is moved by heavenly love and longing when, having clearly beheld the beauty and the fairness of the Word of God, it falls deeply in love with His loveliness and receives from the Word Himself a certain dart and wound of love. For this Word *is the image* and splendor *of the invisible God.* (29)

With the virgin body a link between heaven and earth, erotic imagery is employed in language, but physical passion is denied; desire is to be directed away from the body and toward God.

Catholic mysticism therefore had a long pedigree in European thought, having grown out of pagan philosophy, Judaism, the earliest Christians, and the monastic tradition. Medieval mystical thought occupied two interlinked locations in the hierarchy of piety: the intellectual and the affective. The intellectual mysticism of the most influential of the German mystics, Master Eckhart, for example, was based on a mind/body dualism in which the goal was an ecstasy of higher knowledge, achieved by detachment from the body and its demands. His discourses are described as being "directed to the intellect rather than to the will and are remarkable for their depth of mystical teaching, which only those who were advanced in the spiritual life could fully appreciate"

(McMahon n. pag.). Eckhart's mysticism is therefore gendered male, for women were assumed incapable of such higher intellectual achievement. This type of mysticism had no emphasis on Christ's role, whereas the affective type was based on an ardent love of Christ, especially Christ crucified (Jantzen 117–23).

It was this affective mysticism that was espoused by Bernard of Clairvaux, whose Christocentric emphasis is clearly to be seen in his influential sermons on the Song of Songs. For example, when he speaks of the first verse of the Song, "Let him kiss me with the kisses of his mouth," he tells the monks: "[T]he text we are going to study is the book of our own experience. . . . Anyone who has received this mystical kiss from the mouth of Christ at least once, seeks again that intimate experience, and eagerly looks for its frequent renewal" (3.1.1). Nevertheless, in spite of Bernard's insistence on the erotic imagery of the Song as a basis for his understanding of union with God, the imagery is always intended to be converted to the spiritual dimension. As Jantzen eloquently explains it, the weft of his sermons is hunger for the beloved's presence and for sexual consummation, but the warp is a sharp denial of the body as having any part in it. The love is purely spiritual and there should be no connection with bodiliness or sexuality (128). This may be the ideal, but to heighten sexual tension merely to deny it raises questions as to how sinfully enjoyable this masochistic behavior might become. Furthermore, while men may have indulged or denied themselves thus, the extremely bodily and experiential nature of women's *a lo divino* (applied to the sacred) love poetry, Carvajal y Mendoza's in particular, describes a spirituality that is highly physical and in which the body participates in the glorious experience.

Carvajal y Mendoza's poetic mysticism is of the affective type espoused by Bernard: the soul becomes the beloved of the divine lover, Christ. Her sonnets express the supernatural and transcendent transformations that take place in the heart and soul as a result of the fervent love of her anagrammatic persona, "Silva," for her Pastor. However, as I shall argue in greater detail below, Carvajal y Mendoza's emphasis lies in bodiliness and in this her mysticism is imbued with the same connotations of physicality seen in the works of the German women mystics of the High Middle Ages, particularly Hadewijch of Antwerp. Erotic mysticism for Hadewijch is passionate, embodied mysticism; the erotic is not merely metaphorical but rather a focus for integration of the body into spiritual mysticism. The same can be said for Carvajal y Mendoza's divine sonnets which, unlike those of the other poets in this study, are frankly erotic in their linking of the human soul, more specifically her own soul, with Christ in her intense focus on the relationship between Silva and Christ. However, in spite of the personal and exclusive nature of Carvajal y Mendoza's poetry, her works clearly proved of spiritual benefit to other women. Moreover, they provided comfort to her Jesuit male supporters, as her letter from London to Doña Leonor de Quirós on 31 August 1607 clearly shows: "El librillo de las poesías espirituales que di a mi señóra la Condesa me haga merced VM de dar por algunos días al padre Espinosa, que me pide unas canciones que están allí, y no puedo ahora escribirlas" (*Epistolario* 87; Would Your Honor do me the favor to give the little book of spiritual poems that I gave to my lady the Countess to Father Espinosa for a few days? He has asked me for some songs from it and I cannot write them now).

In her discussion of the works of women visionaries, Ruth El Saffar has noted that the key to the mystic's encounters with Christ's image is surrender to the brokenness represented by his Passion, a masculine imaged as vulnerable rather than powerful (100). However, although Carvajal y Mendoza's biography and letters frequently express her desire to die for and as Christ, her visions of him are strong images of a beautiful Christ. Even as she wishes to share his torments, his wounds are displayed in her poetry as a victor's trophies. All of her poetry reflects her intensely emotional and spiritual dedication to Christ, addressed as her "Pastor" (shepherd), her "esposo" (husband) and her "amado" (beloved). Of the fifty extant poems by Carvajal y Mendoza, only ten percent bear some resemblance to conventional poetry of the type found in the convent and even then her five poems on the Nativity focus on the Christ child to the exclusion of the divine mother. This is in direct contrast to Sor Violante's sonnets, discussed in Chapter 2, where the power of the Virgin Mary is celebrated most in her role of human mother.

Christian teaching emphasized the person of Christ as the natural conduit to God the Father. Christ had expressed his love for humankind through his Incarnation, his preaching, and, ultimately, through his sacrifice on the cross. Renaissance and Baroque art is filled with images of a physically beautiful Christ preaching, teaching, tending the poor and the sick, suffering, dying, and returning from the dead. It is not, then, surprising that women religious, bound by spiritual marriage to Christ, should become particularly enamored of Christ's body. Although Carvajal y Mendoza eschewed the restrictions of the convent in favor of dangerous independence in Madrid, Valladolid, and finally London, she wrote and adhered to her own vows and never deviated from her desire for Christ, especially his embodiment in the host. Cruz, in writing of Carvajal y Mendoza's eucharistic poetry, felicitously describes it as a "poetics of transubstantiation" as she employs pastoral convention and dialogue to bind herself to Christ ("Words Made Flesh" n. pag.).[5]

Carvajal y Mendoza expresses the love between soul and savior as a tight and indivisible knot, in a sonnet entitled "Soneto espiritual de Silva al Santísimo Sacramento; en que habla el Divino Verbo inmenso con el alma que le está recibiendo de las manos del sacerdote" (Silva's spiritual sonnet on the Holy Sacrament, in which the immense Divine Word speaks to the soul receiving it at the hands of the priest). This sonnet will be discussed more fully below, but part of the second quartet is worth noting here because its bodily and sensual language is also used by male religious in describing the bond between the soul and God: "[Y] abrásate en amor tan abrasado, / que hasta que el fuerte nudo haya apretado, / no sea posible quede satisfecho" (6–8; [And] to burn yourself in such burning love / that until that strong knot is tightened / it is impossible to be satisfied). The similarity of expression in her sonnet to the thoughts of Luís de León can be seen in his text *De los nombres de Dios* (On the names of God). Where Carvajal y Mendoza's interest is in the body, Luis de León utilizes this same imagery in describing the tight knot of spiritual devotion:

[Y] es nudo por muchas maneras dulce, . . . que con ser nuestro Padre, y con hacerse nuestra Cabeza y con regirnos como Pastor . . . añadió a todos ellos aqueste nudo y aqueste lazo también, y quiso decirse y ser nuestro *Esposo*. Que para lazo es el más apretado lazo; . . . y el más encendido de todos. . . . [T]oda

---

5. In this same publication Cruz also discusses a number of the sonnets I read here; see "Words Made Flesh," no pagination.

la estrecheza de amor y de conversación y de unidad de cuerpos, que en el suelo hay entre dos, marido y mujer, comparada con aquella con que se enlaza con
nuestra alma este Esposo, es frialdad y tibieza pura. Porque en el otro ayunta-
miento no se comunica el espíritu, mas en éste su mismo espíritu de Cristo se da
y se traspasa a los justos (1 Corinthians: 6,17; *Obras* 619)

[And] it is a knot that is sweet in many ways . . . what with being our Father
and making himself our Head and guiding us as our Shepherd . . . he added to
all those this knot and this bond as well and wanted to announce himself and
be our *Husband.* That bond is the tightest bond . . . and the most inflamed of
all. . . . All the closeness of love and conversation and unity of bodies that exists between two, husband and wife, on earth, when compared with that which
binds our soul to this Husband, is pure coldness and tepidness. Because in that
joining the spirit does not participate but in this, the very spirit of Christ is giv-
en and pierces the just.

For Carvajal y Mendoza, this tight, sweet, delightful, burning embrace
of union with the divine was experienced via the communion bread. She
was not alone in this notion. The importance of the host in the divine
poetry of women religious stems from its significance as the transubstantiated real flesh of Christ, and the opportunity thus provided for women
to partake of his male body. Under the hypostatic union Christ is present both in substance and in spirit in the communion bread and it is unusual, indeed unnecessary, to receive communion under both kinds. The
bread, therefore, embodies the entire spiritual experience of the communion meal.[6] Carvajal y Mendoza's close relationship with the sacrament
is expressed in the several versions of her life that reveal her almost path-
ological need to receive communion daily.

The extraordinarily erotic nature of much of Carvajal y Mendoza's
poetry, the dwelling on pain, piercing, and flaming love, and Petrarchan tropes rendered *a lo divino,* was also apparent in works of female religious of the High Middle Ages. There was at that time a considerable difference between the erotic nature of female mystical poetry and that of
men, which was grounded in intellectual and spiritual inquiry. Women,

---

6. That communion under both kinds was unnecessary was determined at the Council of Trent, Session 21, when it was decreed that Christ was wholly and really present in
both bread and wine (Trent, Sess. 21, c., 3); see P. J. Toner, *Communion under Both Kinds,*
2003, Catholic Encyclopedia Online, available at http://www.newadvent.org/cathen/04175a.
htm.

denied higher education, were dealing at an altogether more bodily level, not based on the mystical meaning of Scripture, but on an unmediated and passionate encounter with Christ. Citing medieval female mystics' relationship with the embodied Christ, Walker Bynum records that their experiences included the physical sensation of eating his flesh, playing with him as a child, feeding at his breast, and, most commonly, pressing themselves to his body. Women's efforts to imitate Christ involved fusing with the body on the cross through both asceticism and eroticism (*Fragmentation* 130–33). Carvajal y Mendoza's erotic fusing with Christ employs imagery of her own torture, as in "Esposas dulces, lazos deseados" (Sweet shackles, desired bonds). In other sonnets she joins with Christ in divine marriage, rendered through the language of the Song of Songs.

It is not surprising that so many sixteenth-century mystics were female since mysticism gave them the singular opportunity to escape from a life in which their choices of action were always limited by the patriarchy that surrounded and ruled them, a patriarchy that often accused them of dangerous heresy and illuminism. There were two ways, according to Margarita Nelken, in which to transcend one's life: either through giving oneself totally to it, the "tipo del conquistador" (the conqueror type), or through total denial with maximum exaltation. Rather than the conquest of life, an avenue scarcely open to them, these women sought its renunciation: "[L]a conquista de sí mismas hasta el punto más extremo, el que despoja el espíritu de la materia" (51; Conquest of themselves to the most extreme level that despoils spirit of matter). The ritualized torture of the young Carvajal y Mendoza by the marquis inspired a similarly pain-centered personal disciplinary practice that was intended to remove spirit from matter. However, although her disciplinary practice, both voluntary and imposed, aspired to the paradigm of renunciation or conquest revealed by Nelken, her poetry and her experience reveal instead a model that seeks both. Efforts to remove spirit from matter founder in Carvajal y Mendoza's poetry. It is there that she manifests her thirst for personal union with Christ and her desire for martyrdom, as well as her employment of Jesuit methods of meditation. Furthermore, when Carvajal y Mendoza abandoned the life of a medieval ascetic in Spain to embark instead on her apostolic mission to London, she converted her quest for Christomimesis into the "tipo del conquistador." As

Cruz has observed, her letters show political and moral awareness and determination that belie her self-ascribed humility, and are social documents that belong to the male tradition of epistolary style ("Chains" 104).

In addition to personal experience, however painful, the appropriation of the language of love or of works of art also assists in the process of achieving the mystical state. Orozco Díaz, for example, draws a parallel between the mystical experience and the creative process of poetry writing. Discussing first the essence of the mystic phenomenon as infused grace, he determines that there is more than one way to achieve this status. Citing St. John of the Cross, he refers to the active and passive principles at work: the soul either works actively to enter the mystical state or it remains passive, allowing God to enter (*Mística* 60). Orozco Díaz regards the creative urge as a more earthbound miracle: "Aunque con la enorme distancia de lo humano a lo divino, pero rodeando otro misterio—en cierto modo otro milagro, pues es convertir la materia en vida y espíritu—las vías, prácticas o métodos del poeta son paralelos a los del místico" (although with the enormous distance between the human and the divine, but enclosing another mystery, in a certain manner another miracle, since it is to convert matter into life and spirit—the ways, practices, or methods of the poet are parallel to those of the mystic). When the mystical and the creative are combined in one soul, as they are in St. John of the Cross, the search for mystical truth becomes one with the search for the Beloved, a fusion of "lo dado" (the given) and "lo buscado" (the sought). He cites the saint directly: in response to a question about the magnificent words of the *Cántico espiritual*, he replied "unas veces me las daba Dios y otras las buscaba yo" (*Mística* 61–62; sometimes God gave them to me and other times I sought them).

The achievement of the mystical experience is not arrived at only through poetic inspiration. In writing of the mysticism of St. Teresa, Victor Stoichita notes the importance of choral and visual imagery to her visions, despite the fundamental otherness of the sacred. On the eve of St. Sebastian, in her first year as prioress of the Encarnación, at the moment of the *salve,* St. Teresa had a vision of the Mother of God, who appeared in the place of her painted image. St. Teresa describes the vision as "looking, I think, a little like the picture the Countess had given me as a present." The vision lasted for the whole of the *salve,* which is significant, for, as Stoichita points out, it is the chanting and the adornment of holy places with symbols that are important to the visionary experience (56–57).

In the case of Carvajal y Mendoza, although she does not appear to have specific imagery or sounds in mind when she composes her poetry, it seems instead that she engages in a Jesuit spiritual meditation exercise, creating a picture for herself, a "composition of place" on which to focus her inner gaze. She once described a vision in her soul of the divine child, with the Virgin and St. Joseph on either side, with the face of the child covered with a delicate veil of light (Abad, *Misionera* 107). This vision recalls many of the Nativity paintings of the Renaissance and early modern periods and may well have been prompted by such a painting. In the same manner, she writes of her experience after taking communion in February 1599, when she saw a vision of the open wounds of Christ's head and hands as she prayed. His visualized suffering, which suggests an Ignatian meditation on the Crucifixion, does not cause her pain but instead the feeling of gently penetrating love that she also writes of occasionally from London. Here she feels that Christ gives himself to her exclusively, but in her poetry it is she who seeks Christ and desires to press herself to his body. Carvajal y Mendoza herself denies any special divine treatment or mystical phenomena when she goes on to affirm that she did not take account of such sensory perceptions, preferring pursuit of the essence of virtue and a pure and strong love of God (108). This rejection supports my contention that what is often regarded as her ecstatic mysticism comes rather from her own strong determination as to the course of her life and her pathologically intense focus on Christ, as well as from the influence of Jesuit meditative practices. The first power of the soul in a Jesuit meditation is memory; the memory of religious paintings would have assisted her "visions."

The ability to create a memory or a mental picture is particularly apparent in Carvajal y Mendoza's "Soneto espiritual de afectos de amor encendidísimo y deseos de martirio" (Spiritual sonnet of the transports of impassioned love and desires for martyrdom), in which she envisages her own longed-for agony and martyrdom. In the first quartet she sets the composition of place on which she will form her meditation:

Esposas dulces, lazo deseado,
ausentes trances, hora victoriosa,
infamia felícisima y gloriosa,
holocausto en mil llamas abrasado.

5   Di, Amor, ¿por qué tan lejos apartado
se ha de mí aquesta suerte venturosa,
y la cadena amable y deleitosa
en dura libertad se me ha trocado?

¿Ha sido, por ventura, haber querido
10   que la herida que al alma penetrada
tiene con dolor fuerte desmedido,

no quede socorrida ni curada,
y, el afecto aumentado y encendido,
la vida a puro amor sea desatada?

(*Epistolario y poesías* 449)

Sweet shackles, desired bonds,
absent moments of death, victorious hour,
most happy and glorious infamy,
burning in a holocaust of a thousand flames.

Tell me, Love, why have you taken so far
from me that most fortunate fate, and
the beloved and delightful chains, and
exchanged them for my harsh liberty?

Could it be, perhaps, through having wanted
that the wound the penetrated soul
endures in measureless agony

should not be succored nor treated
and that augmented and inflamed passion
should unshackle the soul to pure life?

Unusually, "Silva" or the *zagala* (shepherdess) do not appear in this sonnet, suggesting that the poet has emerged from behind her persona. Carvajal y Mendoza is transported with the pleasure of her sacrifice, willingly separated from her entranced body as she is consigned to the flames. She plays with the negative nature of fame for women; the "in-famia" that brings her martyrdom is exquisitely joyous. Having now es-tablished the meditative vision in her mind, the turn occurs here, rather than at the eighth line, and Carvajal adds the faculties of understand-ing and will to that of memory. At first she complains that this felicitous death has been denied her, but by the tercets her reason and understand-ing begin to formulate an answer, although she frames the entire sestet in a question of her beloved. The tercet imagery of piercing, reminiscent of St. Teresa, foregrounds a mystical union that denies the body. Paradoxi-cally, however, the language brings the body forward into a prominent role. As the body suffers, the soul seeks to unite with Christ, but the in-sistent body intrudes, as the "afecto, aumentado y encendido" describes the ecstasy of orgasm. A contemporary dictionary describes *afecto* as "the passion of the soul" but the symptoms described are demonstrated in the body, "que redundando en la voz, la altera y causa en el cuerpo un par-ticular movimiento" (Covarrubias; which, redounding in the voice, alter it and cause a particular movement in the body).

Although the poem begins with an explicit depiction of the martyr consigned to the flames, it ends in a determination that she is destined to die instead through the wounds of love, as the final application of will to her meditation asks: "¿y, el afecto aumentado y encendido, / la vida a puro amor sea desatada?" (13–14). The clear word-pictures that Carvajal y Mendoza creates in meditative sonnets like this one owe more to Jesuit practice than to an attempt to express the ineffable experience of mys-tical ecstasy. Her sonnets are not dialogic, as the writings of medieval women mystics about their spiritual encounters often are; the speaking voice, whether it is Silva, Carvajal y Mendoza, or her Pastor, is permit-ted to express poetic emotion, divine love, or the pleasures of the envis-aged union with Christ, but without response. Carvajal y Mendoza's lone speaking voice is clearly an indication that she creates her own mental picture, rather than that she experiences visions. However, this single, meditative voice of the sonnets is less apparent in her other lyric, as Cruz has noted in writing of one of Luisa's *romances* in "Willing Desire" (183). When the Pastor speaks in her poetry it is at a distance, so that she envis-ages the Pastor addressing her persona, Silva. In this manner she creates a mental picture on which to focus.

In spite of her unusually thorough intellectual development and education, Carvajal y Mendoza does not seek an intellectual rationalization of her experience; like the medieval female religious, communion was a direct, emotionally charged communication between her body and the body of Christ. It is therefore probable that for women religious of any period, emotional and physical expression more clearly conveyed their devotion to Christ than specific explication of the mystery of biblical texts that so occupied both the Fathers of the Church and the men who had control of Carvajal y Mendoza's early life.

As Walker Bynum has argued, the humanity of Christ, by which was meant his full bodily participation, was central to the religiosity of late medieval women, often with erotic or sensual overtones. The change in attitude to the Eucharist between the twelfth and fourteenth centuries saw hunger for mystical union become a metaphor for desire; the emphasis moved from heavenly manna to meat and blood: "To eat God was to take into one's self the suffering flesh on the cross. . . . That which one ate was the physicality of the God-man" (*Holy Feast* 67). Margery Kempe, Angela of Foligno, and Catherine of Siena are three well-attested examples of medieval women whose intense attraction to Christ's human maleness included marriage to Christ in eucharistic visions. A common thread in their experience is their orgasmic bliss at the joining with Christ in the Eucharist. The experience produces both sublime joy and satiation but also, as the moment fades, extreme hunger and emptiness.

Although Walker Bynum writes of women's desire for mystical union with the actual body of Christ in the medieval period, Carvajal y Mendoza's sonnets show that this was not an entirely medieval phenomenon. While Cruz regards Carvajal y Mendoza's sonnets as particularly baroque for their time, at the end of the sixteenth century, which in their overwrought excess they certainly are, they also share the bodily characteristics of the German mystics of the High Middle Ages, previously discussed, in the intensity of their desire for Christ's revealed body and for the sweet pain of the *imitatio crucis.*[7] Carvajal y Mendoza is not alone in

7. Cruz's remarks refer more specifically to Carvajal y Mendoza's imagery: "[Her poems] dwell on concrete images of wounds, shackles, and chains that evoke the material suffering of Christ's Passion. Although imagery of this kind was to appear frequently in later Baroque devotional poetry, its usage in the sixteenth century is quite uncommon

this yearning; another seventeenth-century poet to embrace the symbolism of St. John of the Cross and Luis de León in her divine verse is Cecilia del Nacimiento. She too expresses the insatiable nature of her hunger for Christ's presence and the paradoxical feeling of satiation and emptiness that the divine meal engenders:

> En una fiesta que hizo
> Dios al alma enamorada
> le dio una dulce comida
> de sí y de su cuerpo y alma.
>
> . . .
>
> Ella con amor le come
> y nunca se ve bien harta.
>
> (qtd. in Arenal and Schlau 146)
>
> In a feast that God made
> for the beloved soul
> he gave her a sweet meal of
> himself and of his body and soul.
>
> . . .
>
> She eats him with love
> and sees that she can never have enough.

For Carvajal y Mendoza and for many other religious women, love and reverence for the host was a wholly involving experience of mutual joy and pain, caused by the real sense of Christ's bodily presence and of his suffering. Carvajal y Mendoza had been imbued from childhood with the requirement to purge the spirit of the body. Her sonnets were written when she was also making her vows of poverty, obedience, chastity, the pursuit of spiritual perfection, and martyrdom by any means not repugnant to God. Yet, paradoxically, her sonnets celebrate the body of Christ and the union of that body with her whole being, body and soul, as, for example, in the sonnets which begin "En el siniestro brazo recostado" and "De inmenso Amor aqueste abrazo estrecho."

Carvajal y Mendoza also writes two sonnets that specifically express

---

and cannot be attributed merely to the poet's awareness of religious rhetoric"; see Cruz, "Chains," 98.

the painful nature of love for an absent Savior and the keenly felt loss of Christ's physical presence. One of these, entitled "Soneto espiritual de Silva de sentimientos de amor y ausencia profundísimos" (Silva's spiritual sonnet of profound feelings of love and absence), holds up a mirror to her own nature, as she at once experiences the agony of absence and the transports of divine love, yet clinically observes the changes wrought in her frail body by the experience. This sonnet may, as the second assuredly is, also be specifically related to a four-year period in the 1590s when her confessor refused her permission to take communion more than twice a week and on principal religious feast days:

Aun en los cuatro primeros años de aquella vida heroica, su confesor—un padre de la Compañía—ateniéndose a las reglas y ordenaciones de los superiores mayores, no la permitió comulgar sino dos veces por semana. . . . Obedecía ella sin replicar. . . . Esta obediencia tan sumisa era tanto más admirable, cuanto era mayor el sacrificio que le exigía del ansia de unirse con Dios en el sacramento del amor. Porque era tan grande su ardor y hambre de este divino bocado, que decía muchas veces que, si viera el Santísimo Sacramento rodeado de picas y lanzas, rompiera por medio de ellas, para ir a comulgar, aunque quedara allí muerta. (Abad, "Semblanza" 28)

Even in those first four years of that heroic life, her confessor—a father of the Company—cleaving to the rules and orders of his superiors, did not permit her to take communion more than twice a week. . . . She obeyed without demur. . . . This submissive obedience was all the more admirable given the greatness of the sacrifice he demanded of her given her desire for union with God in the sacrament of love. Because her ardor and hunger were so great for this divine meal, she often said that if she were to see the Holy Sacrament surrounded by pikes and lances she would break through the midst of them to go and take communion, though she were to fall dead there.

Carvajal y Mendoza's custom of taking communion daily was a practice made possible, in Abad's view, by God himself. However, there was no doctrinal reason why Carvajal y Mendoza should have been denied communion. The frequency of communion had been a subject for discussion at the Council of Trent following differences of opinion and practice over the centuries, but in 1587 the Congregation of the council forbade any restriction and ordered that "no one should be repelled from the Sacred Banquet, even if he approached daily" (Scannell n. pag.). A new confessor proved kinder in granting her request, but even then she had to beg it daily and it could always be refused her.

The first sonnet begins on a note of astonishment, framed within a series of rhetorical questions in which the persona, Silva, is expressed as a monster of nature:

> ¿Cómo vives, sin quien vivir no puedes?
> Ausente, Silva, el alma, ¿tienes vida,
> y el corazón aquesa misma herida
> gravemente atraviesa, y no te mueres?
>
> 5   Dime, si eres mortal o inmortal eres:
> ¿Hate cortado Amor a su medida,
> o forjado, en sus llamas derretida,
> que tanto el natural límite excedes?
>
> Vuelto a tu corazón cifra divina
> 10   de extremos mil Amor, en que su mano
> mostrara quiso destreza peregrina;
>
> y la fragilidad del pecho humano
> en firmísima piedra diamantina,
> con que quedó hecho alcázar soberano.
>
> (Epistolario y poesías 437)

> How can you live, without whom you cannot live?
> Your soul being absent, Silva, you live
> with a grave wound that pierces
> your heart, and you do not die?
>
> Tell me, are you mortal or are you immortal?
> Has Love cut you to his measure,
> or forged you, melted in his flames,
> that you so exceed nature's limits?
>
> Your heart was turned into a divine code
> of a thousand extremes by Love, in which
> his hand sought to reveal its rare dexterity,

> turning the fragile human heart
> into firmest, diamantine stone,
> with which he built his sovereign castle.

The questions of the first quartet reflect and elaborate on the "Muero porque no muero" (I die because I do not die) theme of St. Teresa's and St. John of the Cross's poetry, and suggest the transverberation so memorably depicted by Bernini in his statue of the ecstatic Teresa in the Capella Cornaro in Rome. The difficult first line questions the nature of Silva's existence: a body that continues to live, although the soul is transported by love to seek that mystical marriage, the transcendent experience also expressed by St. Teresa and St. John. The beatific vision is afforded only rarely, is fleeting, never forgotten, and leaves a feeling of ineffable emptiness in its wake, while the body that she addresses is an encumbrance that prevents a more permanent union of the soul with the divine. In this sonnet the "quien" without whom Carvajal y Mendoza cannot live is both Christ and the host that is denied her. She questions her ability to survive without spiritual sustenance, without the direct communication that she feels in her heart and soul as she takes the transubstantiated body of Christ into her mouth.

What begins in the sonnet in generalization becomes more specific as the narrative focus turns from Silva's suspended state between mortality and immortality to the absent soul and its empty case, the heart. The rational in the speaker seeks an explanation in the second quartet, surmising that the transformative nature of mystical love has wrought a metamorphosis in Silva. Now made in Love's likeness, the language expresses Silva's physical pain in imagery of cutting, forging, and melting: "¿Hate cortado Amor a su medida, / o forjado, en sus llamas derretida, / que tanto el natural límite excedes?" (6–8). This is not the only sonnet in which Carvajal y Mendoza turns from the pastoral to the industrial to express the effect of divine love on her soul. Where she employs the pastoral "Silva" to link Christ the shepherd and the soul as a lamb, the tortuous imagery of the forging and cutting of metal evokes the painful tortures of Carvajal y Mendoza's youth, both imposed and self-inflicted, and reflects the true nature of the persona as Carvajal y Mendoza herself.

Carvajal y Mendoza wishes to exceed the limits of nature, as her chosen mode of existence reveals. Deprived of the comforts of the body by her own will, the pain that her speaker feels is both physical and spiritual. Her spirit, however, is directed to the absent Pastor/host and not to her despised body. The sonnet becomes a work of self-examination, part of the Jesuit meditative experience functioning under the organizing principles of memory, intellect, and will, and here intellect and the will, figured as the body, clash. The polysemous "will" is utilized as part of the meditative experience, to control the passions, but it also often figures the willful body. This is so, for example, in many of William Shakespeare's sonnets, in which he puns on his own name and makes "will" a synonym for sexual power in determining to exercise his will over the beloved's body. As Carvajal y Mendoza probes the meaning of her physical experience, both body and mind become locked in the process and the sonnet becomes part of Carvajal y Mendoza's perpetual struggle to dominate the body and release the soul.

It is at the beginning of the tercets that the sonnet ceases its ambiguously Petrarchan nature. Until this point, Amor could be either the son of Venus or the son of God. The heart is ritually pierced by the pain of love, and Cupid forges it to his own pattern; the soul has departed on a Neoplatonic journey in search of eternal truth embodied in the beloved object. At the turn, however, Silva's intellectual excursion determines that the heart has been divinely encoded by Amor/Christ: "Vuelto a tu corazón cifra divina / de extremos mil Amor, en que su mano / mostrara quiso destreza peregrina" (9–11). Furthermore, Christ uses Silva as a means to demonstrate this divine dexterity, converting her weak, soft, feeling, and altogether human heart into his "alcázar soberano" (14). The heart of Silva becomes a model of what Christ seeks to achieve in all hearts, and this gives a purpose to her pain that enables the diamantine hardening of her breast. The imagery also suggests her knowledge of Teresa of Avila's *The Interior Castle*.

Although she tries to deny the body, Carvajal y Mendoza's military imagery again reflects the parallels between the palpable, earthly world and human determinations of the divine, in a country where Catholicism imbued every part of state administration and individual daily life. As this Spanish Catholic heart is fortified by Christ's love to defend it from the onslaught of heresy and Protestantism, so the female body is required to be the "alcázar" that protects personal and family reputations from disgrace and dishonor. Carvajal y Mendoza besmirched her own family's reputation in her willing determination to abase herself in public, to the extent that her family refused to acknowledge her once she actively sought disparagement and began her life of poverty in Madrid.[8] As the sonnet ends in the "alcázar" the transformation is completed; the heart becomes the New Jerusalem of the Revelation, set upon a fundament of stone. Her meditation has cleared all uncertainty and questioning and firmed her resolve to endure. She justifies her stance in affirming that the "alcázar" created in her heart is divine in nature. The sonnet moves through intellectual inquiry from ignorance to clear understanding of her role as a tool of God, a self-appointed task frequently alluded to in her correspondence. For example, in February 1606, she writes in a letter to a nun at the court in Flanders, Magdalena de San Jerónimo: "Si Nuestro Señor quiere que haya servido de sólo ponerme en el palenque, y desde él poderle decir: *Adsum, Domine, non recuso laborem,* yo no pretendo exceder de su voluntad y dulce gusto un solo punto" (*Epistolario* 165; If Our Lord wants me to serve him simply by putting myself on the scaffold, and from there be able to tell him: *Adsum, Domine, non recuso laborem,* I shall not attempt to exceed his will and sweet desires one jot). This same nun appears to have written repeatedly urging her to leave England. In March 1606, Carvajal y Mendoza wrote informing her of her long-held desire to go to England: "que ésta de venir aquí estaba en mi pecho desde los 18 años de mi edad, aguardando abriese Nuestro Señor camino de su mano" (165; for this matter of coming here was in my heart since I was eighteen years old, waiting for Our Lord to open the way with his hand). In April 1607, she wrote to her friend, Inés de la Asunción, now a cloistered nun: "No se me puede descubrir qué quiera Su Majestad de mí en Inglaterra, aunque parece querer la perseverancia en ella, hasta ahora a lo menos" (78; I cannot work out what His Maj-

---

8. Abad notes that she was in the Plaza Mayor, when her cousin the Marquis de Almazán passed by, "a caballo . . . con sus criados. . . . el marqués disimuló conocerla. Los criados que la conocieron comenzaron a discurrir sobre el verla en tan abatido traje y ocupación tan humilde" (on horseback . . . with his retinue . . . the marquis pretended not to recognize her. The servants who knew her began to gossip about seeing her in such ragged clothing and in such a humble occupation). Abad further observes that this determination to ignore her existence was general among her relatives; see *Misionera,* 77–78.

esty wants of me in England, although he appears to want me to perse-
vere here, at least until now). Like St. Teresa, by claiming God's control
over her movements Carvajal y Mendoza was able to deflect criticism of
her activities.

Despite her avowed silent obedience to her confessor's restrictions on
the Eucharist, Carvajal y Mendoza's second sonnet of loss and absence
explicitly confirms, in its title, that it is written in mourning for the loss
of daily communion:

Soneto espiritual de Silva a la ausencia de su dulcísimo Señor en la Sagrada Comunión

¡Ay soledad amarga y enojosa,
causada de mi ausente y dulce Amado!
¡Dardo eres en el alma atravesado,
dolencia penosísima y furiosa!

5   Prueba de amor terrible y rigurosa,
y cifra del pesar más apurado,
cuidado que no sufre otro cuidado,
tormento intolerable y sed ansiosa.

Fragua, que en vivo fuego me convierte,
10 de los soplos de amor tan avivada,
que aviva mi dolor hasta la muerte.

Bravo mar, en el cual mi alma engolfada,
con tormenta camina dura y fuerte
hasta el puerto y ribera deseada.

(Epistolario y poesías 437)

Silva's spiritual sonnet to the absence of her sweetest Lord in the Holy Communion

Oh bitter and wearisome loneliness,
caused by my sweet, absent Beloved!
You are a dart piercing my soul, with
furious and unbearable suffering,

A terrible and rigorous test of love,
and a symbol of crushing sorrow,

a care that suffers no other care,
an intolerable torment and anxious thirst;

A forge that converts me into living fire
with its gusts of increased love,
that enliven my suffering unto death;

a wild sea, in which my drowning soul
travels through a harsh and fierce storm
to the desired harbor and shore.

The title reveals that what Silva grieves for is the real body of Christ, and she repeats this in the opening lines. The well-known dart of the beatific experience is here turned to a weapon that evokes both Silva's loss and Christ's Crucifixion. For Carvajal y Mendoza, however, this is not the awareness of the soul leaving the impure body to fuse with the divine. As usual, it is the loss of the physical pleasure of contact with the bread of communion that causes her pain. She is penetrated, not with Christ's body, but with the emptiness of his absence. At the same time, her terminology evokes the piercing pleasure that communion represents for her, in receiving the body of Christ into hers: "y cifra del pesar más apurado, / cuidado que no sufre otro cuidado, / tormento intolerable y sed ansiosa" (6–8).

The quartets therefore tell two stories in one: the experience of communion and the experience of its lack. The magnitude of her suffering also appears in two ways: through the overflowing of her catalogue of grief into the tercets, and in the multitude of superlatives with which she attempts to express her inexpressible suffering: "penosísima," "furiosa," "terrible," "rigurosa," and "cifra que no sufre otro cuidado, / tormento intolerable y sed ansiosa" (7–8). That "sed ansiosa" points to the same insatiable hungering for God's physical presence discussed by Walker Bynum in relation to the medieval mystics (*Holy Feast* 58–68).

Silva determines that the withholding of communion is a trial of her faith: "Prueba de amor terrible y rigurosa" (5). Figuring herself as a countertype to Job, pierced through the heart, and with her emotions cruelly tested in the quartets, the tercets apply further torture in Petrarchan imagery of fire and water. The burning pain becomes a furnace, "fragua, que en vivo fuego me convierte" (9), breathed on and inflamed by love, and herein begins her path to understanding.[9] Carvajal y Mendoza, unusually well-schooled in the test of faith by physical suffering, discovers that the tempering of Silva's soul in the fire of love proves her faith, and the sonnet ends in hope as she passes her test of divine love. Like the blacksmith's burning iron, plunged into water to set its altered shape, Carvajal y Mendoza's tested soul is cooled, soothed, and reformed, enabling her to survive the wild sea of despair: "Bravo mar, en el cual mi alma engolfada, / con tormenta camina dura y fuerte" (12–13). The placing of the adjectives enables Carvajal y Mendoza again to double her message. The test is "dura y fuerte," but so is she. Faith keeps Silva on course toward the source of all her desire, "hasta el puerto y ribera deseada" (14). Carvajal y Mendoza is not alone in regarding suffering as a trial of faith. The testing and hardening nature of physical pain on the spirit was also often expressed and glorified in songs of the nuns' profession ceremonies that celebrated physical pain as the means to the rebirth of the soul in spiritual perfection (Arenal and Schlau 145).

Anne Cruz regards Carvajal y Mendoza's pastoral persona, Silva, as the means by which Carvajal y Mendoza distances herself from the pain of her lifelong submission to physical discipline ("Chains" 105). However, as far as her meditative sonnets are concerned, I contend that Silva, a barely disguised anagram of Luisa, makes a poor hiding place from memory. Instead, she reflects Carvajal y Mendoza's vision of herself as willingly possessed by the divine Shepherd. Silva serves not only to figure forth Carvajal y Mendoza's own character, but also allows the distanced and objective self-analysis sought by the spiritual exercises of Jesuit religious practice. Carvajal y Mendoza was versed in the spiritual exercises, having completed them before her departure for England in 1604. However, even before this, she was urged to practice the exercises as a young girl by her uncle (Abad "Semblanza" 33). When Carvajal y Mendoza identifies with Christ's physical torment, this is due more to her determination toward Christomimesis and her recourse to the meditative composition of place than to a commemorative linking to her youthful experience. Car-

---

9. Covarrubias's description of the *fragua* (forge) illustrates Carvajal y Mendoza's imagery: "La hornaza del herrero . . . está siempre ardiendo para poder domar el hierro" (The oven of the blacksmith . . . it is always burning so as to be able to manipulate the iron). For Carvajal y Mendoza, the "hierro" is a metaphorical rendering of the soul.

vajal y Mendoza's "eye" and her "I" are just far enough apart to accomplish her meditative desires.

Moreover, although Carvajal y Mendoza's wholly admiring descriptions of her uncle imply a psychological dependence engendered by his extraordinary activities, I suggest that Carvajal y Mendoza did not wish to forget either her tortured youth or her determination to endure self-abasement and martyrdom that fuelled her determination to go to England. It was her vow of absolute obedience and her willingness to embrace physical suffering that paradoxically released her from both her psychological bondage and her disciplinary practices. In a letter to Magdalena de San Jerónimo in March 1606 she revealed that the English Customs had confiscated her disciplinary instruments: "Tomáronme los lindos cilicios y otras cosas, con que se han entretenido y reído bien; y a mí me ha sido de mortificación el verlo en tales manos" (*Epistolario* 165–66; They took from me my beautiful hair shirts and other things, with which they entertained themselves and laughed a lot and it was a great mortification to me to see them in such hands).

Carvajal y Mendoza's mission to England afforded her an extraordinary level of independence, enabling her to pursue her ambitions: to die for Christ and to succor the suffering recusant Catholic population. By claiming that she was doing God's will, she was able to deflect criticism at home of her unusually independent stance. In England she was regarded as an extremely successful supporter of the Catholic cause and a source of immense anger and irritation to Abbott, the archbishop of Canterbury (Senning 46). Certainly, she appears in a highly negative light in Abbot's correspondence with William Trumbull, English ambassador to the Low Countries: "She hath spent much time in visiting Popish priests and giving alms to prisoners, not refusing to go into Newgate itself." In the same letters he describes her arrest, ordered by him in 1613: "I privately directed Mr Recorder of London to seize on her and her young ones. Who, going thither . . . apprehended her and brought her to me, who sent her to the Gatehouse" (Hinds 239). Her activities were also known to the king, who ordered severe punishment for the jailers who admitted her, after a suitable bribe, to take supper with the condemned priests, Roberts and Somer, in 1611 (CSP 8: 10).

If Carvajal y Mendoza's denial and punishment of the troublesome body were excessive, the healing balm provided by her spiritual union with Christ is equally strongly revealed in two sonnets expressing joy at her relationship with her Pastor. Furthermore, the degree of grief expressed in her sonnet "¡Ay soledad, amarga y enojosa!" on the withholding of daily communion is better understood when read in the light of her sonnet on the experience of receiving communion at the hands of the priest:

Soneto espiritual de Silva Al Santísimo Sacramento; en que habla el divino Verbo inmenso con el alma que le está recibiendode las manos del sacerdote

De inmenso amor aqueste abrazo estrecho
recibe, Silva, de tu dulce Amado,
y por la puerta de este diestro lado
éntrate, palomilla, acá en mi pecho.

5   reposa en el florido y sacro lecho,
y abrásate en amor tan abrasado,
que hasta que el fuerte nudo haya apretado,
no sea posible quede satisfecho.

Mira cómo te entrego, amiga mía,
10   todo mi ser y alteza sublimada;
estima aqueste don que amor te ofrece;

tendrás en mí glorioso compañía,
y entre mis mismos brazos regalada
gozarás lo que nadie no merece.

(Epistolario y poesías 438)

Silva's spiritual sonnet to the Holy Sacrament; in which the immense, divine Word which she receives from the hand of the priest speaks to her soul

Silva, receive this tight embrace of
immense love from your sweet Beloved,
and through the door in this right flank
enter, little dove, here into my breast.

Repose in the flowery and sacred marriage bed
and burn yourself in such scorching love,

> that until that strong knot has been tightened
> it will be impossible to remain satisfied.
>
> See how I surrender to you, oh friend of mine,
> all of my being and sublimated might;
> esteem this gift that love offers you;
>
> you shall have in me glorious company,
> and in the embrace of my gentle arms
> you shall enjoy that which nobody deserves.

The title fully expresses the spiritual nature of the encounter that takes place between the divine Word and the human soul.[10] The only bodily contact is the mediating hand of the priest, yet, paradoxically, the terminology of the sonnet renders the experience into an epithalamion. Silva is welcomed into the "florido y sacro lecho" of her Creator's embrace by his embodied voice; the all-powerful priest is relegated merely to the title. Again, Carvajal y Mendoza is harking back to an earlier period. For medieval women to receive the Eucharist was *imitatio crucis;* one ate the physicality of God (Bynum, *Holy Feast* 67). The experience was both extremely pleasurable and very painful and the union involved all the senses. One example is the revealed experience of Hadewijch, who wrote poetry in Flemish at the beginning of the thirteenth century: "[H]e gave himself to me in the shape of the Sacrament, in its outward form. . . . After that he came himself to me, took me entirely in his arms, and pressed me to him; and all my members felt his in full felicity, in accordance with the desire of my heart and my humanity" (*Holy Feast* 156).

Some two hundred and fifty years later, in her sonnet, Carvajal y Mendoza expresses exactly this sensation. She combines the Passion and the Eucharist, the two main foci of her prayer and meditation since childhood, in a single passionate image of amatory union. As her Esposo's arms are spread wide in the Crucifixion, embodied in the bread of the Eucharist, they are also open to invite Carvajal y Mendoza's soul into his embrace, and into the open wound in his side: "Éntrate, palo-

---

10. Muñoz, who published the first *vida* in the eighteenth century, insisted that "'los argumentos' o notas en prosa que preceden a muchas de ellas [las poesías], 'también son suyos'" (the arguments or notes in prose that precede many of hers [the poems] are also hers); quoted in Abad, "Nota," 425.

milla, acá en mi pecho" (4). Ambiguity resides in the image of the dove, which represents Christ, the Holy Spirit, and Silva herself. The dove has a long history in pagan literature, both Greek and Latin, associating it with Aphrodite/Venus. This dual image continued into the medieval period; Chaucer, for example, has doves hovering around the head of Venus in the "Knight's Tale." Hence, Carvajal y Mendoza simultaneously celebrates a purely spiritual embrace between the "Paloma" and the "palomilla" and the passionate embrace of physical desire.

The sonnet works throughout, therefore, on two levels: the sacred and the sexual. As Christ enters Silva in the bread, he invites her also to enter him, hence entwining two bodies, as well as the soul and the divine. The religious sacrifice of the Crucifixion and the corporeal sacrifice of sexual coupling become one, while the encounter is rendered in both pain and pleasure, presence and lack: "y abrásate en amor tan abrasado" (6). As the inviting Esposo declares, until husband and wife are joined there can be no satisfaction for that burning hunger: "que hasta que el fuerte nudo haya apretado, / no sea posible quede satisfecho" (7–8). Again, the tight knot that Luis de León describes binds soul and Redeemer together, part of this same embrace. Furthermore, Christ offers himself to Silva as a divine bride, when he invites her to invade the body he offers: "éntrate, palomilla, acá en mi pecho" (4).

This imagery of surrender and the invitation to love is repeated in the sestet: "Mira cómo te entrego, amiga mía, / todo mi ser y alteza sublimada; / estima aqueste don que amor te ofrece" (9–11). Here, Carvajal y Mendoza recurs to the Eucharist itself, for when the host is elevated before the altar in the mass the bread is changed and raised into the body and blood of Christ. For Carvajal y Mendoza, Christ, although raised to sit at the right hand of God, still offers himself to her soul. What he promises, what Carvajal y Mendoza will enjoy, is the divine grace of the beatific vision: "estima aqueste don que amor te ofrece" (11). The divine gift of himself and of sanctifying grace is accentuated by the emphatic double negative, "lo que nadie no merece," that expresses both the unworthiness of sinful humankind and the singular qualities of Silva as Christ's bride. It also emphasizes Catholic dogma, for grace is a rare divine gift that nobody "deserves." Carvajal y Mendoza's sonnet insists that this gift has been offered to her, bringing forth the exclusive nature of her relationship with Christ. The sonnet is a further evocation of her inner feelings and her security in her favored status, and has none of the didactic and inclusive qualities of Sor Violante's poetry.

Carvajal y Mendoza's intense physical and emotional attachment to her Savior is seen more clearly in the sonnet that begins "En el siniestro brazo recostada" (1):

> En el siniestro brazo recostada
> de su amado Pastor, Silva dormía,
> y con la diestra mano la tenía
> con un estrecho abrazo a sí allegada.
>
> 5   Y de aquel dulce sueño recordada,
> le dijo: "El corazón del alma mía
> vela, y yo duermo; ¡ay, suma alegría,
> cual me tiene tu amor tan traspasada!
>
> Ninfas del Paraíso soberanas,
> 10   sabed que estoy enferma y muy herida
> de unos abrasadísimos amores.
>
> Cercadme de odoríferas manzanas,
> pues me veis como fénix encendida;
> y cercadme tambíen de amenas flores."
>
> (*Epistolario y poesías* 438)

> Reclining within the left arm of
> her beloved Pastor, Silva was sleeping,
> and with his right hand he held her
> to him in a tight embrace.
>
> And remembering that sweet dream she
> said to him "The heart of my soul
> keeps vigil and I sleep; ah, fullest joy,
> since your love holds me transfixed!
>
> Sovereign nymphs of Paradise,
> know that I am very sick and wounded
> with scorching, burning love.

Surround me with sweet-smelling apples,
for I see myself like an inflamed phoenix;
and surround me also with pleasant flowers."

Silva is now securely in her Pastor's embrace in "un estrecho abrazo a sí allegada" (4). Carvajal y Mendoza utilizes the sensual language
of the Song of Songs to express her ineffable joy and certainty that she
is Christ's chosen bride. The music of the words is important; Carvajal y Mendoza employs internal rhyme within the first quartet: "siniestro / diestra," bringing both left and right arms into a continuum within
which Silva is held, while recurrent synelephas in the fourth line, "estrecho abrazo a sí allegada," emphasize the closeness of the embrace.[11]

Silva breaks the silence of the embrace, and speaks to her Pastor: "El
corazón del alma mía / vela, y yo duermo; ¡ay, suma alegría, / cuál me
tiene tu amor tan traspasada!" (6–8). The body sleeps but the eternal
soul awakens and is pierced by love in a now-familiar image of mystical union;[12] the magnitude of the experience leaves her weakened physically but strengthened spiritually in her rebirth as a phoenix: "Cercadme
de odoríferas manzanas, / pues me veis como fénix encendida; / y cercadme tambíen de amenas flores" (12–14). This vision clearly evokes Carvajal y Mendoza's yearning for a martyrdom that would literally enable
the rekindling of her spirit into eternal life as her body is burned away,
but, at the same time, the inclusion of the garden as *locus amoenus* and
of the apples returns to the Song of Songs. Sick and wounded with love
though she is, the destructive principle is dispelled by the phoenix imagery. Hence, the wounds and flames bring only delight, as the phoenix
also symbolizes both her regenerated love and the risen Christ. Similarly, the garden imagery restores the imbalance of the Fall, with the apple
becoming a positive image of the fruitful relationship between the soul
and Christ. The sweetness and harmony of her imagery is reflected in the

11. The embrace is both given and returned in the Song of Solomon: "Oh that his
left hand were under my head and that his right hand embraced me [2: 6]. . . . [W]hen I
found him whom my soul loves. I held him, and would not let him go until I had brought
him into my mother's house, and into the chamber of her that conceived me" [3:4].

12. The dream accords almost exactly with the Song: "I slept, but my heart was
awake. . . . My beloved put his hand to the latch, and my heart was thrilled within me"
(5: 2).

structure of evenly distributed short and long words, musical sound and rhythm. Having accepted her Esposo's invitation to the embrace in the earlier sonnet, she now expresses her certainty in its continuing bliss.

Not content to express merely her own soul as transfixed by the dart of divine love, Carvajal y Mendoza demonstrates the mutuality of this relationship in a sonnet expressing Christ's experience of being shot through with love for "la naturaleza humana" (humankind). Its subtext, however, remains one of love for herself, for although her title suggests an inclusive redemption of humankind, the sonnet is again ambiguous, through the recurrent figures of the "zagala," and of Christ as the loving Pastor:

> *Soneto espiritual de Silva del encendido amor con que*
> *Nuestro Señor deseó y esperó el día en que había de dejar*
> *restaurada la naturaleza humana, a costa de su inestimable*
> *vida temporal, acabada entre innumerables oprobios*
>
> En las ardientes llamas encendido
> de amor, y de su flecha atravesado,
> el Príncipe de gloria disfrazado
> en traje pastoril desconocido,
>
> 5   muchos más de catorce años servido,
> sin dar punto de alivio a su cuidado
> por su zagala había, y no cansado,
> le han poquísimos días parecido.
>
> Y su excesivo amor no satisfecho,
> 10   porque sangre en las venas le quedaba,
> causaba angustias mil dentro en su pecho.
>
> Y vuelto a la que en tanto extremo amaba,
> decía: "¿Qué ha por ti tu Pastor hecho,
> mientras la vida y sangre no te daba?"
>
>   (*Epistolario y poesías* 438)

*Silva's spiritual sonnet about the inflamed love with which
Our Lord desired and waited for the day in which he would be
able to leave human nature restored at the cost of his inestima-
ble temporal life, finished among immense opprobrium*

Burning in the ardent flames of
Love, and pierced by his arrow,
the Prince of glory, disguised in
the pastoral raiment of an unknown,

served his shepherdess many more
than fourteen years without relief
for his cares, and untiring, it seemed
to him not more than a few days.

And, his excessive love, not satisfied
because the blood still flowed in his veins,
caused a thousand anguishes in his heart.

And turning to her whom he so extremely loved,
he said "What has your Pastor done for you,
when he has not yet given his life and blood for you?"

Role-reversal in the first stanza causes the Pastor to suffer the pangs
of love: "En las ardientes llamas encendido / de amor, y de su flecha
atravesado" (1–2). Similarly, the words she ascribes to the Pastor in the final tercet appear to belong not to a generalized "naturaleza humana" but
to herself "la que en tanto extremo amaba" (11). Like St. Bernard, who
would see the Pastor's words as intended for the human soul, Carvajal
y Mendoza's title and terminology may also embrace this image. Underlying it, however, is the insistent demand of Carvajal y Mendoza as an
independent noblewoman, who, in giving everything away and seeking
martyrdom, gained that most precious of gifts seldom experienced by
women: freedom of choice.

In an age of female enclosure, when the small freedoms of the previous century had largely disappeared under the strictures of the Council
of Trent, Carvajal y Mendoza achieved a remarkably independent existence through sheer force of her own personality and determination. Her
sonnets to her "Esposo" are similarly single-minded in their devotion to

the person of Christ. They differ markedly from Sor Violante's didactic and meditative works on Christ's earthly ministry, discussed in the previous chapters. Carvajal y Mendoza's personal relationship with Christ is not an inclusive celebration of shared devotion, as convent poetry frequently is, nor, when she directs her sonnets to the host, do they celebrate the mystery of transubstantiation as an important part of Church dogma. Instead, they are further evocations of her attachment to the body of Christ.

In the sonnet entitled "Soneto de Silva al Santísimo Sacramento: ¡Hostia!" (Silva's sonnet to the Holy Sacrament: Host!) Silva praises the host, more specifically her divine Esposo in the form of the bread. She returns to the familiar images of fire and water, affirming that only when she partakes of Christ in the communion bread can she find peace. Nevertheless, the sonnet opens in some ambiguity:

> Contra los hostes soberano y fuerte
> amparo, do tu nombre se deriva:
> de cristalinas aguas fuente viva
> que templa la abrasada ansia de verte.
>
> 5   Muerte eres, vida eterna, de mi muerte,
> y de aquella manzana tan nociva
> remedio contrapuesto que la esquiva
> fortuna nos volvió en dichosa suerte.
>
> Ambrosia y néctar, que su ser inmenso
> 10   al alma comunica en tanto grado,
> que queda hecha soberana diosa,
>
> y de amor encendida tan intenso,
> que no puede vivir ya sin su Amado,
> ni, fuera dél, amar ninguna cosa.
>
>   (*Epistolario y poesías* 437)

> Sovereign and strong shelter against
> enemies, from which your name derives:
> living fountain of crystalline waters
> that tempers the burning anxiety to see you.

Death you are, eternal life, of my death,
and to that so noxious apple
a counterposed remedy that devious
fortune turned into our happy fate.

Ambrosia and nectar, which your great
being communicates to the soul in high degree,
leave her changed to a sovereign goddess,

and with such intense burning love
that she can no longer live without her Beloved,
nor, away from him, love any thing at all.

The editors of *Tras el espejo la musa escribe* deduce that Carvajal y Mendoza confused the etymology of *hostia*, the host, and *hostes*, hostile forces. Given her broad education and knowledge of Latin, and her own unambiguous dependence on the host, it seems more certain that she deliberately used this structure to emphasize the protection and favor it offered. For Carvajal y Mendoza, *hostia* is not derived grammatically from the homonymic *hostes* but semantically, from *amparo*. The host/Christ is Carvajal y Mendoza's shield and defender against all ills and enemies, who gives her divine favor at the moment of communion. Similarly, Cruz links the sacrificial term "hostia" to both the victim and its symbol, the communion wafer, in her consideration of this sonnet ("Words Made Flesh" n. pag.).

For Carvajal y Mendoza, the Eucharist is the only balm that can soothe her burning physical desire: "de cristalinas aguas fuente viva / que templa la abrasada ansia de verte" (3–4). These words reflect the Psalmist's yearning for God: "As a hart longs for flowing streams, so longs my soul for thee, O God. My soul thirsts for God, for the living God. When shall I come and behold the face of God" (Psalm 42: 1). Carvajal y Mendoza, however, is bolstered by the New Covenant of Christian love and salvation, as is revealed in the second quartet, where the first line is a delightful layering of opposites: "Muerte eres, vida eterna, de mi muerte" (5). She reorders the well-known words of John of the Cross and Teresa of Avila: "muero porque no muero." Here, Christ's death and eternal life spell the death of the eternal death with which humankind was threatened as the direct result of the Fall. In the same quartet Christ is portrayed as the antidote to the poisoned apple, a clever line that leaves Eve and her culpability out of it completely. As Christ is the remedy to the "manzana nociva," the curious lines "que la esquiva / fortuna nos volvió en dichosa suerte" (7–8) suggest this poet's belief in the "fortunate fall." Had the sin of Eden never occurred, Christ would not have entered the world; there would have been no Christianity; "Silva" would not have had her "Pastor."

Under the influence of the transubstantiated host, the soul becomes a sovereign goddess in the last line of the first tercet, bride again of the embodied Christ. The experience leaves the soul so inflamed with love that life without him becomes impossible: "que queda hecha soberana diosa, / y de amor encendida tan intenso / que no puede vivir ya sin su Amado" (11–13).[13] A poem that begins in praise of the host becomes personal to Carvajal y Mendoza again by the second quartet: "Muerte eres . . . de mi muerte" (8), and ends in the certainty of her own soul's need for the person of Christ: "ni, fuera dél, amar ninguna cosa" (14).

CONCLUSION

As I have attempted to show in this chapter, Carvajal y Mendoza's active mysticism owes more to the active Martha than to the contemplative Mary. Although her early life of torment was enjoined on her from outside, and undoubtedly colored her own determination toward personal suffering and martyrdom, she was able to take control of her own fate to an extraordinary degree. Her apostolic journey to England was sanctioned by Church authorities, probably, as Elizabeth Rhodes has suggested, due to the near-impossibility of getting male priests into the country, and once there she enjoyed extraordinary freedom ("Journey" 905). Once in England she was able to pursue her own aims and manage her

13. The similarity in approach to the flaming soul between Carvajal y Mendoza and other mystical writers is evident in a poem by John of the Cross: "¡Oh llama de amor viva, / que tiernamente hieres / de mi alma en el más profundo centro! / Pues ya no eres esquiva, / acaba ya si quieres, / rompe la tela de este dulce encuentro" (O living flame of love / that tenderly burns / my soul in its most profound core! / Well now that you do not avoid me / end me, if you wish, / break the thread of this sweet encounter).

own household. She also, at that point, gave away the anachronistic exis-tence of a medieval ascetic, becoming noticeably active in her support of English Catholics.

As far as her mystical poetry is concerned, Carvajal y Mendoza's mys-ticism is, in Dionysian terms, symbolic and cataphatic, concerned with what she can affirm about God, rather than apophatic where, in the pres-ence of God, speech and thought are silenced (Louth 165). She is never silent, never silenced, neither in her sonnets nor in her nine years in Lon-don, which included two terms of imprisonment. Her sonnets eloquent-ly reflect her absolute devotion to Christ in body and soul, a wholly ab-sorbing experience between Carvajal y Mendoza and her Savior that has none of the didacticism and inclusiveness of convent poetry.

Carvajal y Mendoza wrote her poetry in what may be called her "Mary" period when she was living her determination to abase herself utterly, to live and die as Christ, seeking that apophaticism that would lead her into rapt silence before God. This is why her sonnets are intro-spective and meditative in the Jesuit style, precluding any other influence than that which she believed she received directly from Christ. Once able to turn her passionate devotion to more outward expression, Carvajal y Mendoza entered her "Martha" phase, where she comforted the con-demned before the scaffold and enshrined their dismembered remains as saintly relics. She became an able apostle of Christ and an active support-er, educator, and shelter to the oppressed English Catholics. It was in this active role that she finally found her martyrdom. Her death, through ill-ness, was attributed to the trials she suffered in her imprisonments, and her body was returned with great honor to Spain. She would no doubt be astonished to know that the body she despised, mortified, and so de-sired to leave behind is now venerated in the reliquary of the Monasterio de la Real Encarnación in Madrid.

CONCLUSION   *Living the Baroque*

༄

It is another feather, perhaps the finest, in their caps.

They wrote as women write, not as men write.

(Woolf 68)

IN RECENT DECADES, FEMINIST SCHOLARSHIP has revealed a previously almost invisible body of work by women writers and intellectuals who wrote against or in spite of patriarchal restriction, dating back to the far reaches of the Christian era. In presenting
this study of sonnets by women of the seventeenth century in the Iberian Peninsula, I have sought to add to this body of scholarship by drawing together women's poems written at the very seat of power and at the
periphery in both the secular and the religious fields. Such a broad approach provides a spectrum of women's lived experience as it is reflected in their poetic works, for the research is necessarily limited by wom-
en's ability to leave a written trace in the record. Extant literary works
from this period have mainly come from women of the educated elite or
the noble classes, accustomed to command their own servants, schooled
in the niceties of social deportment, always comfortably off, and always
aware of their own value as commodities in the marriage market controlled by their male relatives. While this study has remained within the
realm of aristocratic women's literary production, increasingly research is
being conducted by others into the activities of less fortunate and lower-

class women and those writing to defend themselves against Inquisitional charges.[1]

Women's literary works provide important evidence of contemporary cultural experience. They also require us to reconsider women's place in the literary culture of seventeenth-century Iberia. They not only add to our knowledge of women's experience but also reveal some aspects of men's lives, now seen through a feminine and not always complimentary lens. The scope of the work has caused me to focus specifically on the sonnets since the volume of poetry by these women is considerable. There is therefore much work still to be done in discerning the attitudes and rhetorical skills deployed in their verse. The often acerbic works of Ramírez, for example, provide a rich repository of observed quirks and foibles that were part of daily Spanish life in the upper classes. Nevertheless, through contextually based readings of their sonnets, against the prevalent philosophical, theological, and social background of seventeenth-century Spain, we can broaden the existing picture of women's intellectual achievements and their social role.

As I have shown in Chapter 1, patronage offered women singular opportunities for social advancement if they were prepared to submit to a socially advantageous marriage, and for power, albeit within a limited coterie of other women.[2] However, it also brought rewards, both political and financial, as Sor Violante's patronage sonnets indicate. Her fame as a court poet enabled her to proffer advice to the king, as in one of the last sonnets of her life, written in 1689, where she urges the king to destroy the Turks. This affirmation of female power within the patronage system supports my view that these women did not overtly work to prove themselves "fully human," to borrow Lerner's phrase (*Consciousness* 10). It further suggests that these women did not feel that their capacity for intelligent reasoning was under question. Their works proceed from the natural assumption that they are important members of their community and of their families. They are not apologetic about putting their

1. I refer here to such works as Vollendorf's *The Lives of Women*, Poska's *Women and Authority in Early Modern Spain*, and Perry's *The Handless Maiden*.

2. The extent of women's activities in the patronage of and in managing convents and convent estates, for example, has been explored by Elizabeth Lehfeldt in *The Permeable Cloister*.

thoughts and feelings into verse. They write confidently, secure in their social position and their education, and they strongly affirm women's capacity for abstract thought and reason. This ability is particularly noticeable in the sonnets of *desengaño* that form part of Chapter 5, on the love poetry, where they treat failed courtships as an educative experience. They learn of the duplicity and moral failings of men whom they have been encouraged to believe are of a higher order of intelligence and honor than it is possible for women to achieve due to their supposed humoral fallibility. In this chapter we also see criticism, not of direct oppression of women by men, but of a system that permits men freedom of movement that would be unthinkable for women. The demands and opportunities of empire were available to women only as part of the train of the men who went to make new lives in the New World. For instance, when Ramírez's brother, Lorenzo, sailed away to Guatemala, he went alone, in spite of much evidence in her poetry of his willingness to pay court to young women in his immediate environs. It was Lorenzo who left behind a bastard son, Manuel, fathered on a *pastelera,* possibly the "Aminta" of Ramírez's sardonic poem (Carrasco García 112–13).

In spite of the inadequacies of the less than honorable lover, which may account for the fact that none of these women wed, what remains clear in the verse explored in this work is that the family was of central importance in this period. The value of family life as an aspect of social control and financial and emotional support is well known. What is new in this study is the degree of love, warmth, and informality that existed between daughters and their fathers, as well as between siblings. These attitudes are manifested in verse directed specifically to family members and therefore not intended to be representations of abstract thought or contributions to an established genre. It is commonly stated that the early modern father, as head of the household and responsible for all within it, was an austere figure. Such an imposing patriarch, it has been supposed, could not inspire love in daughters, who presented little more than opportunities for a socially desirable marriage. Even this possibility was always coupled with the burden of providing a dowry. Ramírez is one poet who clearly shows her fondness for her father in her concern for his health and her delight in presenting him with poetic petitions for gifts from Madrid. While Cueva does not pen such informal poetry as

Ramírez, her sad poem marking her father's death strongly suggests genuine affection. These poetic inscriptions of filial devotion are amply supported by the anecdotal evidence provided by Lady Fanshawe's memoirs and the reports of English visitors to Spain, detailed in Chapter 3.

However surprising the father's role may appear in these works, in the light of historical evidence to the contrary the mother occupies a pivotal role of her own. As the center of the household, the mother had full control of the children in their early years, but, at least theoretically, lost control of her sons once they reached an age where male family members took command of their education. The intention was to turn the child into a man who would be capable of demonstrating the requisite level of *hombría* appropriate to his high social status. The works of Sor Violante del Cielo, I have contended, stand in complete opposition to this picture. Sor Violante shows that the strong bond of love between a son and his mother remains a constant source of moral and emotional support within the family. Sor Violante strengthens her argument by applying it to the unanswerable figures of the Virgin Mary and Jesus Christ. As I have argued in Chapter 2, Sor Violante does not make of the Virgin Mary an impossible figure of parthenogenesis, beyond the ability of ordinary women to emulate. Rather, the Virgin Mary stands in for all women, regardless of rank, and for the importance of their maternal role.

Familial love is not restricted by these poets to their parents. There is ample evidence of friendship and warmth among siblings. Furthermore, Ramírez is one poet who does not hesitate to lampoon and criticize the behavior of her brothers. There is no sense of rebellion in these works; she simply observes their failings and points them out in verse, surely an acceptable manner of delivering a mild rebuke. For Cueva, her brother provides yet another opportunity to further family renown, as she praises his efforts in the train of the cardinal-prince. Nevertheless, there is pride and affection in works that speak of a relationship that supersedes the advantages of rank and honor. Although Luisa de Carvajal y Mendoza penned no poetry to her brother, her *Epistolario* includes a number of letters to him in which she offers advice on family and spiritual matters. Similarly, she writes of her experiences in London to her cousins, and attempts through these letters to sway the foreign policy of her king in the interests of the oppressed English Catholics. The span of this study has not afforded opportunities for a detailed study of her letters, which provide much information of interest to a social historian and which merit further investigation. For all her avowed obedience and self-abasement, Carvajal y Mendoza's strongly worded letters do not suggest that she was in awe of her brother, who was the titular head of her family. Where in her view she saw a family member in danger of spiritual annihilation she did not hesitate to commit her thoughts to verse, as in the sonnet admonition to the cousin who shared her early life, discussed in Chapter 3. This is one of only three sonnets by Carvajal y Mendoza that did not directly address a divine figure or event, pointing to the importance to her of maintaining the spiritual purity of her bloodline.

Notwithstanding the independent stance and proud intelligence demonstrated in these sonnets, the fact remains that repressive societal norms sought to limit women's freedom to act in the early modern period, through long-held opinions regarding women's physiological unsuitability for responsibility or for philosophical or political thought. However much women desired independence and to have their intelligence recognized and encouraged, they too had to live within the confines of the political and philosophical system that governed everybody, rich and poor, regardless of sex. What my investigation of their works reveals is that while these women sought avenues to express themselves and demonstrate their capacity for independent thought, this was not a politically motivated attempt to change women's status. They lived within the system which, at their elevated social level, had much to offer them in terms of patronage, advantageous marriages, and social status. However slight these advantages may appear in twenty-first-century terms, it would be anachronistic to suggest that the benefits they received from manipulating the system to their own ends were not rewarding to them. There were no democracies in the seventeenth century; every western European country had its own form of patriarchal and hierarchical governing system. This philosophy was particularly irksome to intelligent women, as the works of María de Zayas or of the English writer Aphra Behn, reveal. Nevertheless, an ability to live within the system and to make it work to the best advantage possible was the only solution available. Women retained a degree of independence by not marrying or by entering a convent that would permit them a modicum of social intercourse, as well as the opportunity to continue with their studies, as is the case with Sor Violante and Marcia Belisarda. The solitary exception to this situation was Luisa de Carvajal y Mendoza, whose extraordinary life of religious devotion and sacrifice, coupled with a frequently repeated determination to adhere to absolute obedience, granted her greater independence than any of the women in this study. However, she achieved this independence by going over the heads of the human hierarchy and citing God as her motivating force.

The greatest support to writing women, outside their own families, was their network of friendships. As I have revealed in Chapter 4, nuns like Marcia Belisarda welcomed novices into the convent with verse that stressed the communal nature of the convent life and the benefits to be derived from marriage to Christ. Similarly, sonnets written by Cueva, Ramírez, and Sor Violante to friends that express longing for their companionship show that seventeenth-century women had sufficient opportunities, in spite of the often-repeated strictures of moralists like Juan de Zabaleta or Fray Luis de León, to meet and share confidences and to support and reassure each other. Nevertheless, as the life story of Ramírez also shows, friendship could turn to enmity when presumptions of social status within the hierarchical order, even at the provincial level, were upset. In the light of these poems, therefore, although women did not seek to upset the social order, they did make determined efforts to rise within it to a position where greater status could afford them more independence and power.

While friendship and family were important in seventeenth-century Spanish society, religion dominated every aspect of life, as the appearance of religious verse in almost every chapter shows. The religious fervor of Counter-Reformation Spain was evident in the art and literature of the period and among these poets is most clearly seen in the poetry of Sor Violante and Carvajal y Mendoza.[3] As Sor Violante's sonnets to the Virgin Mary celebrate motherhood and the Virgin's humanity, they also remind her readers of the exalted status of this most divine of mothers, through her position at the side of God. However, neither Sor Violante nor any of the poets in the study regards the Virgin as an intercessory figure. On the contrary, she is a figure of feminine power in her own right, as is clear in

---

3. Marcia Belisarda's religious verse is not found in great quantity in her sonnets, although religious thought abounds in other poetry in her manuscript.

Sor Violante's sonnet on her coronation as Queen of Heaven, explored in Chapter 2. Carvajal y Mendoza, on the other hand, although she named her little sisterhood in London "La Congregación de la Soberana Virgen María Nuestra Señora" (The Congregation of the Sovereign Virgin Mary Our Lady), writes no sonnets to the Virgin. She venerated the Virgin and writes of having her at her side in London, but her sonnets, indeed almost all her poems, are directed to her *esposo*, Christ. While the most erotic love poetry of all five women is that directed by Carvajal y Mendoza to Christ, her adaptation of Juan de la Cruz's and Teresa de Avila's poetry as well as the Song of Songs, grounds her work in writings dating back to the earliest Christians, in proposing her soul as Christ's bride.

For all her courage, determination, and independence, Carvajal y Mendoza remains a solitary and unusual figure in the landscape of feminine endeavor in the seventeenth century. What comes through above all in the poetry of the other four poets is a robust enjoyment of the opportunities they created for themselves. Sor Violante saw her poetry in print and it is significant that, in spite of her large portfolio of religious verse, it was her secular works that were published in her lifetime. Similarly, the poetry that Marcia Belisarda prepared for publication included both secular and religious works. That these works were intended for a wider audience, together with the large number of sonnets written by women for *certámenes,* indicates women's pride in their literary skill and a determination to share their thoughts beyond the walls of the home or convent.

The sonnets reproduced and explored in this study represent cultural expressions of women's own sociohistorical paradigm. Furthermore, they enhance our understanding of the Baroque by presenting their own attitudes and a joyous expression of female thought and reason. These women lived the Baroque and made the most of every opportunity presented to them to show their skill. In doing so, they demonstrated that literature and art cannot be entirely separated from other aspects of social practice, for they harnessed their intellectual skills and education to existing poetic modes formed in a masculine system of self-expression. Though the degree of autonomy they achieved in writing their own thoughts and exercising their education and wit may be small by today's standards, it is a significant demonstration that these privileged members of Spanish society found life sufficiently rewarding, varied, and interesting to preserve it in verse.

BIBLIOGRAPHY

PRIMARY SOURCES

Arteaga, Inarda de. ms. 3890 Biblioteca Nacional de España. Madrid.

Belisarda, Marcia. ms. 7469. Biblioteca Nacional de España. Madrid.

Carvajal y Mendoza, Luisa de. *Epistolario y poesías.* Biblioteca de Autores Españoles. Ed. Jesús González Marañon, completada y revisada por Camilo María Abad. Vol. 179. Madrid: Atlas, 1965.

Cueva y Silva, Leonor de la. ms. 4127. Biblioteca Nacional de España. Madrid.

del Cielo, Sor Violante. *Rimas varias de la Madre Sóror Violante del Cielo, Religiosa en el Monasterio de la Rosa de Lisboa. Dedicadas al Excelentissimo Señor Conde Almirante y por su mandado, sacadas a luz.* Ruán (Rouen): Maurry, 1646.

————. *Parnaso lusitano de divinos e humanos versos, compostos pela Madre Soror Violante do Ceo, Religiosa Dominica no Convento da Rosa de Lisboa, dedicado a' Senhora Soror Violante do Ceo, Religiosa no convento de Santa Martha de Lisboa.* Primeyro tomo. Lisboa: Miguel Rodrigues, 1733.

do Ceo, Sor Violante. *Obras Varias poeticas.* Additional Ms. 25353. British Library. London.

Ramírez de Guzmán, Catalina Clara. mss. 3884, 3917. Biblioteca Nacional de España. Madrid.

Vieira, Fray Antonio de, et al. *Memorias funebres. Sentidos pellos ingenhos portugueses na morte da Senhora Dona Maria de Attayde Offerecidas a Senhora Dona Luiza Maria de Faro Condessa de Penaguiam.* Lisboa: Officina Craesbekiana, 1650.

SECONDARY SOURCES

Abad, Camilo María. "Nota preliminar a las poesías." *Luisa de Carvajal y Mendoza: Epistolario y poesías.* Ed. Camilo María Abad and Jesús González Marañon. Biblioteca de Autores Españoles 179. Madrid: Atlas, 1965.

————. "Semblanza biográfica de Doña Luisa de Carvajal y Mendoza (1566–1614)."

Luisa de Carvajal y Mendoza: Epistolario y poesías. Ed. Camilo María Abad and Jesús González Marañon. Biblioteca de Autores Españoles 179. Madrid: Atlas, 1965. 15–63.

———. *Una misionera española en la Inglaterra del siglo XVII (1566–1614)*. Santander: Universidad Pontificia, 1966.

Aguiar e Silva, Vítor Manuel. *Maneirismo e barroco na poesia lírica portuguesa*. Coimbra: Centro de Estudos Romanicos, 1971.

Alcalá Zamora, José. *La vida cotidiana en la España de Velázquez*. Madrid: Temas de Hoy, 1989.

Alzieu, Pierre, Robert Jammes, and Yvan Lissorgues, eds. *Poesía erótica del Siglo de Oro*. Barcelona: Crítica, 1983.

Aquinas, Thomas. *The Summa Theologica*. Chicago: Encyclopaedia Britannica, 1952.

Arenal, Electa, and Georgina Sabat de Rivers, eds. *Literatura conventual femenina: sor Marcela de San Félix, hija de Lope de Vega, Obra completa*. Barcelona: Promociones y Publicaciones Universitarias, 1988.

Arenal, Electa, and Stacey Schlau. *Untold Sisters: Hispanic Nuns in Their Own Works*. Albuquerque: University of New Mexico Press, 1989.

Ariès, Philippe. *Centuries of Childhood*. Trans. Robert Baldick. London: Cape, 1962.

Aristotle. *Nicomachean Ethics Books VIII and IX*. Trans. Michael Pakaluk. Clarendon Aristotle Series. Ed. J. L. Ackrill and Lindsay Judson. Oxford: Clarendon Press, 1998.

Armon, Shifra. *Picking Wedlock*. Lanham: Rowman Littlefield, 2002.

Armstrong, Nancy, and Leonard Tennenhouse, eds. *The Ideology of Conduct*. New York: Methuen, 1987.

Augustine, of Hippo. *The City of God*. London: Dent, 1931.

———. "Tractate on the Gospel of John," 119.2. 2003. Catholic Encyclopedia Online. Available at *www.newadvent.org/fathers/1701119.htm*. Retrieved 22 April 2004.

Bacon, Francis. *The Essays*. Harmondsworth: Penguin Books, 1985.

Baker, Edward. "Patronage: The Parody of an Institution in Don Quijote." *Culture and the State in Spain 1550–1850*. Ed. Tom Lewis and Francisco J. Sánchez. New York and London: Garland, 1999. 102–125.

Bennassar, Bartolomé. *Historia de los Españoles*. Vol. 1. Trans. Bernat Hervàs. Barcelona: Crítica, 1989.

———. *La España del Siglo de Oro*. Barcelona: Crítica, 2001.

———. *The Spanish Character: Attitudes and Mentalities from the Sixteenth to the Nineteenth Century*. Berkeley and Los Angeles: University of California Press, 1979.

Bergmann, Emilie, and Leah Middlebrook. "La mujer petrarquista: 'hollines y peces.' Poética renacentista a través de la óptica de Sor Juana." *Breve historia feminista de la literatura española (en lengua castellana). Tomo II: La mujer en la literatura española, modos de representación desde la Edad Media hasta el siglo XVII*. Ed. Iris M. Zavala. Vol. 2: Editorial Universidad de Puerto Rico, 1995. 145–151.

Bernard, of Clairvaux. *On the Song of Songs.* Trans. Kilian J. Walsh and Irene M. Edmonds. Spencer: Cistercian Publications, 1971–1980.

Brownlee, Marina Scordilis, and Hans Ulrich Gumbrecht. *Cultural Authority in Golden Age Spain.* Baltimore: Johns Hopkins University Press, 1995.

Burt, Donald X. *Friendship and Society: Introduction to Augustine's Practical Philosophy.* Grand Rapids: Eerdmans, 1999.

Butler, Christopher. "Numerological Thought." *Silent Poetry: Essays in Numerological Analysis.* Ed. Alistair Fowler. London: Routledge, 1970. 1–31.

Bynum, Caroline Walker. *Fragmentation and Redemption: Essays on Gender and the Human Body in Medieval Religion.* New York: Urzone, 1991.

————. *Holy Feast and Holy Fast: The Religious Significance of Food to Medieval Women.* Berkeley and Los Angeles: University of California Press, 1987.

————. *Jesus as Mother: Studies in the Spirituality of the High Middle Ages.* Berkeley and Los Angeles: University of California Press, 1982.

Carrasco García, Antonio. *La Plaza Mayor de Llerena y otros estudios.* Valdemoro: Tuero, 1985.

Carvajal y Mendoza, Luisa de. *This Tight Embrace: Luisa de Carvajal y Mendoza (1566–1614).* Trans. Elizabeth Rhodes. Ed. Elizabeth Rhodes. Milwaukee: Marquette University Press, 2000.

Catholic Truth Society. *A Spanish Heroine in England: Doña Luisa de Carvajal.* 1905.

Chaucer, Geoffrey. *The Knight's Tale.* Ed. A. C. Spearing. Cambridge: Cambridge University Press, 1966.

Cicero. *On Friendship and The Dream of Scipio.* Trans. and ed. J. G. F. Powell. Warminster: Aris & Phillips, 1990.

Clarke, Danielle, and Elizabeth Clarke. *This Double Voice: Gendered Writing in Early Modern England.* Basingstoke: Macmillan, 2000.

Costa e Silva, José María. *Ensaio biográfico sobre os melhores poetas portugueses.* Vol. 8. Lisboa: Silviana, 1854. 57–92.

Cruz, Anne J. "Chains of Desire: Luisa de Carvajal y Mendoza's Poetics of Penance." *Estudios sobre escritoras hispánicas en honor de Georgina Sabat-Rivers.* Ed. Lou Charnon-Deutsch. Madrid: Castalia, 1992. 97–112.

————. "Challenging Lives: Gender and Class as Categories in Early Modern Spanish Biographies." *Disciplines on the Line: Feminist Research on Spanish, Latin-American, and U.S. Latina Women.* Ed. Anne J. Cruz, Rosalie Hernández-Pecoraro, and Joyce Tolliver. Newark: Juan de la Cuesta, 2003. 103–23.

————. "Feminism, Psychoanalysis, and the Search for the M/other in Early Modern Spain." *Indiana Journal of Hispanic Literatures* 6–7 (Spring–Fall 1995): 31–54.

————. "Juana and Her Sisters: Female Sexuality and Spirituality in Early Modern Spain and the New World." *Recovering Spain's Feminist Tradition.* Ed. Lisa Vollendorf. New York: MLA, 2001. 88–105.

————. "Willing Desire: Luisa de Carvajal y Mendoza and Female Subjectivity." *Power and Gender in Renaissance Spain: Eight Women of the Mendoza Family, 1450–1650.* Ed. Helen Nader. Urbana and Chicago: University of Illinois Press, 2004. 177–94.

————. "Words Made Flesh: Luisa de Carvajal's Eucharistic Poetry." *En desa-*

gravio de las damas: Women's Poetry of the Golden Age. Ed. Julián Olivares and Elizabeth Boyce. Asheville: Pegasus. Forthcoming.

Custodio Vega, Angel. *La poesía de Santa Teresa.* 2nd ed. Madrid: Católica, 1975.

Defourneaux, Marcelin. *Daily Life in Golden Age Spain.* Trans. Newton Branch. Stanford: Stanford University Press, 1970.

Deleito y Piñuela, José. *La mujer, la casa y la moda (en la España del rey poeta).* Madrid: Espasa-Calpe, 1946.

———. *La vida religiosa española bajo el cuarto Felipe: santos y pecadores.* Madrid: Espasa Calpe, 1963.

Derrida, Jacques. *Politics of Friendship.* Trans. George Collins. London and New York: Verso, 1997.

Díaz, José Simón, ed. *Siglos de Oro: Índice de Justas Poéticas.* Madrid: CSIC, 1962.

Díaz-Plaja, Fernando. *La vida cotidiana en la España de la Inquisición.* Madrid: EDAF, 1996.

———. *La vida cotidiana en la España del siglo de oro.* Crónicas de la historia 9. Madrid: EDAF, 1994.

———. *La vida y la época de Felipe III.* Barcelona: Planeta, 1998.

Domínguez Ortiz, Antonio. *La sociedad española en el siglo XVII.* Vol. 1. 2 vols. Granada: Universidad de Granada, 1992.

Donne, John. *The Complete English Poems of John Donne.* Ed. C. A. Patrides. London: Dent, 1985.

DuBois, Page. *Sowing the Body: Psychoanalysis and Ancient Representations of Women.* Chicago: University of Chicago Press, 1988.

Ellington, Donna Spivey. *From Sacred Body to Angelic Soul: Understanding Mary in Late Medieval and Early Modern Europe.* Washington, D.C.: The Catholic University of America Press, 2001.

El Saffar, Ruth. *Rapture Encaged: The Suppression of the Feminine in Western Culture.* New York: Routledge, 1994.

Entrambasaguas y Peña, Joaquín de. "Estudio preliminar." *Poesía de doña Catalina Clara Ramírez de Guzmán.* Ed. y notas por Joaquín de Entrambasaguas y Peña. Badajoz: Centro de Estudios Extremeños, 1930. 5–41.

Evans, Robert C. *Ben Jonson and the Poetics of Patronage.* Lewisburg and London: Bucknell University Press, 1989.

Fanshawe, Lady Ann. "The Memoirs of Ann, Lady Fanshawe." *The Memoirs of Anne, Lady Halkett and Ann, Lady Fanshawe.* Ed. John Loftis. Oxford: Clarendon Press, 1979.

Ferguson, Margaret, ed. *Rewriting the Renaissance: The Discourses of Sexual Difference in Early Modern Europe.* Chicago: University of Chicago Press, 1986.

Flynn, Maureen. *Sacred Charity: Confraternities and Social Welfare in Spain, 1400–1700.* Houndmills, Basingstoke, Hampshire: Macmillan, 1989.

Forster, Leonard W. *The Icy Fire: Five Studies in European Petrarchism.* London: Cambridge University Press, 1969.

Foucault, Michel. *The History of Sexuality.* London: Penguin Books, 1990.

Fra-Molinero, Baltasar. "The Condition of Black Women in Spain during the Renaissance." *Black Women in America.* Ed. Kim Marie Vaz. Thousand Oaks: Sage, 1995. 159–78.

Fullerton, Lady Georgiana. *The Life of Luisa de Carvajal*. Leipzig: Tauchnitz, 1881.

García Verdugo, M. *Luisa de Carvajal: Aventurera y escritora*. 2004. Universidad Complutense de Madrid. Available online at *http://www.ucm.es/info/especulo/numero26/carvajal.htm*. Retrieved 8 September 2004.

Gazul, Arturo. "La familia Ramírez de Guzmán en Llerena." *Revista de Estudios Extremeños* 15, no. 3 (1959): 499–577.

Gilbert, Sandra M., and Susan Gubar. *The Madwoman in the Attic: The Woman Writer and the Nineteenth-Century Literary Imagination*. 2nd ed. New Haven: Yale University Press, 2000.

Goody, Jack. *The Development of the Family and Marriage in Europe*. Cambridge: Cambridge University Press, 1983.

Haseldine, J., ed. *Friendship in Medieval Europe*. Stroud: Sutton, 1999.

Helmholz, R. H. *Marriage Litigation in Medieval England*. London and New York: Cambridge University Press, 1974.

Hinds, A. B., ed. *Report on the Manuscripts of the Marquess of Downshire Preserved at Easthampstead Park, Berks*. Vol. 4. 6 vols. London: HMSO, 1938.

Horace. *The Odes of Horace*. Rev. ed. Trans. James Michie. London: Folio Society, 1987.

Howatson, M. C., and Ian Chilvers, eds. *The Concise Oxford Companion to Classical Literature*. Oxford and New York: Oxford University Press, 1993.

Hyatte, Reginald. *Arts of Friendship: The Idealisation of Friendship in Medieval and Early Renaissance Literature*. New York and Leiden: E. J. Brill, 1994.

Ibero, Alba. "Imágenes de maternidad en la pintura barroca." *Las mujeres en el Antiguo Régimen: Imagen y realidad*. Barcelona: Icaria, 1994.

Irigaray, Luce. *This Sex Which Is Not One*. Ithaca: Cornell University Press, 1985.

Janés, Clara. *Las Primeras poetisas en lengua castellana*. Madrid: Ayuso, 1986.

Jantzen, Grace. *Power, Gender, and Christian Mysticism*. Cambridge Studies in Ideology and Religion 8. Cambridge and New York: Cambridge University Press, 1995.

Jauralde Pou, Pablo. *Francisco de Quevedo (1580–1645)*. 2nd ed. Madrid: Castalia, 1999.

Jesús, Teresa de. *Obras completas*. 4th rev. ed. Ed. Otger Steggink and Efrén de la Madre de Díos. Madrid: Editorial Católica, 1974.

Jones, Ann Rosalind. *The Currency of Eros*. Bloomington: Indiana University Press, 1990.

———. "Nets and Bridles: Early Modern Conduct Books and Sixteenth-Century Women's Lyrics." *The Ideology of Conduct*. Ed. Nancy Armstrong and Leonard Tennenhouse. New York: Methuen, 1987. 39–72.

———. "New Songs for the Swallow: Ovid's Philomela in Tullia d'Aragona and Gaspara Stampa." *Refiguring Woman: Perspectives on Gender and the Italian Renaissance*. Ed. Marilyn Migiel and Juliana Schiesari. New York: Cornell University Press, 1991. 263–78.

———. "Surprising Fame." *The Poetics of Gender*. Ed. Nancy K. Miller. New York: Columbia University Press, 1986. 74–95.

Jordan, Constance. *Renaissance Feminism: Literary Texts and Political Models*. Ithaca and London: Cornell University Press, 1990.

Juana Inés de la Cruz, Sor. *Obras completas*. Vol. 1. 4 vols. Ed. Alfonso Méndez Plancarte. Mexico: Fondo de Cultura Económica, 1997.

Kagan, Richard. *Students and Society in Early Modern Spain*. Baltimore: Johns Hopkins University Press, 1974.

Kelly, Joan. "Did Women Have a Renaissance?" *Becoming Visible: Women in European History*. Ed. Renate Bridenthal, Claudia Koonz, and Susan Stuard. Boston: Houghton Mifflin, 1987. 175–202.

Kettering, Sharon. *Patronage in Sixteenth- and Seventeenth-Century France*. Aldershot: Ashgate, 2002.

King, Margaret L. *Women of the Renaissance*. Chicago and London: University of Chicago Press, 1991.

Kristeva, Julia. "Stabat Mater." Trans. León S. Roudiez. *The Kristeva Reader*. Ed. Toril Moi. Oxford: Basil Blackwell, 1986. 160–86.

Labalme, Patricia H. *Beyond Their Sex: Learned Women of the European Past*. New York: New York University Press, 1980.

Larson, Donald. *The Honor Plays of Lope de Vega*. Cambridge: Harvard University Press, 1977.

Lehfeldt, Elizabeth A. "Discipline, Vocation, and Patronage: Spanish Religious Women in a Tridentine Microclimate." *Sixteenth Century Journal* 30, no. 4 (1999): 1009–30.

———. *Religious Women in Golden Age Spain: The Permeable Cloister*. Aldershot: Ashgate, 2005.

Leitão de Barros, Teresa. *Escritoras de Portugal. Génio feminino revelado na literatura portuguesa*. Vol. 1. 2 vols. Lisboa: Imprensa Lucas & Cie, 1924.

León, Fray Luis de. *La perfecta casada*. Madrid: Libsa, 1998.

———. *Obras completas castellanas*. Madrid: Editorial Catolica, 1959.

Lerner, Gerda. *The Creation of Feminist Consciousness: From the Middle Ages to Eighteen-Seventy*. New York: Oxford University Press, 1993.

———. *Why History Matters: Life and Thought*. New York: Oxford University Press, 1997.

Lesko Baker, Deborah. *The Subject of Desire: Petrarchan Poetics and the Female Voice in Louise Labé*. West Lafayette: Purdue University Press, 1996.

Locke, John. *Some Thoughts upon Education*. 1693. NetLibrary. Electronic Reproductions, 1999. Available at *www.netlibrary.com.ezproxy.aucklandac.nz/Reader*. Retrieved 22 May 2004.

Loomie, Albert J. *Spain and the Jacobean Catholics*. Vol. 2. 2 vols. London: Catholic Record Society, 1978.

López, Carlos María. *Malón de Chaide*. 1991. Internet website. Hispánica. Available online at *http://poesiadelmomento.com/hispanica/43misticos.html*. Retrieved 2 September 2004.

Louth, Andrew. *The Origins of the Christian Mystical Tradition from Plato to Denys*. Oxford: Clarendon Press, 1981.

Loyola, Ignatius of. *Ignatius of Loyola: The Spiritual Exercises and Selected Works*. Ed. George E. Ganss. New York: Paulist Press, 1991.

Maclean, Hugh. *Ben Jonson and the Cavalier Poets: Authoritative Texts, Criticism*. New York: Norton, 1974.

Maclean, Ian. *The Renaissance Notion of Woman: A Study in the Fortunes of Scholasticism and Medical Science in European Intellectual Life.* Cambridge and New York: Cambridge University Press, 1980.

Malón de Chaide, Pedro. *La conversión de la Magdalena.* Madrid: Espasa-Calpe, 1957.

Marotti, Arthur. "John Donne and the Rewards of Patronage." *Patronage in the Renaissance.* Ed. Guy Fitch Lytle and Stephen Orgel. Princeton: Princeton University Press, 1981. 207–35.

Martín, Adrienne. "The Rhetoric of Female Friendship in the Lyric of Sor Violante del Cielo." *Caliope* 3, no. 2 (1997): 57–71.

Martín Gaite, Carmen. *Desde la ventana: enfoque femenino de la literatura española.* Madrid: Espasa-Calpe, 1987.

McKendrick, Melveena. *Woman and Society in the Spanish Drama of the Golden Age: A Study of the Mujer Varonil.* London and New York: Cambridge University Press, 1974.

McMahon, A. L. Meister Eckhart. 2004. Catholic Encyclopedia Online. Available online at *http://www.newadvent.org/cathen/05274a.htm.* Retrieved 8 September 2004.

Merchant, Carolyn. *The Death of Nature.* San Francisco: Harper & Row, 1990.

Migiel, Marilyn, and Juliana Schiesari, eds. *Refiguring Woman: Perspectives on Gender and the Italian Renaissance.* New York: Cornell University Press, 1991.

Miller, Beth Kurti. *Women in Hispanic Literature: Icons and Fallen Idols.* Berkeley and Los Angeles: University of California Press, 1983.

Miller, Nancy K. *The Poetics of Gender.* New York: Columbia University Press, 1986.

Montaigne, Michel Eyquem de. *The Complete Essays of Montaigne.* Trans. Donald M Frame. Stanford: Stanford University Press, 1965.

Montrose, Louis Adrian. "'The Place of a Brother' in *As You Like It*: Social Process and Comic Form." *Shakespeare Quarterly* 32, no. 1 (1981): 28–54.

Muñoz, Luis. *Vida y virtudes de la Venerable Virgen Doña Luisa de Carvajal y Mendoza. Su jornada a Inglaterra y sucesos en aquel Reyno. Van al fin algunas poesías españolas suyas, parte de su devoción y ingenio.* Madrid: Imprenta Real, 1632.

Nader, Helen, ed. *Power and Gender in Renaissance Spain: Eight Women of the Mendoza Family, 1450–1650.* Urbana and Chicago: University of Illinois Press, 2004.

Navaro, Ana, ed. *Antología poética de escritoras de los siglos XXVI y XVII.* Madrid: Castalia, 1989.

Nelken, Margarita. *Las escritoras españolas.* Barcelona: Labor, 1930.

Olivares, Julián, and Elizabeth Sievert Boyce. "Sor Violante del Cielo (y de la Tierra): The Subversion of Amorous Lyrical Discourse." *A Ricardo Gullón: sus discípulos.* Ed. Adelaida López de Martínez. Erie: Aldeeu, 1995. 189–201.

———. *Tras el espejo la musa escribe: lírica femenina de los Siglos de Oro.* Madrid: Siglo Veintiuno, 1993.

Oñate, Maria del Pilar. *El feminismo en la literatura española.* Madrid: Espasa Calpe, 1938.

Oppenheimer, Paul. *The Birth of the Modern Mind: Self, Consciousness and the Invention of the Sonnet.* New York and Oxford: Oxford University Press, 1989.

Origen. *The Song of Songs: Commentary and Homilies.* Trans. R. P. Lawson. Westminster: Newman Press, 1957.

Orozco Díaz, Emilio. *Estudios sobre San Juan de la Cruz y la mística del Barroco, edición, introducción y anotaciones: José Lara Garrido.* Granada: Universidad de Granada, 1994.

———. *Expresión, comunicación y estilo en la obra de Santa Teresa (notas sueltas de lector).* Granada: Excma. Diputación Provincial de Granada, 1987.

Ortega Costa, Milagros. "Spanish Women in the Reformation." *Women in Reformation and Counter-Reformation Europe: Public and Private Worlds.* Ed. Sherrin Marshall. Bloomington and Indianapolis: Indiana University Press, 1989. 89–119.

Osuna, Francisco de. *Tercer Abecedario espiritual.* Ed. Melquiades Andrés Martín. Madrid: Biblioteca de Autores Cristianos, 1972.

Ovid. *Heroides and Amores.* 2nd ed. Works, vol. 1. Trans. Grant Showerman. Ed. G. P. Goold. Cambridge, Mass., and London: Harvard University Press/W. Heinemann, 1977.

Pakaluk, Michael, ed. *Other Selves: Philosophers on Friendship.* Indianapolis: Hackett, 1991.

Peck, Linda Levy. *Court Patronage and Corruption in Early Stuart England.* London and Boston: Unwin Hyman, 1990.

Pérez, Louis C. *The Dramatic Works of Feliciana Enríquez de Guzmán.* Valencia: Albatros, 1988.

Pérez Molina, Isabel. *Las mujeres en el Antiguo Régimen: imagen y realidad (s. XVI–XVIII).* Antrazyt. Barcelona: Icaria, 1994.

———. "Las mujeres y el matrimonio en el derecho catalán moderno." *Las mujeres en el Antiguo Régimen: Imagen y realidad.* Barcelona: Icaria, 1994.

Perry, Mary Elizabeth. *Crime and Society in Early Modern Seville.* Hanover: University Press of New England, 1980.

———. *The Handless Maiden: Moriscos and the Politics of Religion in Early Modern Spain.* Princeton: Princeton University Press, 2005.

———. "Subversion and Seduction: Perceptions of the Body in Writings of Religious Women in Counter-Reformation Spain." *Religion, Body and Gender in Early Modern Spain.* Ed. Alain Saint-Saëns. San Francisco: Mellen Research University Press, 1991. 66–78.

Perry, Mary Elizabeth, and Anne J. Cruz, eds. *Culture and Control in Counter-Reformation Spain.* Minneapolis: University of Minnesota Press, 1992.

Pfandl, Ludwig. *Cultura y costumbres del pueblo español en los siglos XVI y XVII.* Barcelona: Araluce, 1959.

———. *Historia de la literatura nacional española en la edad de oro.* 2nd ed. Barcelona: J. Gili, 1952.

Pineda, Juan de. *En las honras de la Doña Luisa de Carvajal difunta en Londres por enero de 1614, sermón funebre por el padre Juan de Pineda en el seminario de los alumnos ingleses de S. Gregorio de Sevilla.* Sig.R/20949 (20). Biblioteca Nacional de España, Madrid.

Pinillos Iglesias, Maria de las Nieves. *Hilando oro: Vida de Luisa de Carvajal y Mendoza.* Madrid: Laberinto, 2001.

Plato. *Plato's Phaedrus.* Trans. R. Hackforth. Cambridge: Cambridge University Press, 1952.

Pociño López, Andrés José, ed. *Sóror Violante do Céu (1607–1693).* Madrid: Ediciones del Orto, 1998.

Poska, Allyson M. *Women and Authority in Early Modern Spain: The Peasants of Galicia.* Oxford: Oxford University Press, 2005.

Powell, Amanda. "'*Oh qué diversas estamos, / dulce prenda, vos y yo!*' Multiple Voicings in Love Poems to Women by Marcia Belisarda, Catalina Clara Ramírez de Guzmán, and Sor Violante del Cielo." *En desagravio de las damas: Women's Poetry in the Golden Age.* Ed. Julián Olivares and Elizabeth Boyce. Asheville, NC: Pegasus. Forthcoming.

Public Record Office. *Calendar of State Papers, Domestic Series, of the Reign of James I, King of England.* Vol. 8. Nendeln, Liechtenstein: Kraus Reprint 1967 [1908].

Quevedo, Francisco de. *Poesía original completa.* Ed. introducción y notas de José Manuel Blecua. Madrid: Planeta, 1996.

Ramírez de Guzmán, Catalina Clara. *Poesías de Doña Catalina Clara Ramírez de Guzmán. Estudio preliminar, edición y notas por Joaquín de Entrambasaguas y Peña.* Badajoz: Centro de Estudios Extremeños, 1930.

Raymond, Janice. *A Passion for Friends.* Reading: Cox & Wyman, 1991.

Rees, Margaret A. *The Writings of Doña Luisa de Carvajal y Mendoza, Catholic Missionary to James I's London.* Lewiston: E. Mellen Press, 2003.

Rhodes, Elizabeth. "Biography." *This Tight Embrace: Luisa de Carvajal y Mendoza (1566–1614).* Ed. and trans. Elizabeth Rhodes. Milwaukee: Marquette University Press, 2000. 1–42.

———. "Luisa de Carvajal's Counter-Reformation Journey to Selfhood (1566–1614)." *Renaissance Quarterly* 51, no. 3 (1998): 887–912.

Rivers, Elías L., ed. *El soneto español en el Siglo de Oro.* Madrid: Akal, 1993.

Robbins, Jeremy. *Love Poetry of the Literary Academies in the Reigns of Philip IV and Charles II.* London: Tamesis, 1997.

Rojas, Víctor Julio. "Vida y obra de Violante do Céu." Doctoral thesis, University of Indiana, 1975.

Romero-Díaz, Nieves. *Nueva nobleza, nueva novela: reescribiendo la cultura urbana del barroco.* Newark: Juan de la Cuesta, 2002.

Sabat de Rivers, Georgina. "Love in Some of Sor Juana's Sonnets." *Colonial Latin American Review* 4, no. 2 (1995): 101–23.

Sabugosa, Conde de. *Neves de antanho.* Lisbon: Portugalia, 1919.

Saint-Saëns, Alain, ed. *Religion, Body and Gender in Early Modern Spain.* San Francisco: Mellen Research University Press, 1991.

Sánchez, Magdalena S. *The Empress, the Queen, and the Nun: Women and Power at the Court of Philip III of Spain.* Studies in Historical and Political Science, Series 2, 116. Baltimore: Johns Hopkins University Press, 1998.

Scannell, T. B. Frequent Communion. 2004. Catholic Encyclopedia Online. Available online at *http://www.newadvent.org/Cathen/06278a.htm.* Retrieved 17 July 2004.

Schiesari, Juliana. *The Gendering of Melancholia: Feminism, Psychoanalysis, and the*

Symbolics of Loss in Renaissance Literature. Ithaca: Cornell University Press, 1992.

Schlau, Stacey. *Spanish American Women's Use of the Word: Colonial through Contemporary Narratives*. Tucson: University of Arizona Press, 2001.

———. *Viva al siglo, muerta al mundo: Selected Works/Obras escogidas by/de María de San Alberto (1568–1640)*. New Orleans: University Press of the South, 1998.

Scott, Joan Wallach. *Gender and the Politics of History*. New York and Chichester: Columbia University Press, 1988.

Segura, Cristina. *Feminismo y misoginia en la literatura española: fuentes literarias para la historia de las mujeres*. Madrid: Narcea, 2001.

Seneca. *Letters from a Stoic: Epistulae Morales ad Lucilium*. Trans. Robin Campbell. Harmondsworth: Penguin Books, 1969.

Senning, Calvin F. "The Carvajal Affair: Gondomar and James I." *Catholic Historical Review* 56, no. 1 (1970): 42–66.

Serrano y Sanz, Manuel. *Apuntes para una biblioteca de escritoras españolas*. Madrid: Atlas, 1975.

Shakespeare, William. *The Merry Wives of Windsor*. Ed. and introd. G. R. Hibberd. London: Penguin Books, 1973.

Shaw Fairman, Patricia. *España vista por los ingleses del siglo XVII*. Madrid: Sociedad General Española de Librería, 1981.

Smith, Paul Julian. *The Body Hispanic: Gender and Sexuality in Spanish and Spanish American Literature*. Oxford: Clarendon Press, 1989.

Smith, Theresa Anne. *The Emerging Female Citizen: Gender and Enlightenment in Spain*. Berkeley and Los Angeles: University of California Press, 2006.

Smuts, R. Malcolm. "Art and the Material Culture of Majesty in Early Stuart England." *The Stuart Court and Europe: Essays in Politics and Political Culture*. Ed. R. Malcolm Smuts. Cambridge: Cambridge University Press, 1996. 86–113.

Soufas, Teresa Scott. "Absence of Desire in Leonor de la Cueva y Silva's *La firmeza en la ausencia*." *Gender, Identity and Representation in Spain's Golden Age*. Ed. Anita K. Stoll and Dawn L. Smith. Lewisburg: Bucknell University Press, 2000.

———. "The Gendered Context of Melancholy for Spanish Golden Age Women Writers." *Spanish Women in the Golden Age: Images and Realities*. Ed. Magdalena S. Sánchez and Alain Saint-Saëns. Westport and London: Greenwood Press, 1996. 171–84.

———. *Women's Acts: Plays by Women Dramatists of Spain's Golden Age*. Lexington: University Press of Kentucky, 1997.

Southey, Robert. *Letters Written during a Journey in Spain and a Short Residence in Portugal by Robert Southey*. 3rd ed. 2 vols. London: Longman, 1808.

Souvay, Charles. St Joseph. 2004. Catholic Encyclopedia Online. Available online at http://newadvent.org/cathen/08504a.htm. Retrieved 8 August 2004.

Stallybrass, Peter. "Patriarchal Territories: The Body Enclosed." *Rewriting the Renaissance: The Discourses of Sexual Difference in Early Modern Europe*. Ed. Maureen Quilligan, Margaret W. Ferguson, and Nancy J. Vickers. Chicago: University of Chicago Press, 1986. 123–42.

Stoichita, Victor. *El ojo místico: pintura y visión religiosa en el Siglo de Oro español.* Madrid: Alianza, 1996.

Stone, Lawrence. *The Family, Sex and Marriage in England 1500–1800.* London: Weidenfeld & Nicolson, 1977.

Stone, Marilyn. *Marriage and Friendship in Medieval Spain: Social Relations According to the Fourth Partida of Alfonso X.* American University Studies, Series 2, Romance Languages and Literature 131. New York: P. Lang, 1990.

Subirats, Marina, et al., eds. *Teatro de mujeres del Barroco.* Madrid: Asociación de Directores de Escena de España, 1994.

Surtz, Ronald E. *The Guitar of God: Gender, Power, and Authority in the Visionary World of Mother Juana de la Cruz (1481–1534).* The Middle Ages Series. Philadelphia: University of Pennsylvania Press, 1990.

Toner, P. J. Communion Under Both Kinds. 2003. Catholic Encyclopedia Online. Available online at *http://www.newadvent.org/cathen/04175a.htm.* Retrieved 15 December 2003.

Torres Sánchez, Concha. *La clausura femenina en la Salamanca del siglo XVII: Dominicas y Carmelitas Descalzas.* Acta Salmanticensia. Estudios históricos y geográficos 73. Salamanca: Universidad de Salamanca, 1991.

Valency, Maurice. *In Praise of Love: An Introduction to the Love Poetry of the Renaissance.* New York: Macmillan, 1958.

Vega Carpio, Lope Felix de. *Colección escogida de obras no dramáticas de Frey Lope Felix de Vega Carpio, por don Cayetano Rosell.* Biblioteca de Autores Españoles 38. Madrid: Atlas, 1950.

Vickers, Nancy. "Diana Described: Scattered Woman and Scattered Rhyme." *Critical Inquiry* 8, no. 2 (1981): 265–79.

Vieira Mendes, Margarida. "Apresentação." *Violante do Céu: Rimas varias.* Ed. introdução notas e fixação do texto: Margarida Vieira Mendes. Lisboa: Editorial Presença, 1993. 7–17.

Vigil, Mariló. *La vida de las mujeres en los siglos XVI y XVII.* México: Siglo Veintiuno Editores, 1986.

Vives, Juan Luis. *The Education of a Christian Woman: A Sixteenth-Century Manual.* Ed. and trans. Charles Fantazzi. Chicago: University of Chicago Press, 2000.

Vollendorf, Lisa. *The Lives of Women: A New History of Inquisitional Spain.* Nashville: Vanderbilt University Press, 2005.

———. "'No Doubt It Will Amaze You': María de Zayas's Early Modern Feminism." *Recovering Spain's Feminist Tradition.* Ed. Lisa Vollendorf. New York: MLA, 2001. 103–22.

———, ed. *Recovering Spain's Feminist Tradition.* New York: MLA, 2001.

Voltes, María José, and Pedro Voltes Bou. *Las mujeres en la historia de España.* Barcelona: Planeta, 1986.

Voros, Sharon D. "Fashioning Feminine Wit in María de Zayas, Ana Caro and Leonor de la Cueva." *Gender, Identity and Representation in Spain's Golden Age.* Ed. Anita K. and Dawn L. Smith Stoll. Lewisburg: Bucknell University Press, 2000. 156–77.

Warner, Marina. *Alone of All Her Sex.* New York: Random House, 1983.

———. *Monuments and Maidens: The Allegory of the Female Form.* London: Picador, 1985.

Wayne, Valerie. "Some Sad Sentence: Vives' *Instruction of a Christian Woman.*" *Silent But for the Word: Tudor Women as Patrons, Translators and Writers of Religious Works.* Ed. Margaret P. Hannay. Kent: Kent State University Press, 1985. 15–29.

Weber, Alison. *Teresa of Avila and the Rhetoric of Femininity.* Princeton: Princeton University Press, 1990.

Wilkins, Ernest H. "The Invention of the Sonnet." *Modern Philology* 13 (1915–1916): 79–112.

Woolf, Virginia. *A Room of One's Own; Three Guineas.* Ed. and introd. Michel Barrett. London: Penguin Books, 1993.

Yarbro-Bejarano, Yvonne. *Feminism and the Honor Plays of Lope de Vega.* Purdue Studies in Romance Literatures 4. West Lafayette: Purdue University Press, 1994.

Zabaleta, Juan de. *El día de fiesta por la mañana y por la tarde.* Clásicos Castalia 130. Ed. Cristóbal Cuevas García. Madrid: Castalia, 1983.

Zavala, Iris M., ed. *Breve historia feminista de la literatura española (en lengua castellana): La mujer en la literatura española: Modos de representación desde la Edad Media hasta el siglo XVII.* Vol. 2. 6 vols. Madrid and Barcelona: Anthropos, 1995.

GENERAL INDEX

INDEX OF FIRST LINES

INDEX OF FIRST LINES IN
TRANSLATION

Subtle Subversions: Reading Golden Age Sonnets by Iberian Women was designed and typeset in Adobe Garamond by Kachergis Book Design of Pittsboro, North Carolina. It was printed on 60-pound Natures Natural and bound by Thomson-Shore of Dexter, Michigan.